IMAGES
of America

BOWIE

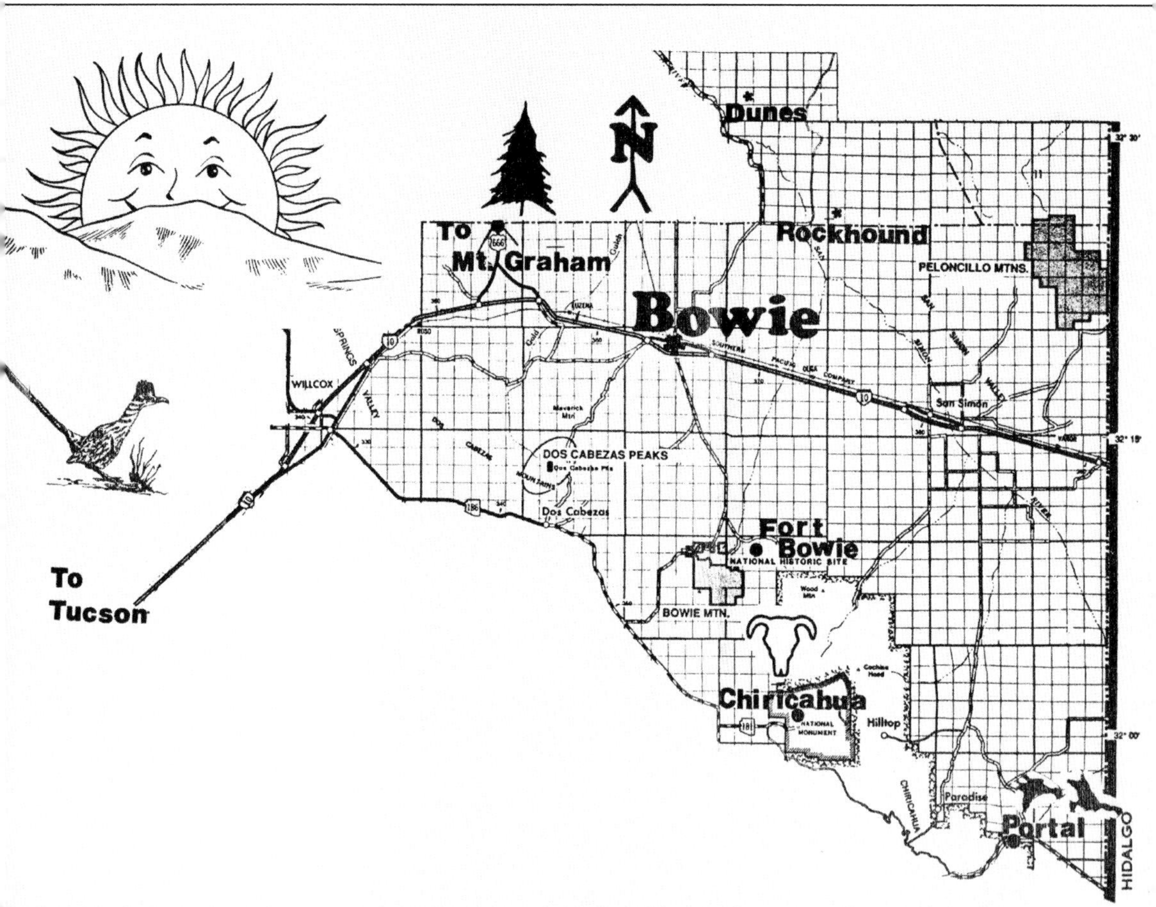

This map shows the town of Bowie, Arizona, located along Interstate 10 in the southeast corner of the state, near the New Mexico state line. At an elevation of 3,758 feet, Bowie is in the San Simon Valley, near the base of the Dos Cabezas Mountains of the Chiricahua Mountain Range. (Courtesy of Bowie Chamber of Commerce.)

On the Cover: Standing in front of Bowie High School, which was built in 1922, are the school band members of 1946. It was comprised of students from grades seven through 12. They received excellent ratings in band competitions and marched in parades in Arizona and New Mexico. Page 85 includes individual student identifications. (Courtesy of Janice Grizzle.)

IMAGES
of America

BOWIE

Kathy Klump and Peta-Anne Tenney for
Sulphur Springs Valley Historical Society

ARCADIA
PUBLISHING

ISBN 978-0-7385-8509-3

Published by Arcadia Publishing
Charleston, South Carolina

Printed in the United States of America

Library of Congress Control Number: 2011931723

For all general information, please contact Arcadia Publishing:
Telephone 843-853-2070
Fax 843-853-0044
E-mail sales@arcadiapublishing.com
For customer service and orders:
Toll-Free 1-888-313-2665

Visit us on the Internet at www.arcadiapublishing.com

To Evelyn Spikes Lathram, who had the vision, encouraged alumni to participate, relentlessly searched for images and news items, and was so generous in her support

Contents

ACKNOWLEDGMENTS

We are indebted to the people of Bowie, Arizona—former residents, business owners, and school alumni—who shared their photographs and memories of their hometown. Special thanks to Evelyn Lathram, who first approached us about doing the book. She spent over a year making contacts to encourage the sharing of historic photographs, family stories, yearbooks, and documents. We appreciate Janice Grizzle for sharing her many photo albums and her foresight in saving the Lois Blake Tomlinson collection. Thanks also to Barbara Welker Blandin, Nancy-Jean Welker, and Bill Hoy, former ranger for Fort Bowie. We also thank postmistress Marisela Gonzalez and Judge Michael Skiles, for their assistance. We thank Jill McCleary and the staffs of the Arizona Historical Society, University of Arizona Special Collections, and Arizona State Archives and Public Records.

We thank alumni Dewain and Katharine Lockwood, Delbert and Raymond Fousel, Sam McKee, Bill Allen, Bobby Montana, Carisa Fulkerson, Ed and Ernestine Harmon Crews, Vic Boll, Melvin "Dutch" Grusendorf, Guy Clerc, Gary Royster, Luiza Amodeo, and Jeanette Engler Burcham. Thank you to those who shared their school yearbooks and many others, as noted by each courtesy line.

Images in this volume appear courtesy of the Sulphur Springs Valley Historical Society (SSVHS), and the Arizona Historical Society (AHS).

We wish to thank Kristie Kelly and Stacia Bannerman, our editors at Arcadia Publishing, for their expert guidance. To our husbands, Keith Klump and Todd Tenney, thank you for all your encouragement and support.

Introduction

James Henry Tevis arrived in the Arizona wilderness as station manager for the Butterfield Overland Stage, from 1857 to 1859. The Chiricahua Apaches, led by famous Chief Cochise, roamed this land, which contained the only permanent water source for miles. Apache Pass, called El Puerto del Dado (Pass of Chance) by the Spanish, was known as being one of the most dangerous locations for encounters with Indians in all of Arizona. Fort Bowie was established in 1862 as protection to the early settlers. Many bloody skirmishes with the Apaches were fought before the soldiers obtained control of the spring. Rogue Apaches continued hostilities until Geronimo and his band surrendered in 1886.

In 1880, Captain Tevis returned and opened a sutler store in the old stage station at Fort Bowie. He invented a type of windmill that he sold to the early ranchers. He hired soldiers Michael E. Kinchala and Aaron Evans to help him locate 50 gold and silver mining claims, which began the Tevis Mining District. When Tevis learned the railroad was being built, he placed his homestead in the projected path and donated a right-of-way to Southern Pacific. Then, Tevis, Kinchala, Evans, and Julian Navarette dug a well to supply water to the railroad workers and the projected town. Tevis built a store and a hotel. Soon, Southern Pacific built a depot with a telegraph office, freight house, and hotel. Bowie Station was the forwarding point for military troops and livestock. A large number of freighters were constantly on the go, transporting soldiers, Indian scouts, thousands of cavalry horses, pack and team mules, and supplies. Wells Fargo had offices here from 1883 to 1912.

Before there was any settlement, this spot in the San Simon Valley was called Tres Cebollas (Three Onions). The first to make land claims were Capt. James Tevis, Mary Marringer, and O. Campbell. A post office was established as Teviston on July 25, 1881, first in a tent and later in Tevis's store. William L. Martin was postmaster. In September 1881, Superintendent Bean, of the Southern Pacific Railroad, changed the name to Bean, after himself, with Henry A. Smith as postmaster. Tevis said to him, "Damn it, man, we have beans three times a day, every day of the year, and are damned tired of even the name *Bean*." So, Bean changed it to Bowie Station, after Fort Bowie. Captain Tevis later sold his store to the Solomon-Wickersham Company and his townsite property to Cuthbert S. Kellum.

In January 1894, the Gila Valley, Globe & Northern Railroad was incorporated. Later known as the Arizona Eastern, it would carry workers and supplies from Bowie to Fort Thomas and, eventually, to the largest mines in Arizona at Globe and Miami. Bowie became the site for the roundhouse for both railroads, with workers and their families residing in railroad housing. Passenger travel increased dramatically. Besides the freight trains, there would be 10 to 15 passenger trains a day. They stopped for 20 minutes for meals at the hotel dining room, first managed by Mrs. James Campbell and known far and wide for its first-class cuisine. When the Santa Fe Railroad joined the Southern Pacific at Deming, a Harvey House restaurant was established in Bowie with waitresses dressed in black-and-white uniforms.

In 1909, Bowie had one store, several railroad houses, "Dad" Kellum's saloon, a few scattered homes, a one-room schoolhouse, a hotel, and a depot.

By October 1913, Bowie suddenly boomed to include five stores, three hotels, three restaurants, three saloons, a telephone exchange, opera house, blacksmith shop, lumberyard, shoe shop, boardinghouse, veterinary surgeon, livery stable, real estate office, bank, new brick schoolhouse, two newspapers, a barbershop, three pool halls, and the depot.

In 1910, drilling for oil resulted in the opening of artesian wells with water reaching temperatures of 106 degrees. This discovery brought a steady influx of homesteaders to try dry land farming. Practically every quarter section of land had been homesteaded by 1915. The rich soil resulted in a bounty of all kinds of fruits and vegetables of excellent quality and size. Later, with irrigation, farmers raised, among other things, huge crops of tomatoes, onions, and cotton.

The goat ranchers raised angora goats and shipped thousands of pounds of mohair each year. The open range provided rich grasslands for the cattle ranchers who drove their cattle to the pens at the station, shipping them by rail to the rest of the nation.

Several mining operations were active in the area. Most were located in Buckeye Canyon, Apache Pass, and Gold Gulch. The marble quarry shipped marble all over the world beginning in 1909.

After Highway 86 was completed through town, several gasoline service stations, motels, and cafés sprang up to take care of the tourists traveling through.

Bowie continued to prosper with a population that once reached 1,000 people. It became a fine community in which to raise children, with excellent schools, churches, and social organizations.

When the railroad ended passenger service at Bowie in the 1950s, the trains traveled right on through. In 1969, Interstate 10 was built, bypassing the town. Businesses that had relied on tourism could no longer survive. Little by little, the cafés, service stations, and motels closed down.

Today, the town revolves mostly around the school and the three churches. The post office is the general gathering place. The most successful businesses are the pistachio and pecan farms and vineyards with their own vintages of prize-winning wine. The new Bowie Power Station is working towards construction, which will bring many needed jobs to the area. Fort Bowie National Historic Site is only 14 miles away with more than 10,000 visitors a year. The Chiricahua National Monument in the nearby Chiricahua Mountains, once known as the "Wonderland of Rocks," offers a variety of camping, hiking, and sightseeing opportunities.

One

Fort Bowie and the Chiricahua Apaches

The Butterfield Overland Mail established a route across southeast Arizona, through the native lands of the Chiricahua Apaches, led by the famous Chief Cochise. In 1858, a stage station was built west of Apache Pass near the spring and managed by Anthony Elder. This spring, located in the Dos Cabezas Mountains, was the Apache's main reliable source of water; however, Cochise allowed the stage to operate peacefully until 1861. Then came the famous Bascom Affair, in which six of Cochise's people were held hostage and killed over the kidnapping of a young boy, later known as Mickey Free. Cochise had killed the hostages he had captured after efforts to exchange them for his family failed, and so began bloody warfare for the next 25 years.

To protect the pass and allow for the settling of the Southwest, Fort Bowie was established in 1862. After several days of battle with the Apaches, the soldiers secured possession of the spring. In 1872, peace was made with Cochise. The Chiricahua Indian Reservation, which included a huge area of the Apache homeland, was designated. After Cochise died in 1874, the reservation was taken from the Apaches. All, except 400 Apaches led by Juh, were removed to the San Carlos Indian Reservation. Geronimo was one of these 400 who vanished into the surrounding mountains and were considered hostile renegades. Eventually, they were also taken to San Carlos but escaped and continued raiding, stealing cattle and horses, attacking mail carriers, travelers, miners, and soldiers. This small band of warriors outwitted and outfought soldiers many times their number until very few Apaches were left. Geronimo and Cochise's son Naiche finally surrendered to Col. Nelson A. Miles at Skeleton Canyon on September 4, 1886.

Fort Bowie was abandoned October 17, 1894. Soldiers' graves were removed to the National Cemetery in San Francisco. The soldiers and their families boarded the train at Bowie for their new post at Fort Logan, Colorado. In June 1911, the fort was sold at public auction and used for cattle grazing. Finally recognizing the importance the fort had played in the final American Indian war, Congress proclaimed it a National Historic Site on August 31, 1964, with dedication ceremonies on July 29, 1972.

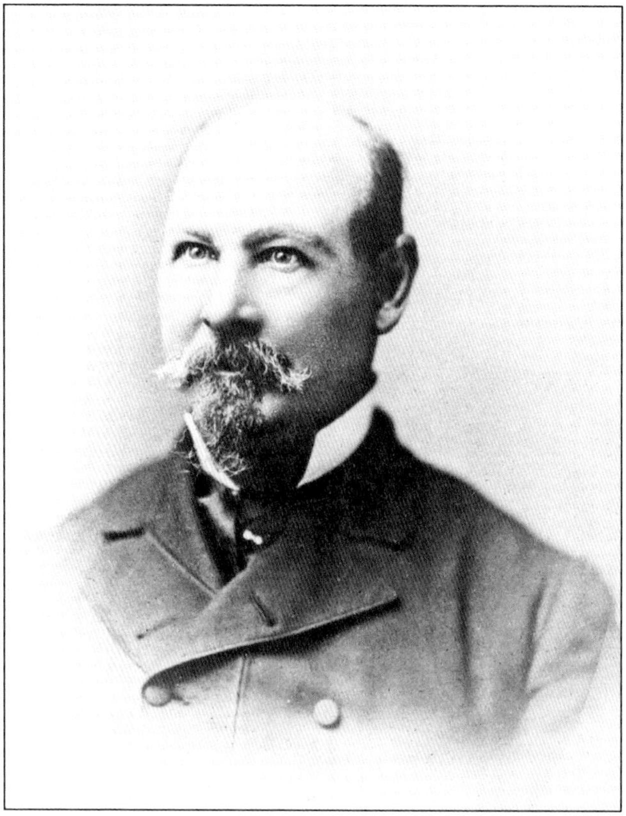

George Washington Bowie was commanding officer of the 5th Regiment California Volunteer Infantry. After the Battle of Apache Pass was won, soldiers began constructing Fort Bowie on July 28, 1862, in his name, to protect the pass and the very important, ever-flowing springs. Bowie was commander of the District of Arizona from January to November 1864. He was brevetted brigadier general of volunteers on March 13, 1865. (Courtesy of Barbara Blandin.)

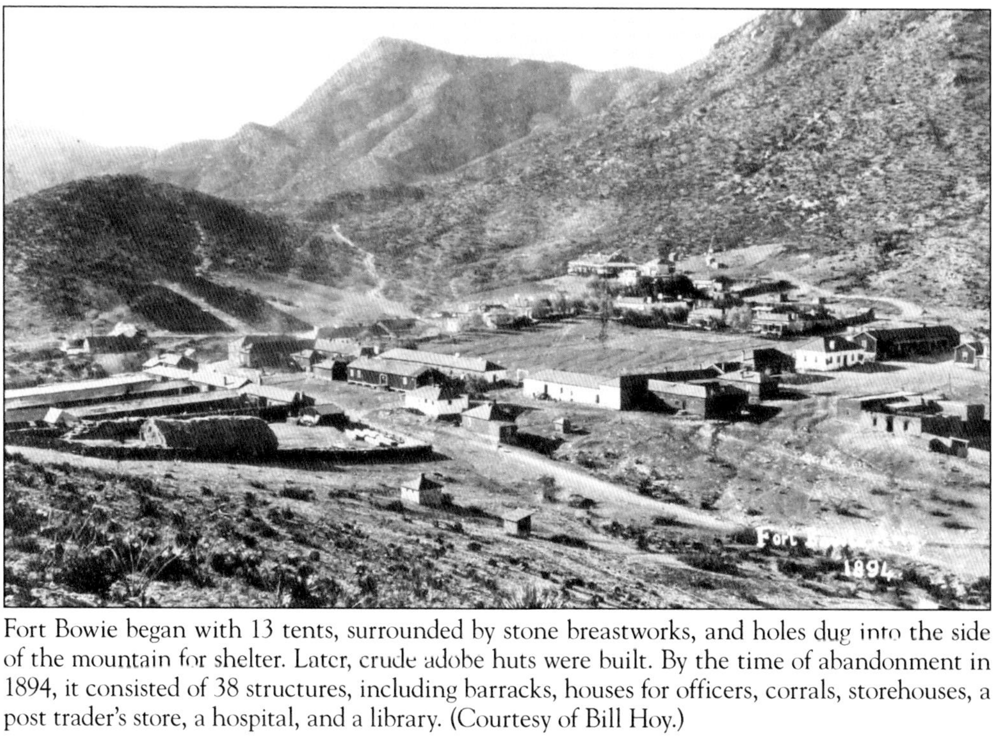

Fort Bowie began with 13 tents, surrounded by stone breastworks, and holes dug into the side of the mountain for shelter. Later, crude adobe huts were built. By the time of abandonment in 1894, it consisted of 38 structures, including barracks, houses for officers, corrals, storehouses, a post trader's store, a hospital, and a library. (Courtesy of Bill Hoy.)

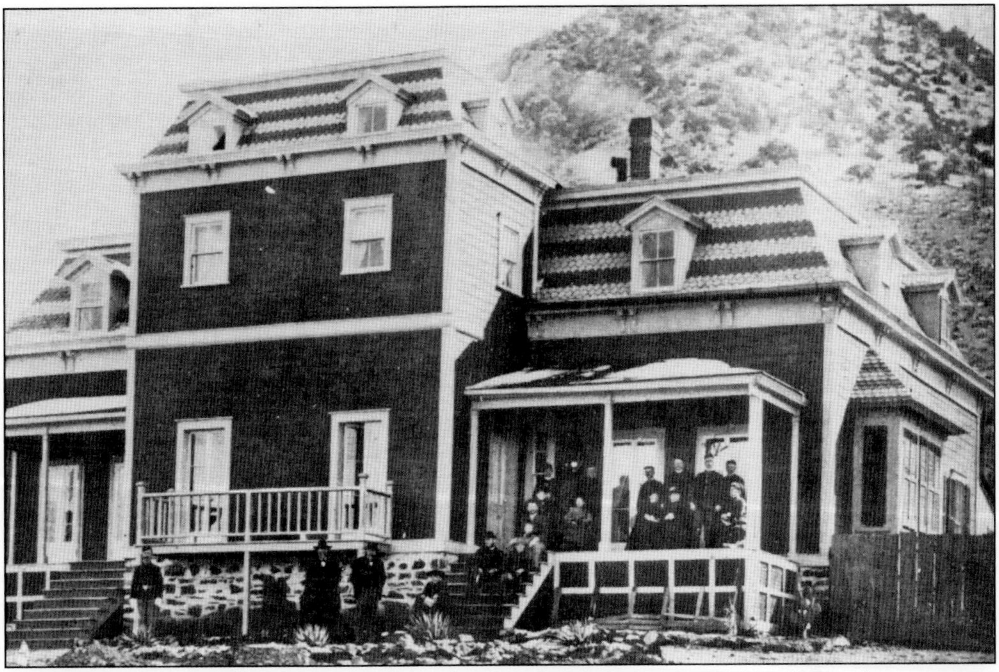

In 1886, the commander complained of the commanding officers quarters' "useless and unnecessary ornamentation." This elegant, two-story, 13-room house was located between the hospital and officers row. In contrast, outside the fort's six-mile square were saloons and other establishments, ready to take the soldiers' money. Jim Barrack, the "king" of the local "hog ranch," and Ada Miller provided rotgut whiskey, gambling, and prostitutes. (Courtesy of SSVHS.)

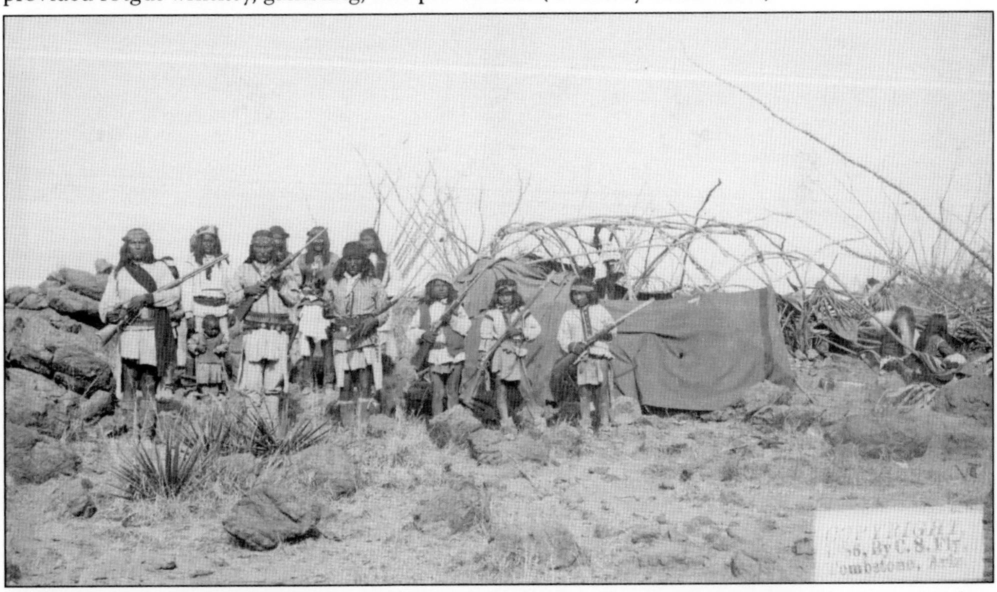

C.S. Fly, the only photographer of Indians as enemies in the field, took this photograph of an Apache camp during the Geronimo campaign. The boys holding rifles could fight, but only became warriors after undergoing certain tests and ceremonies. The wickiup is covered with Army-issue wool blankets. These temporary shelters were made of branches covered with bear grass, canvas, or any available material. (Courtesy of AHS No. 78157.)

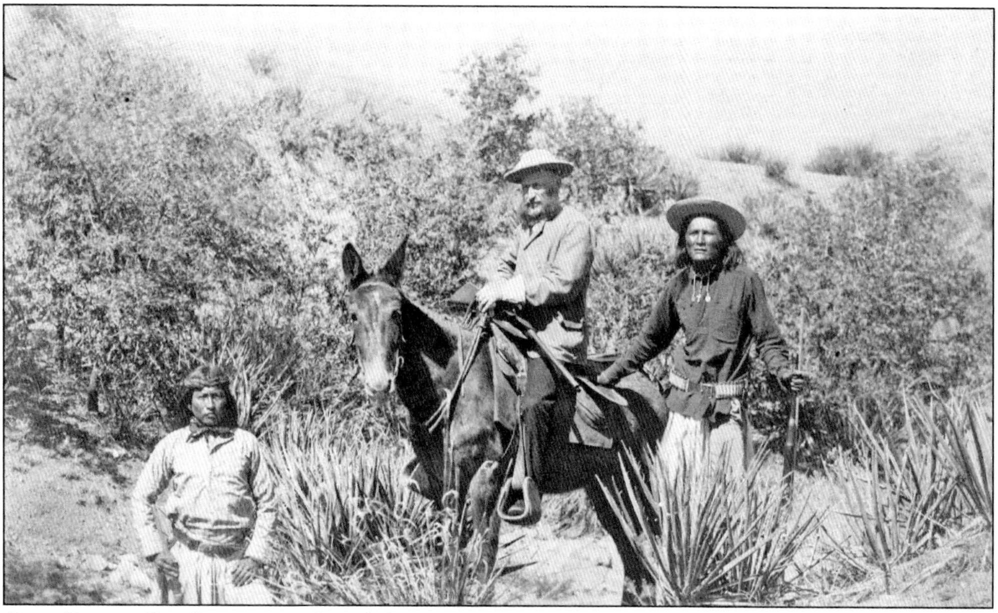

Gen. George Crook, commander of the Department of Arizona in 1871, succeeded in removing the Apaches to the reservation. From 1882 to 1886, he relentlessly pursued the Apaches with an extensive force of Indian scouts. After the planned surrender at Canyon de los Embudos failed, Crook resigned from his command. Scouts were sent to Florida with the other Apaches, with no regard for their service. (Courtesy of AHS No. 25625.)

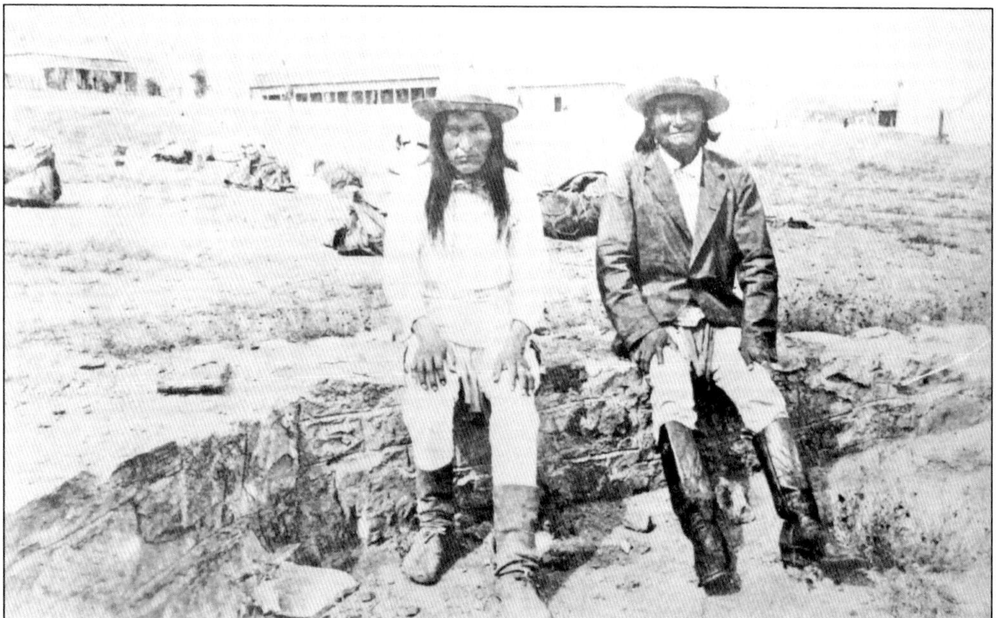

At Fort Bowie, Naiche and Geronimo wait to be taken to Florida via the special train at Bowie Station on September 8, 1886. They were disarmed, dismounted, and escorted out as the 4th Cavalry band played "Auld Lang Syne." Spending 28 years in captivity, the Apaches would have to wait 100 years before returning to their homeland, during a commemoration of the surrender, in September 1986. (Courtesy of AHS No. 17420.)

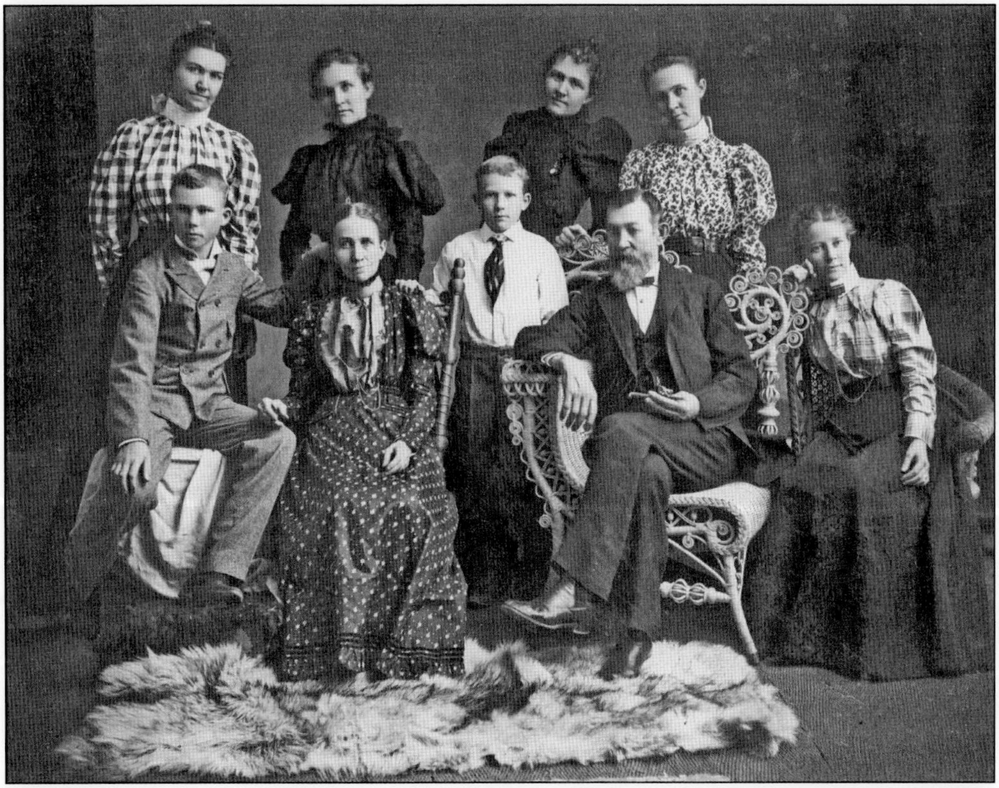

James and Emma Tevis are with their children Minnie, Belle, Josephine, Mary, Louis, Granville, and Lettie; their son Albert died in 1883. The family arrived in Bowie in 1882. Their home was called the Gardens and had 1,400 experimental fruit trees and plants. Their son-in-law, engineer James Boyer, was killed July 4, 1893, when he jumped from a train and the tender turned over and crushed him. (Courtesy of University of Arizona Special Collections.)

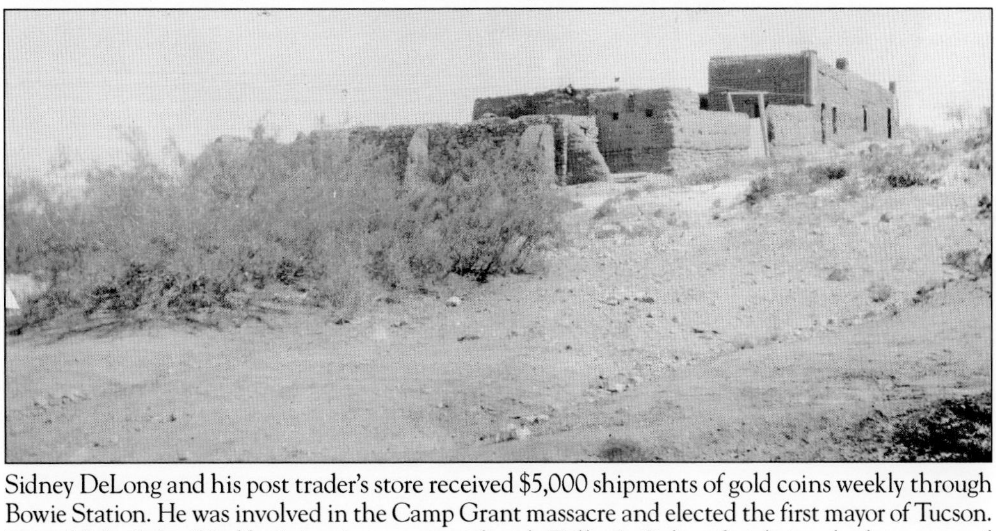

Sidney DeLong and his post trader's store received $5,000 shipments of gold coins weekly through Bowie Station. He was involved in the Camp Grant massacre and elected the first mayor of Tucson. He published the *Weekly Arizonian*, partnered with Tully & Ochoa freighting, had a store and mine at Dos Cabezas, and served as first official historian for the Society of Arizona Pioneers. (Courtesy of AHS No. PC155.)

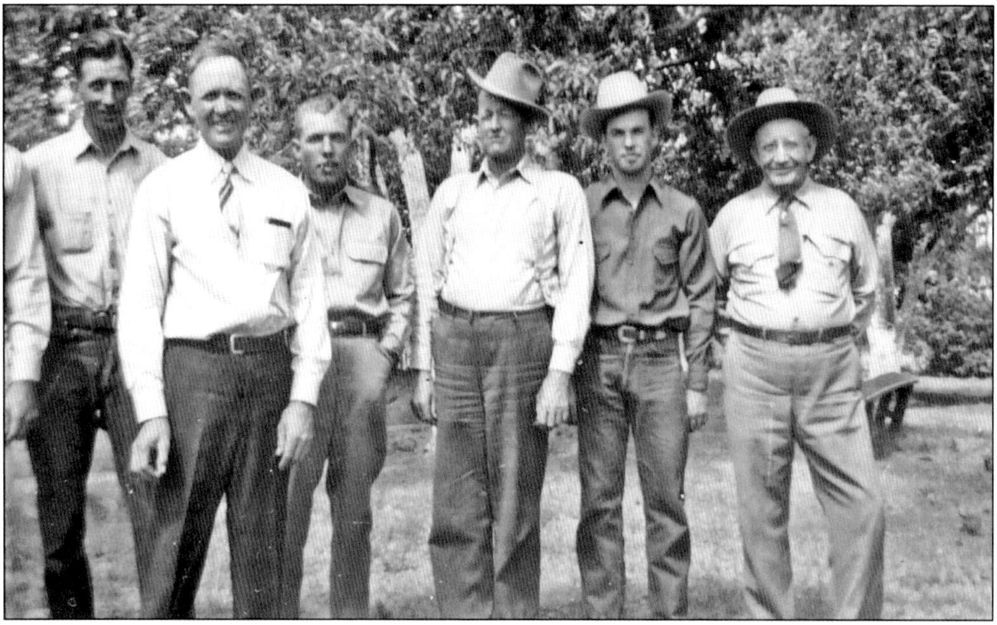

Several families owned ranches near the fort. When the fort closed, it became a popular picnic and hiking area for local residents. Pictured are, from left to right, early pioneers Joseph Schafer (of the HYL Ranch), Donnel Riggs, Thomas Adams, Dana Riggs, Will DeBorde, and Will Cox. (Courtesy of Keith Klump.)

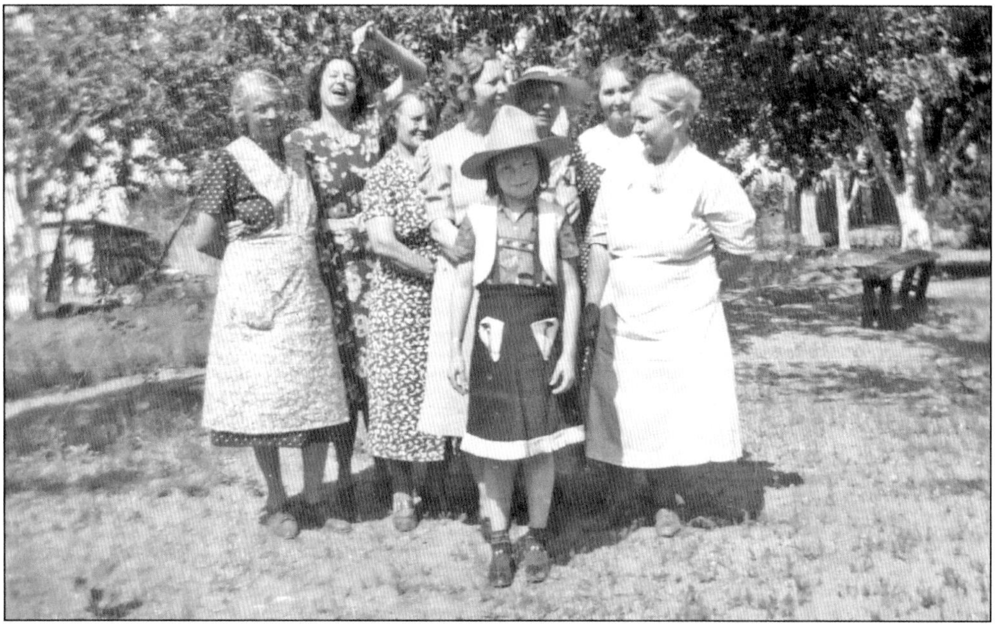

Wives and family members were photographed the same day near the fort. They are, from left to right, Lizzie Schafer, Berta DeBorde, Lizzie Adams, Josie Lawhon, Anna Lawhon, Mrs. Hyatt, Maggie Rumans Cox, and an unidentified young girl. Lizzie Adams and Anna Lawhon are sisters. Anna is the mother of Maggie Cox and Josie Lawhon (later married to Sam Moseley). Josie was inducted into the Cowboy Hall of Fame in 2000. (Courtesy of Keith Klump.)

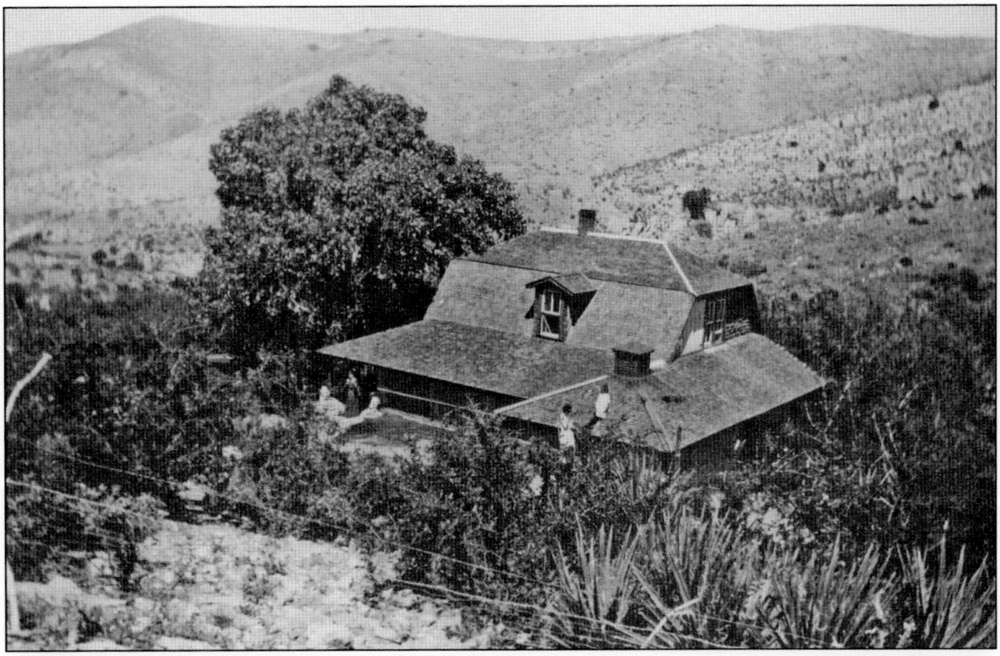

Children are on the roof of the James Dickson house, built with windows and lumber from the abandoned officers' quarters. Located in Bear Springs, it was purchased by Ludwig and Addie Ruth Knape, arriving from Brownwood, Texas, on November 29, 1918. The Knapes raised Angora goats and shipped apples, peaches, pears, apricots, French prunes, and garden produce. This house is now part of a Buddhist retreat. (Courtesy of Keith Klump.)

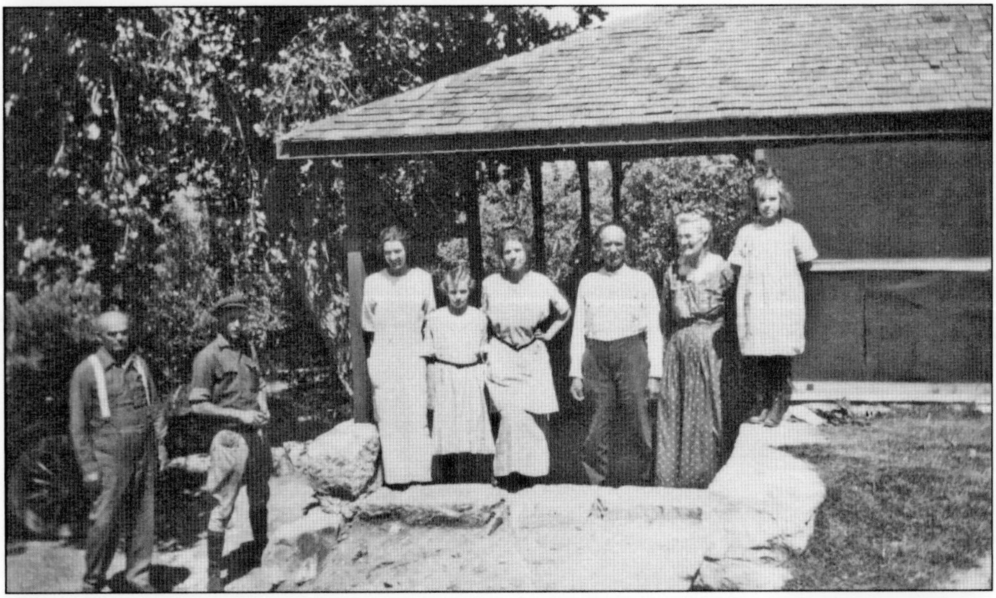

Shown about 1920 at the Knape residence, near Apache Pass, are, from left to right, Thomas Riggs, who owned a ranch just down the canyon; Ed Riggs; Delia Knape; Pauline Riggs; her mother, Anna Mae Riggs; Ludwig and Addie Ruth Knape; and Lillie Mae Riggs. Delia Knape later married cattle rancher John Sherman Klump and never wanted to see another goat in her life. (Courtesy of Keith Klump.)

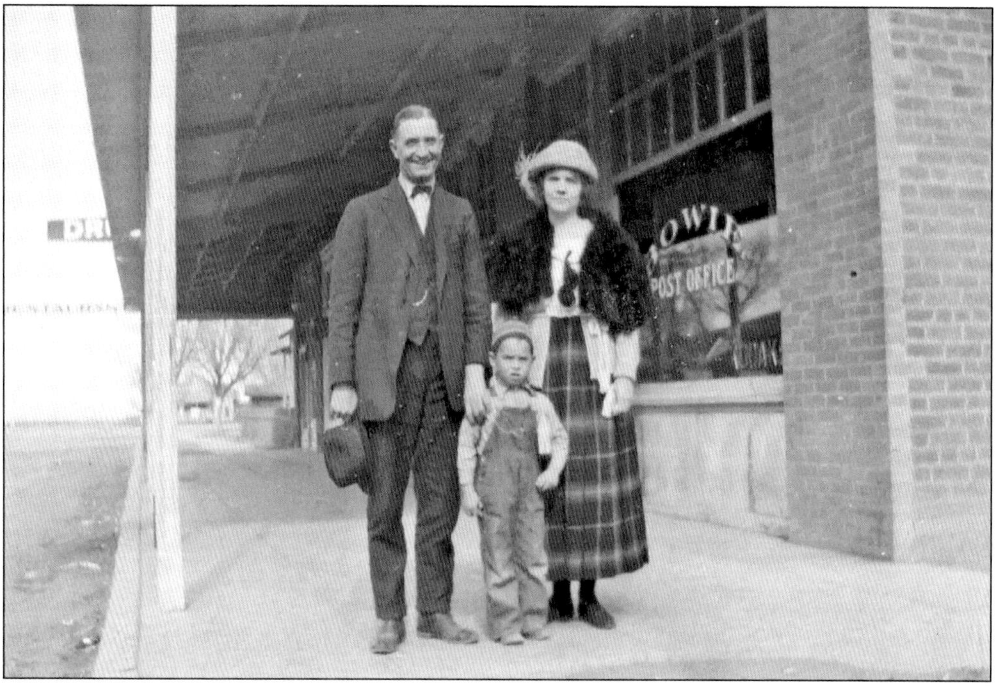

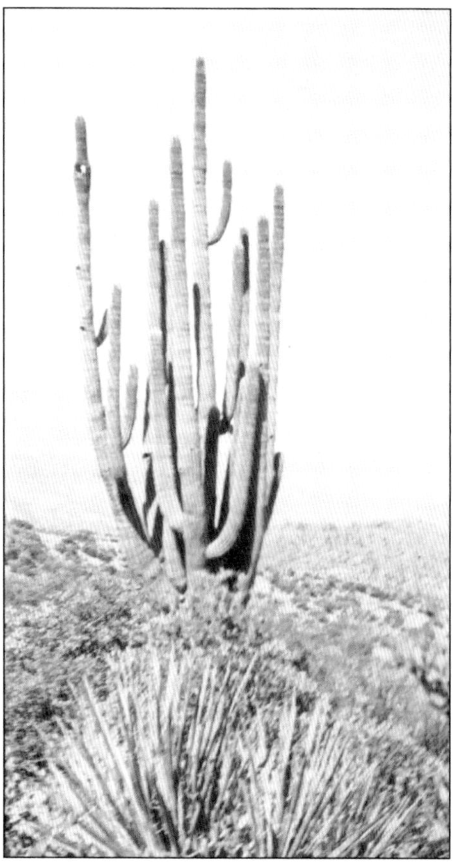

Thomas Riggs strung a telephone line from his place to neighboring ranches, the marble quarry, and into town. He had the first apiary and was president of the Bee Keepers Association. He extracted 1,700 gallons of fine cat's-claw honey in July 1915. He and his wife, Anna Mae Stafford, and their son Donald walk by the post office. Their two-story home burned in May 1922. (Courtesy of Ann Neerings.)

Although none exist there today, this one saguaro grew in Apache Pass. Edmund Wells mentions it in his book *Argonaut Tales.* An Apache boasted, to Sergeant Rodriguez, of torturing the sergeant's friend by binding his naked back against the thorns of the lone saguaro and dismembering him slowly until he died. To retaliate, the sergeant inflicted the same savage treatment upon the Apache. (Courtesy of Keith Klump.)

Two

Teviston and Bowie Station

The Southern Pacific Railroad was completed across Arizona to the New Mexico state line on September 22, 1880. The first depot was constructed in 1881, destroyed by fire the next year, and rebuilt. In 1883, the "Sunset Route" was opened, with daily trains between San Francisco and New Orleans serving southern Arizona. Fare from San Francisco to Tucson was $55. From 1885 to 1886, Charles Renaud, later of Pearce, was in charge of forwarding supplies. By 1885, Norton and Stewart's daily stage line from Bowie Station connected with stage lines for Clifton and Upper Gila, at Solomonville, and then connected with the stage line to Globe, at Camp Thomas. The fare from Bowie to Camp Thomas was $12.50, and from Bowie to Globe was $20. Layton Stage Line carried the US mail. In November 1888, the stage was robbed of mail and $800 between Bowie and Solomonville. Bandits from Mexico held up the stage in 1891. Leslie Webb and Jake Felshaw received 10 years in prison for stage robbery on this route in January 1894, and it was robbed again by W.T. Boyd in December 1894. The Gila Valley, Globe & Northern Railway made stage lines and freighters unnecessary. In 1923, the "Sunset Highway" (Highway 86) forced traffic east and west through town, instead of north and south. As airplane travel became popular, passenger trains were phased out. The last Golden State passenger train passed through on February 20, 1968. Amtrak has operated since May 1, 1971. Well-known people arriving on the train included three-time candidate for US president William Jennings Bryan and Pres. Calvin Coolidge, who visited on his way to attend the grand opening of Coolidge Dam. In 1936, the hotel and restaurant were torn down. The rest of the depot was bulldozed on January 18, 1988.

The town was known as both Teviston and Bowie Station, until it officially became Bowie on June 11, 1908. In 1923, townspeople voted down a movement by old-timers to change the name back to Teviston. Bowie has a justice of the peace but was never incorporated, so it never had a city council or mayor.

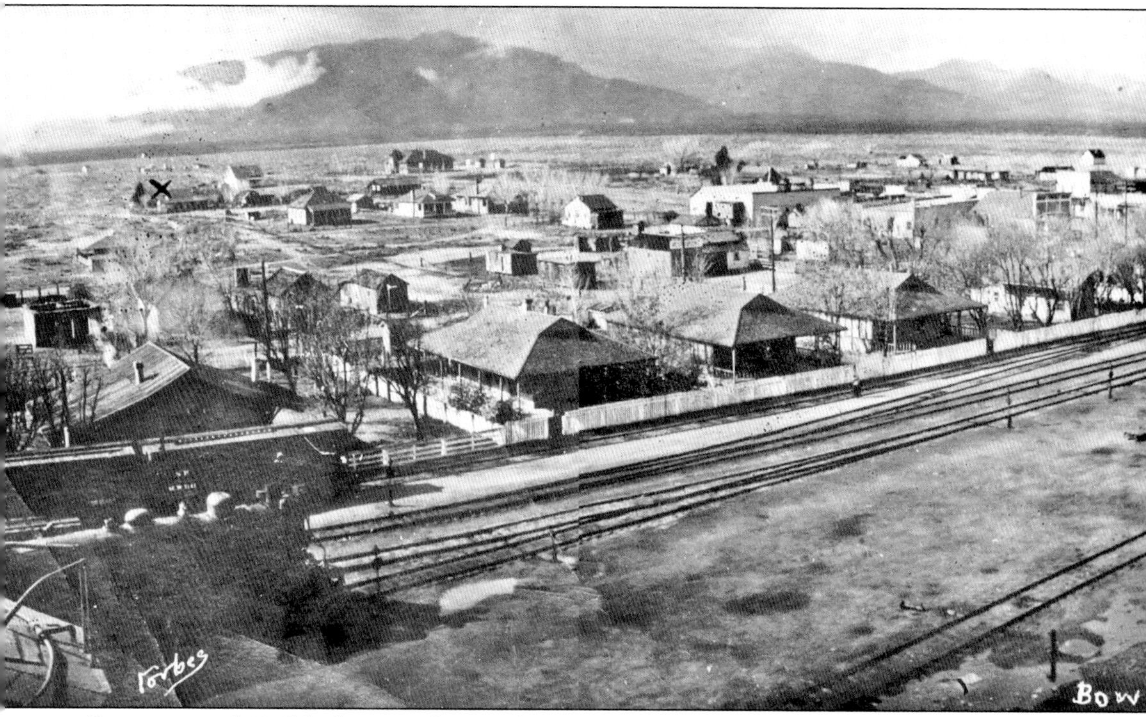

Bowie, around 1915 looking southwest, shows the Methodist church and the grammar school at upper left, at the end of Central Avenue. The railroad depot is at upper right. At lower right is the pump house. Businesses included Gurley's blacksmith shop, offering horseshoeing, plow work, and automobile repair. J.L. Torrence owned Bowie Hay & Grain. Earl Boyd operated Bowie Livery, Transfer, and Storage Company. Miss S.A. Wynn owned the Peoples Variety Store. Fong

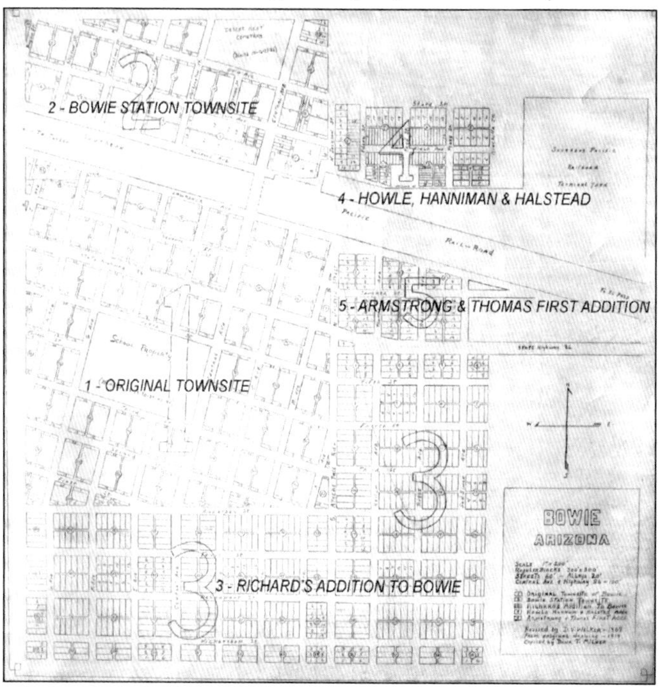

This 1919 map (revised) shows Bowie before Cochise County changed lettered avenues to presidents' names, after 1953. Stop signs were put in, but residents said, "We never stopped there before; we aren't going to stop there now." Kinchilla Street is named after Michael Kinchala, Tevis's partner, but spelled incorrectly. Other additions included the Monk Addition (surveyed by John Rockfellow in 1914), and Morning Side Acres subdivision. (Courtesy of Janice Grizzle.)

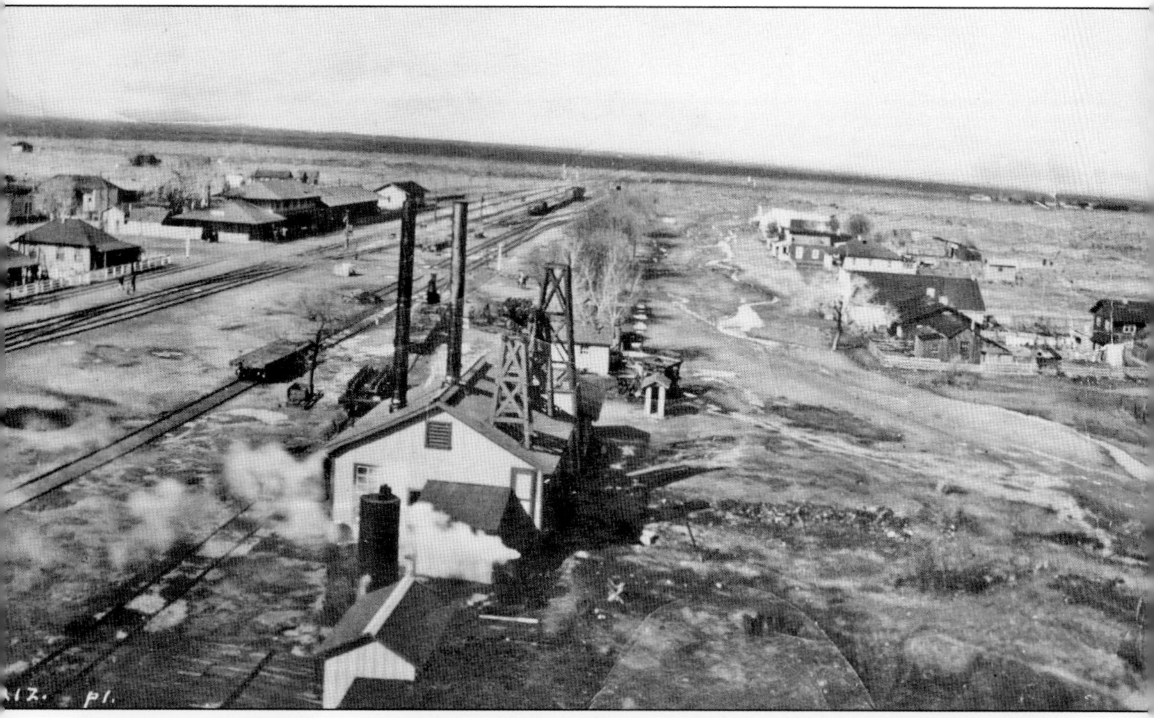

Do Lueng and W.F. Simmons had restaurants. Florence Bunch sold ice-cold drinks and ice cream sodas. There was Jaque Insurance Company, Morris Simon Mercantile, Schafer-Milner Mercantile, Bush and Currier's Lumber Yard, McDaniels' Barbershop, and Louie Wah's laundry, and Mrs. Ellis Wright and her sister Miss Whitaker were proprietors of a dressmaking and millinery establishment. (Courtesy of AHS No. 83145.)

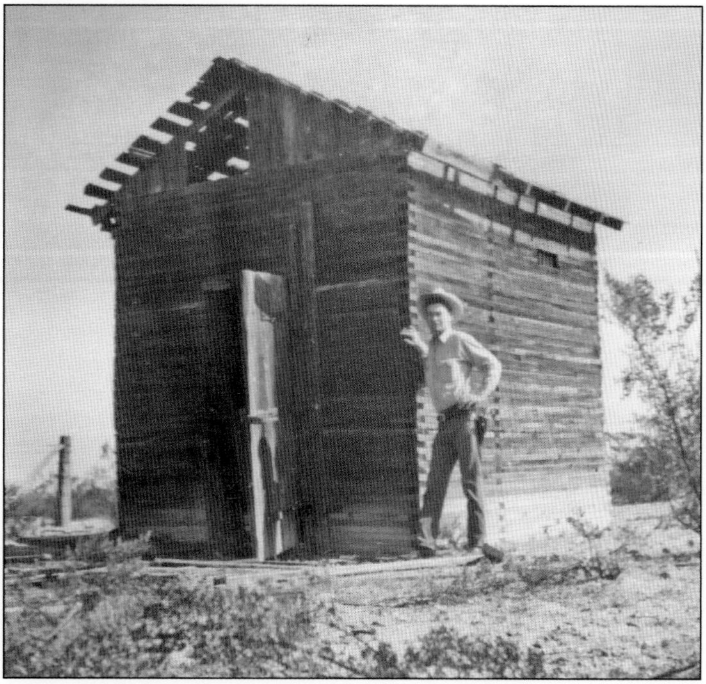

Les Jones, deputy sheriff in the 1950s, stands beside the first jail, built about 1890. Prisoners were chained to a large iron ring in the concrete floor. On July 30, 1915, the new jail was finished, built by G.M. Porter for $685. The Cawood brothers furnished the stone, gravel, and sand. The jailor's wages were $36 a month. The third jail, with the justice of the peace's office, was built in 1957. (Courtesy of Barbara Blandin.)

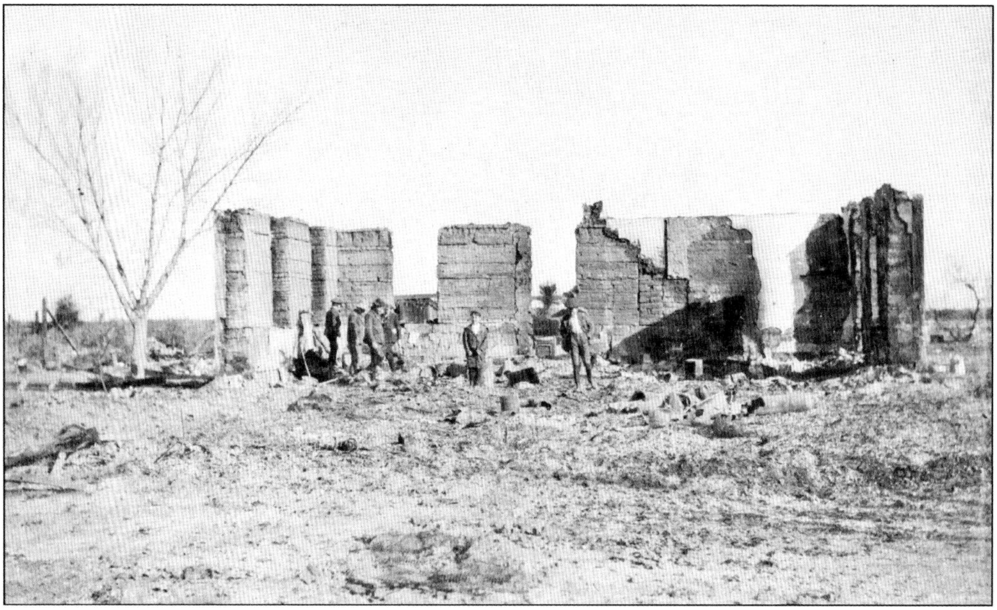

Only ruins remain of the Tevis Hotel, built in 1881 and destroyed by fire from an oil heater in 1908. It was located across the track from the Southern Pacific Hotel. James Tevis and Julian Navarette erected the adobe walls with an upper story containing four rooms. At the rear are portions of a high adobe fence, half a block long. (Courtesy of University of Arizona Special Collections.)

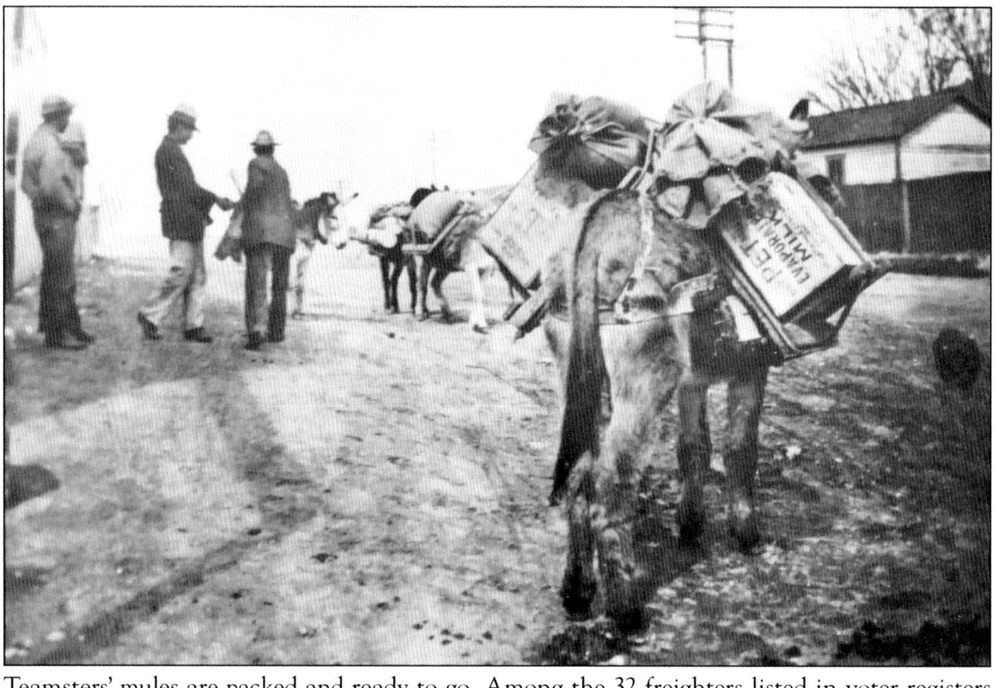

Teamsters' mules are packed and ready to go. Among the 32 freighters listed in voter registers from the 1880s are Alvia Don Alger (mail carrier), David Barney, Shem Wilson, J.W. Dibble, Nick Maringer, Pablo Menendez, Joseph Parrier, Alfred Sapp, John Dooling, William Grey, W.H. Kirkland, Felipe Vialobo, John Clapp, Dan Cordova, Joseph Godin, Peter Granger, John F. Jeffords, Benjamin Minchey, John S. Warren, and John Boyd. (Courtesy of Janice Grizzle.)

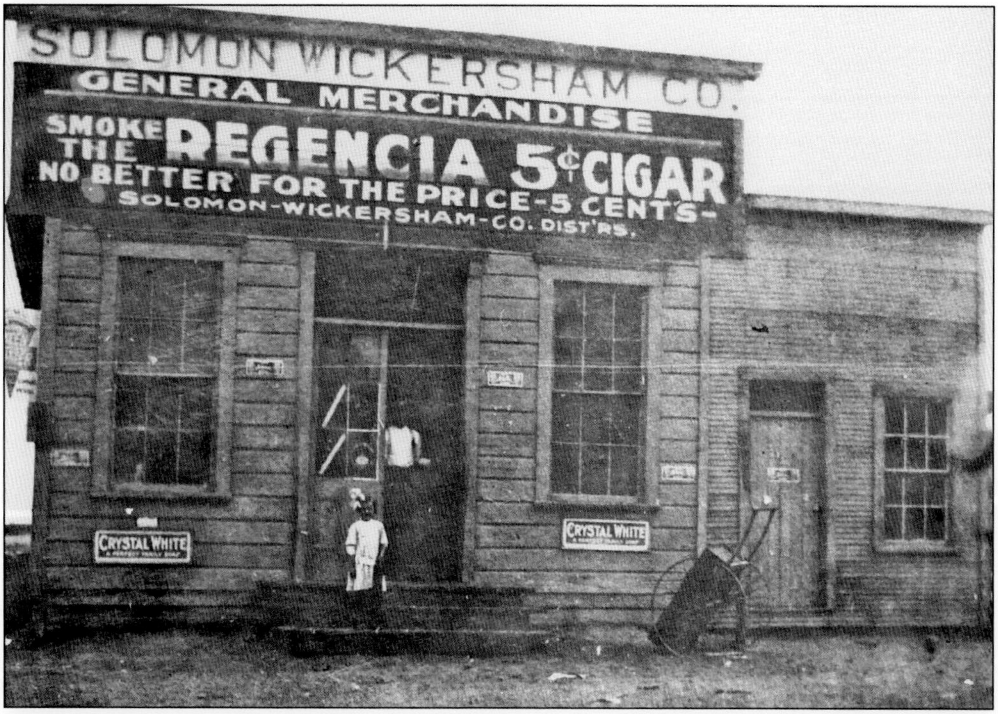

Adolph Solomon and David Wilmot Wickersham operated the most profitable business, the Solomon-Wickersham Company. They held the government freighting contracts and supplied many military posts and businesses in the San Simon Valley, Gila Valley, San Carlos, and Globe with hay, grain, groceries, and supplies. J.W. Weinberger purchased the store in 1918 and sold it to Meyers Brothers on March 2, 1923, with Charles Boll as manager. (Courtesy of William Kelly.)

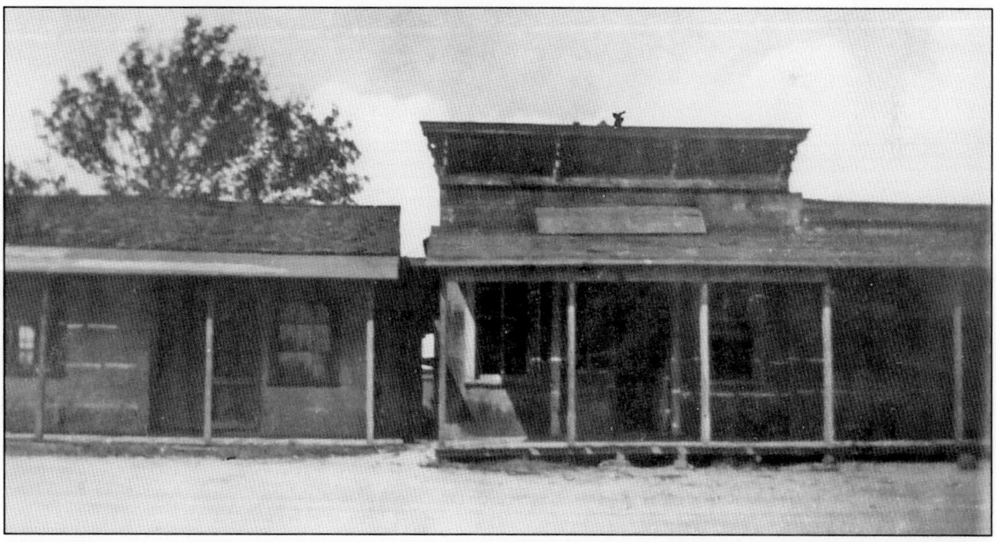

James Tevis gave the land for the very first school (left). Donated by Southern Pacific, railroad carpenters and painters worked on Sundays and after hours to complete it by May 1885. Judge Monk's niece Lizzie Greenwalt taught here in 1889, and Lizzie Hall was teaching in 1893. Mary Marringer's home (right) was 150 feet west of the Tevis Hotel and sold to John Boyd in 1894. (Courtesy of William Kelly.)

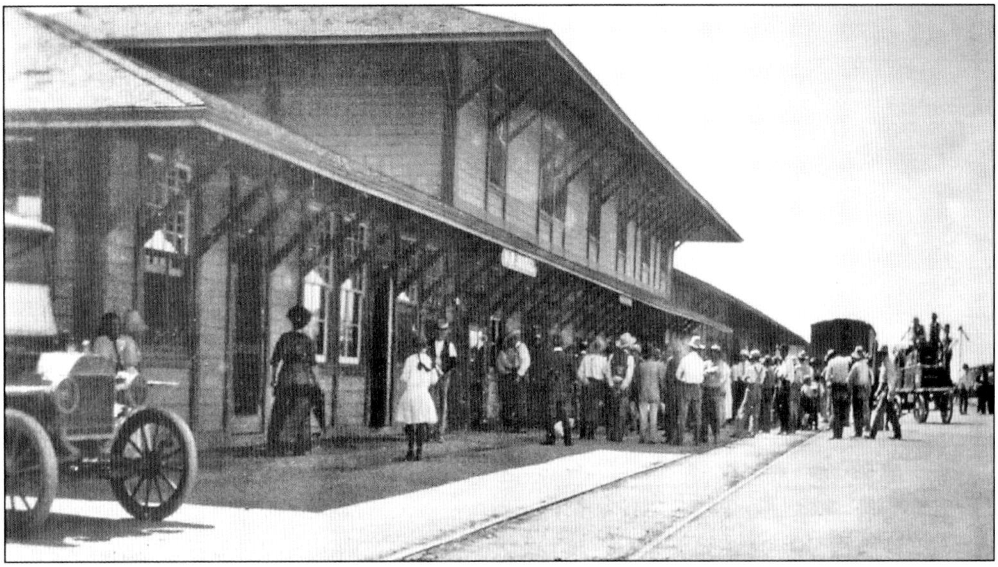

In 1914, people await the arrival of Pancho Villa. The depot, rebuilt about 1883, was 100 feet by 40 feet and included a freight house, agent's office, and upstairs family apartments. The two-story hotel was 80 feet by 40 feet with a wing for the kitchen and pantry and provided dinner for all trains. There was a 15-stall roundhouse, a nine-room bunkhouse, and one bathroom. (Courtesy of Bowie Justice Court.)

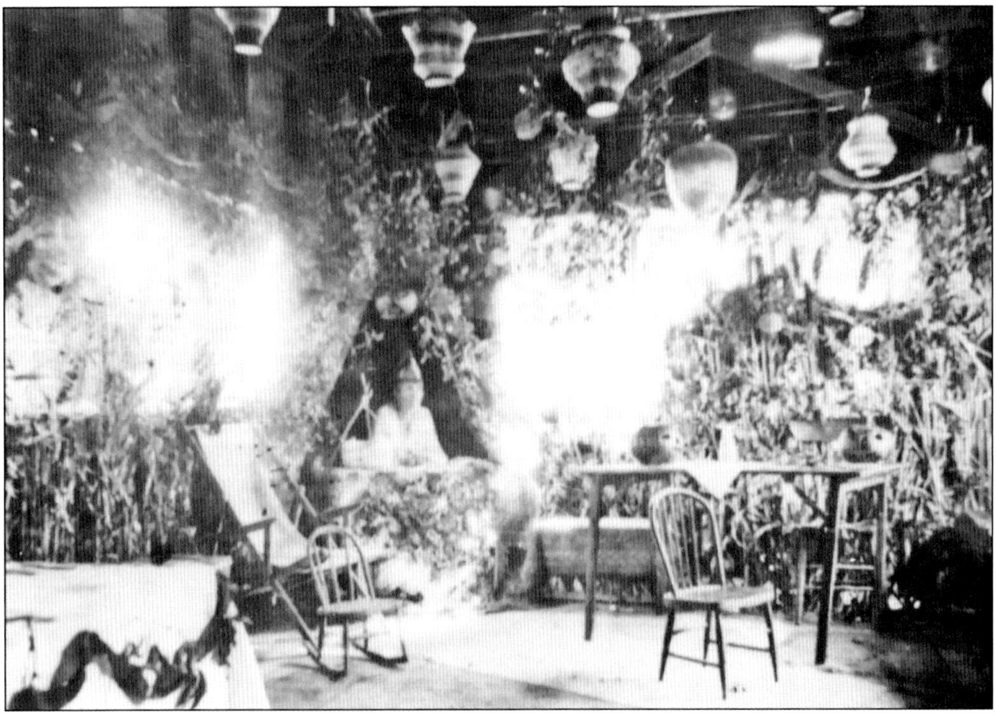

Lola Blake Tomlinson took this photograph of the Beer Garden, the restaurant inside the SP Hotel. The special table was decorated for Pancho Villa. The electric generators in the Southern Pacific yard provided the electricity for the lanterns hanging from the ceiling. The depot was remodeled in 1918, at a cost of $20,000. (Courtesy of Janice Grizzle.)

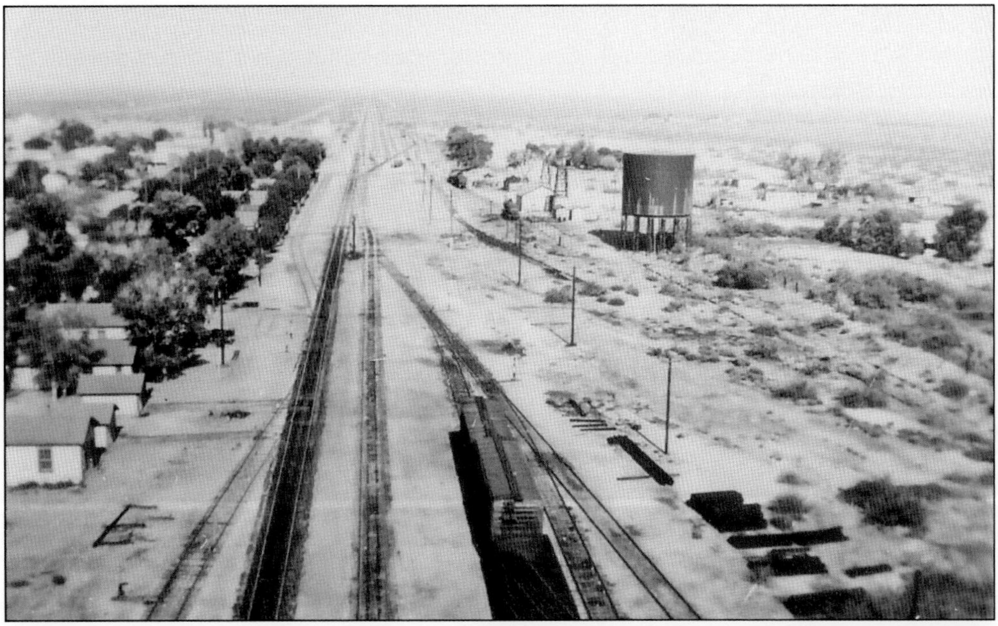

Looking west from the coal chute, the water tank at upper right was built in 1915, doubling the capacity of the original tanks, which were removed. In 1917, the freight division was established with 12 addition crews. The Doodlebug, an engine with two cars, ran on the tracks of Arizona Eastern, carrying passengers, luggage, and freight to Safford and Globe. (Courtesy of Gregory Chavez.)

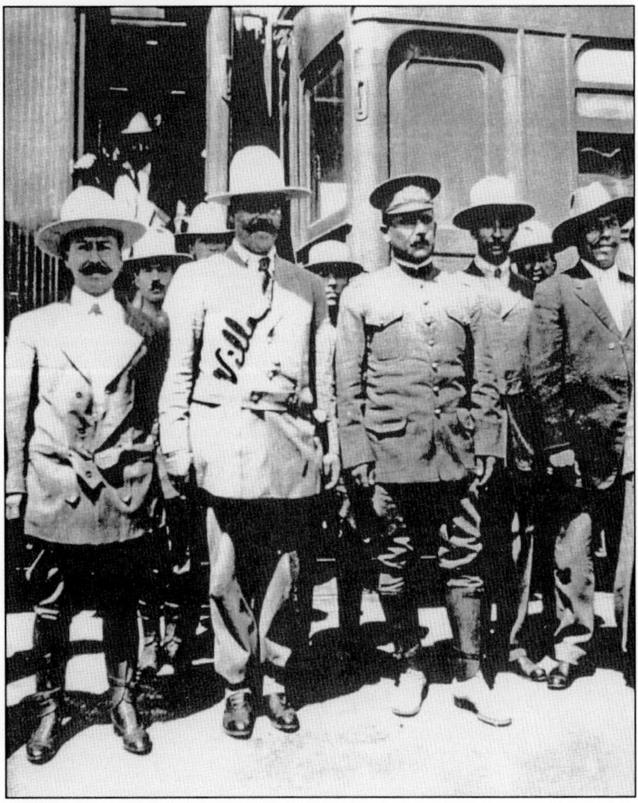

Pancho Villa (second from left), Alvaro Obregon (third from left), and troops were transported, under orders of President Madero, through El Paso to Nogales. On August 27, 1914, the special train had a passenger car, flat cars for artillery, and boxcars for horses. A band played Mexican music while they enjoyed their dinner. Refusing a special table prepared for him, Villa chose to sit with his back to the far wall. (Courtesy of Janice Grizzle.)

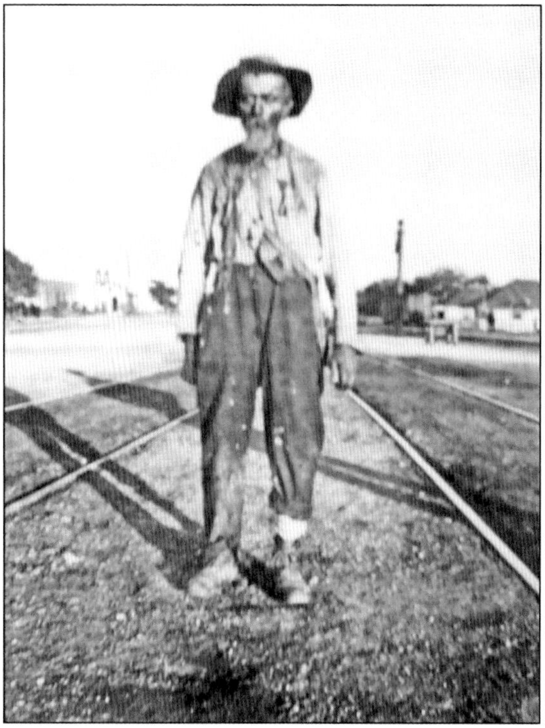

Arizona Charlie (real name never known) imagined he was employed as a railroad trackwalker. For years, tramping back and forth between El Paso, Texas, and Indio, California, his meager supplies were frequently robbed by hobos. He refused offers of housing or rides, concerned that a bad piece of track may be overlooked. Supposedly, he had never mentally recovered from the death of his wife and family at a train crossing. (Courtesy of Janice Grizzle.)

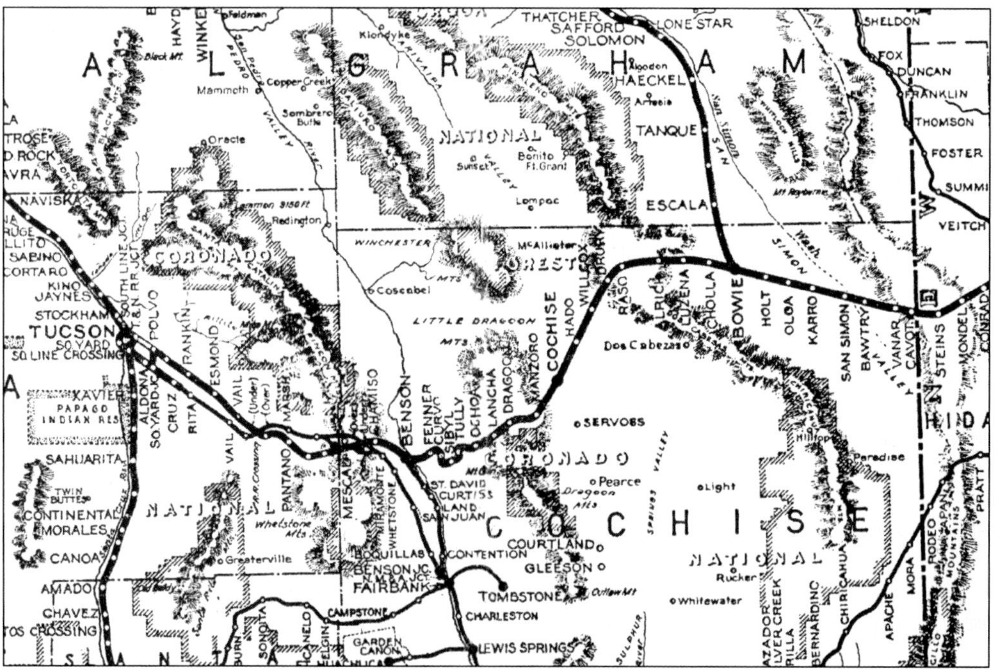

An old railroad map shows the many stations or sidings along the track where the trains would fill up with water and coal. There were six between Willcox and Bowie, three between Bowie and San Simon, and three between Bowie and Solomonville. Sometimes, entire families lived there and at other times, only one overseer. Olga had a school. The depot and pump house at Tanque burned January 14, 1924. (Courtesy of Bob Gaston.)

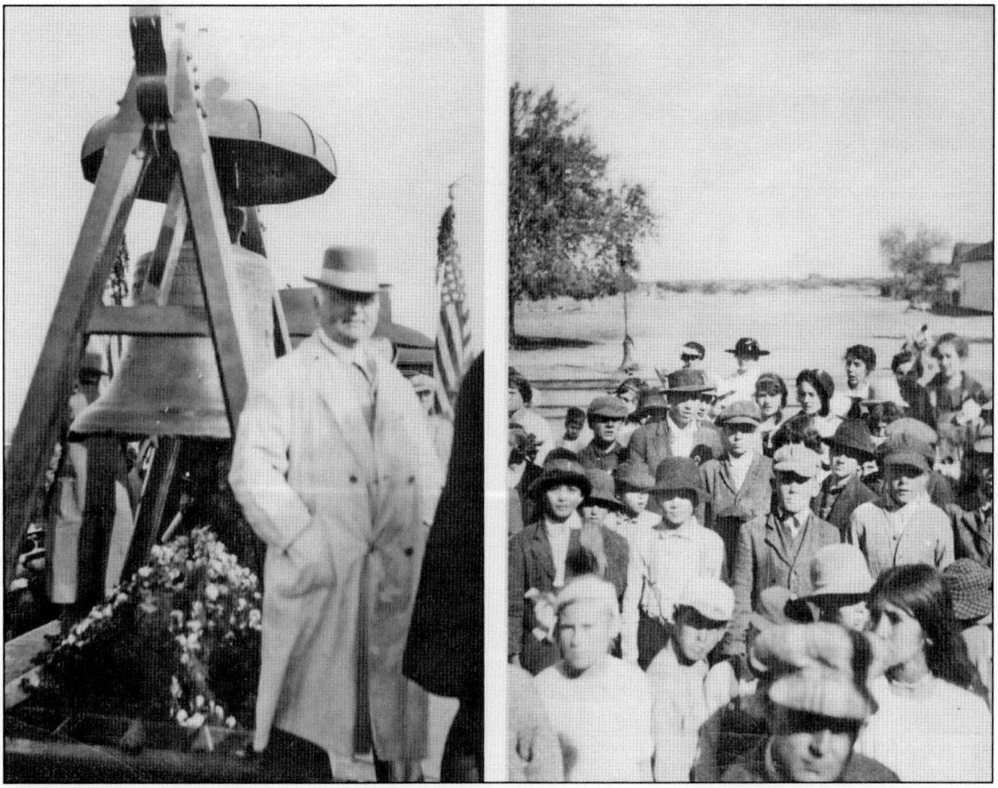

Schoolchildren from Bowie and the Nine-mile School crowd around to see the special train carrying the Liberty Bell, one of America's most cherished relics, on November 16, 1915. The train stopped for only five minutes in each town. Souvenirs were thrown from the train car. Standing by the bell is Lieutenant Governor McClain of Pennsylvania, who accompanied the bell on its trip across America. (Courtesy of SSVHS.)

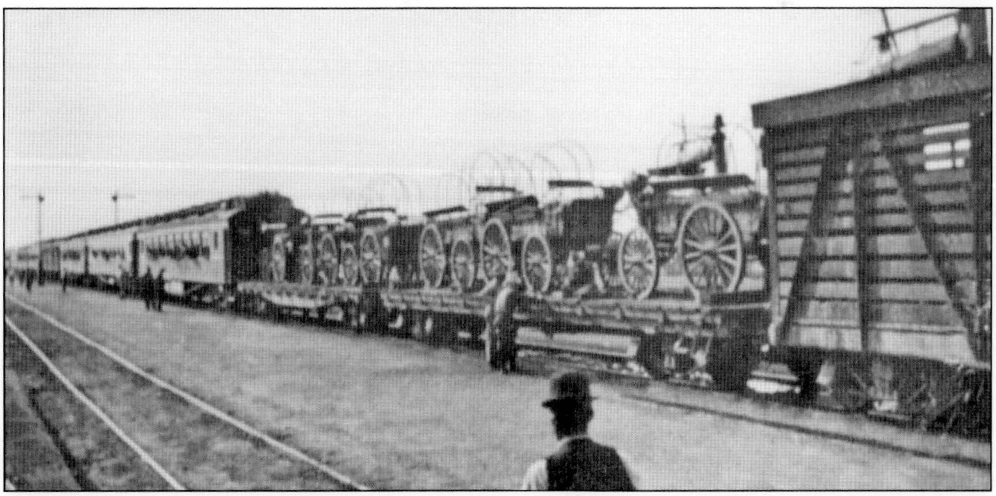

On July 13, 1916, the United States shipped military trucks over the rails for Army forces stationed in Nogales. It was necessary to defend the border during the Mexican Revolution, which began in 1910. Conflicts over the border ended August 27, 1918, at the Third Battle of Nogales with the Mexican army and their German advisors. (Courtesy of Janice Grizzle.)

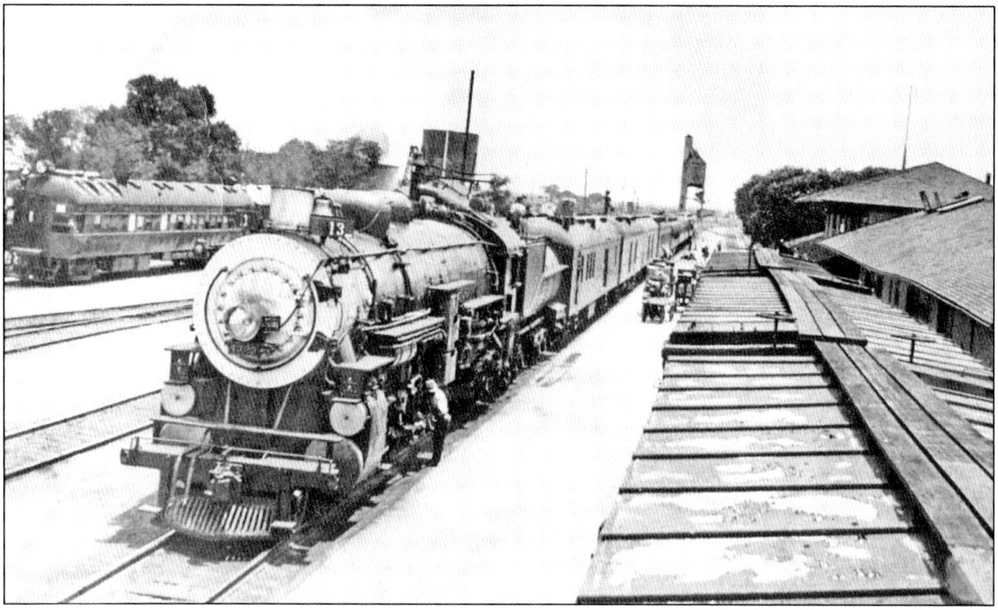

The 12:10 engine No. 4323 pulled into town on July 27, 1930. On March 13, 1935, special officer John Bradberry and immigration agent William Beckstrom were checking a freight train for hobos and illegal immigrants. A hobo named Jack Sullivan had a concealed blackjack. While arresting him, Sullivan stole Bradberry's gun and shot him in the stomach. Sullivan escaped but was later executed for the murder. (Courtesy of Janice Grizzle.)

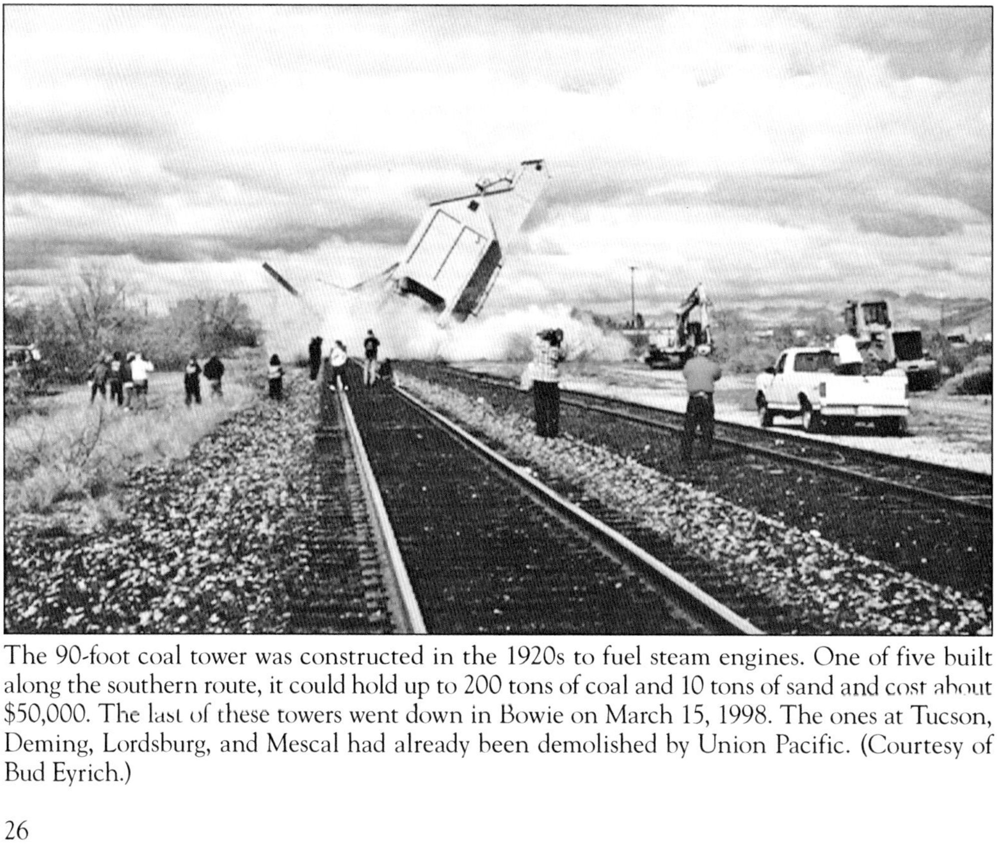

The 90-foot coal tower was constructed in the 1920s to fuel steam engines. One of five built along the southern route, it could hold up to 200 tons of coal and 10 tons of sand and cost about $50,000. The last of these towers went down in Bowie on March 15, 1998. The ones at Tucson, Deming, Lordsburg, and Mescal had already been demolished by Union Pacific. (Courtesy of Bud Eyrich.)

Three

Marble Quarry and Mining

Soldiers from the California Volunteers discovered a ledge containing gold. On October 31, 1868, they filed claim to the Harris Lode, named after one of the discoverers, located three-quarters of a mile south of the Fort Bowie parade ground. The Apache Pass Gold Mining Company later acquired it. This brought a brief boom in placer gold mining. The absence of railroads made it very difficult to move mining equipment into the area, and smelting had to be done in California. There was also the constant threat of the Apaches, who robbed the miners of work animals, tools, and supplies. After the Chiricahua Indian Reservation was closed, two miners named Todenworth and Kehoe thought it would now be safe to look for quartz veins. They were surprised and killed by renegade Apaches. The arrival of the railroad boosted precious metals production in Arizona, from fifth in the nation in 1879 to first by 1882.

Captain Tevis, General Hardiman, Major Dunn, Robert Patterson, and Lieutenant Hancock were partners in the Cochise Mining and Milling Company, which dissolved in 1883. In August 1881, Sheriff Behan filed a writ of attachment on Bowie Mining and Milling Company, including the Tevis claims, for failure to pay Lord Williams and Company $2,425. Other companies included Consolidated Gold Mines, Howle-Hanniman Gold Mining, Bowie Mines Development (in Buckeye Canyon), Kilmurry-Morgan (in Apache Pass), Voltare Mining, and Bowie Copper (the old Pete Simmons mine in Gold Gulch). There was Patrick Courtney's Ardmoniel Mine claim of 1897, William Thompson's Red Jacket Mine (in Happy Camp), the Willie Rose Mine, and the Cowboy Mine.

Besides ores, marble was mined at Marble Camp in Emigrant Canyon. Huge blocks of cut marble are there today, just as they were when the quarry closed.

For many years, developers persisted in drilling for oil. They finally gave up on making it a profitable venture.

Today, chabazite, or zeolite, is being mined. Bowie has the largest known high-grade deposit in the United States—and it is the only type that absorbs mercury.

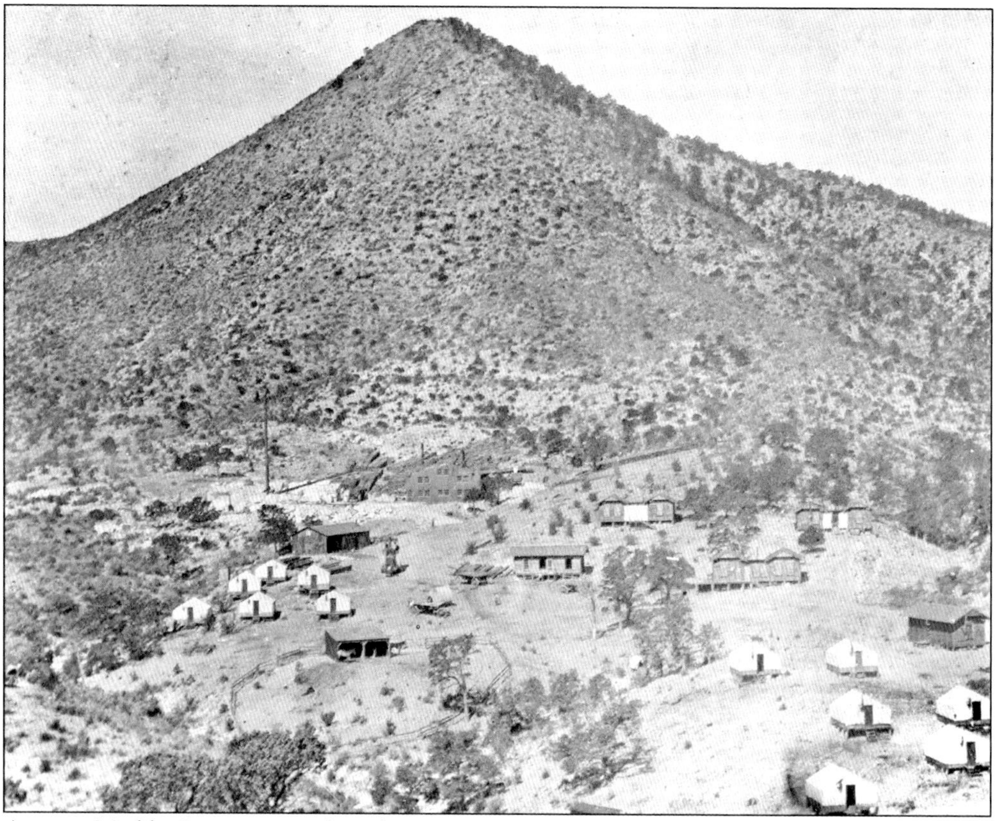

Arizona Marble Company was based in Denver, Colorado. Articles of incorporation were filed December 19, 1908. Coming from Denver were Dana T. Milner, as bookkeeper and office manager; John Kerr, engineer and general supervisor; and John Kaiser, as teamster and "good man Friday." Six wells blasted into the rock provided water. Fourteen miles of road had to be built, three miles of it through the mountains. At Marble Camp, 100 men were hired. Most of them were single and lived in tent houses. John Dickson was master mechanic and ran the blacksmith shop, and his wife, Hester, cooked. Fong Doo, another cook, was awakened by a skunk in his tent, killed it with his bare hands, and had to burn all his possessions. The mine consisted of 11 claims, totaling 1,760 acres. (Both, courtesy of Dewain Lockwood.)

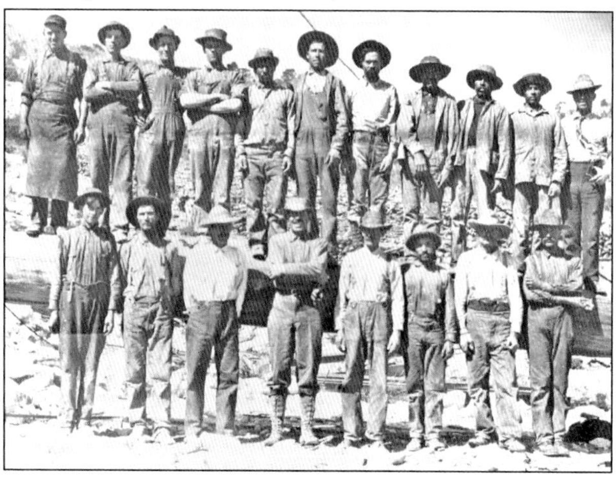

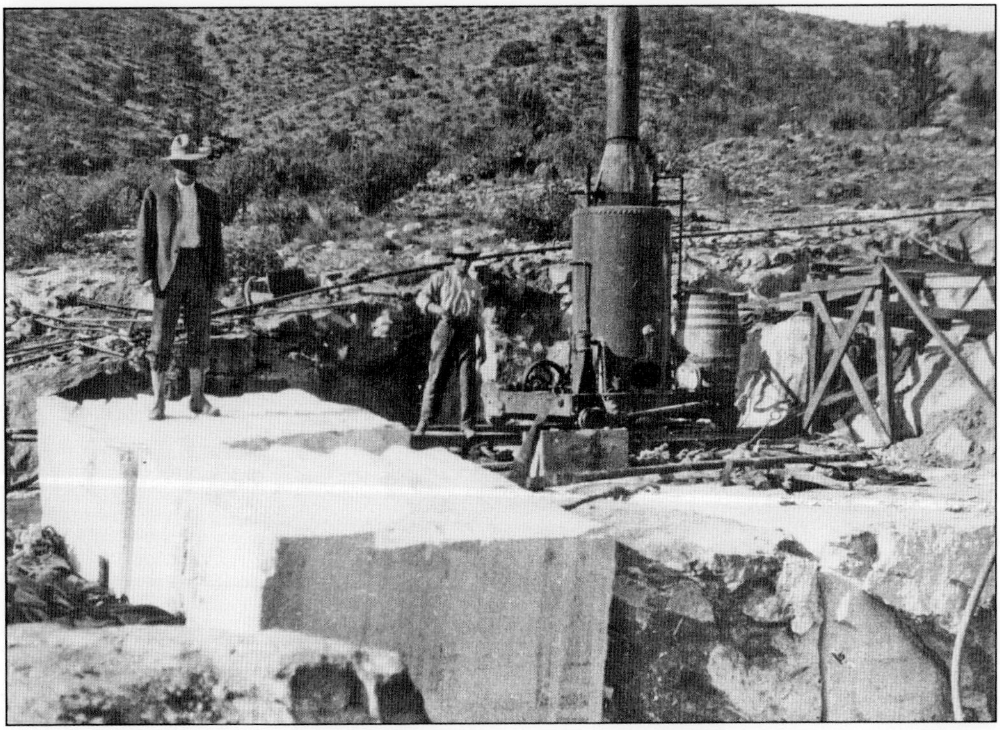

Steam tractors hauled six wagons, each carrying a large marble block. They were loaded on trains at Olga and shipped to Denver, Chicago, New York, and Los Angeles. Buildings in Denver finished entirely from Bowie marble included the First National Bank, International Trust, and the Tramway. Quarry operations were shut down in 1911. The bridges washed out in a flood in 1922, and the corporation closed in 1937. (Courtesy of SSVHS.)

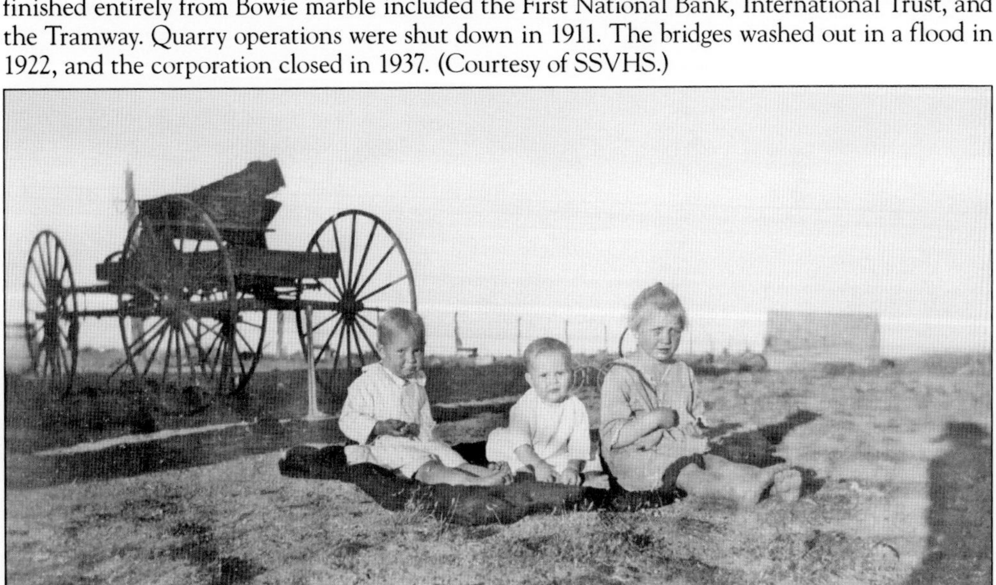

Grace, Neva, and Euline Allen were daughters of Clyde and Mertie Bell Anderson Allen, who made homestead entry on July 16, 1920, in Gold Gulch. Oil derricks from the "oil boom" of 1917 can be seen in the background. Euline married Ernest Harmon, a carpenter and owner of the Home Café. Their children were Charles, Marcia, Ernestine, Thelma, Dora, and Joe. (Courtesy of Bill Allen.)

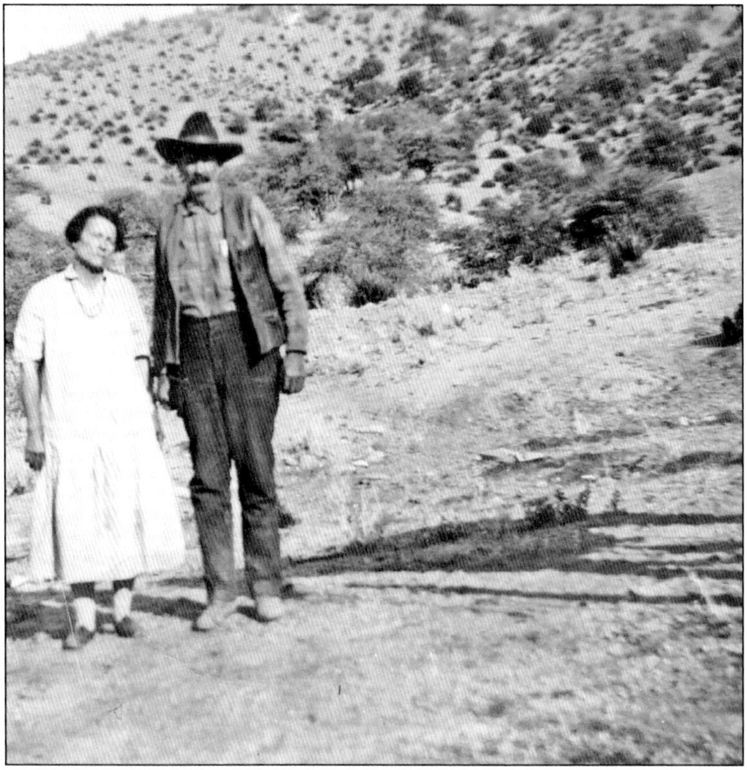

Lula and Tom Quillan, residents since 1904, owned Helen Dome Mine and Apache Pass Gold Mining Company with brothers-in-law J.A. Stanfield and Theophilus K. Mitchell. Two versions exist for changing the name of Cow Peak to Helen's Dome: A girl named Helen was running from Apaches and jumped to her death. Or, it was named after Captain Hackett's wife, Helen, who often climbed the peak with friends. (Courtesy of Keith Klump.)

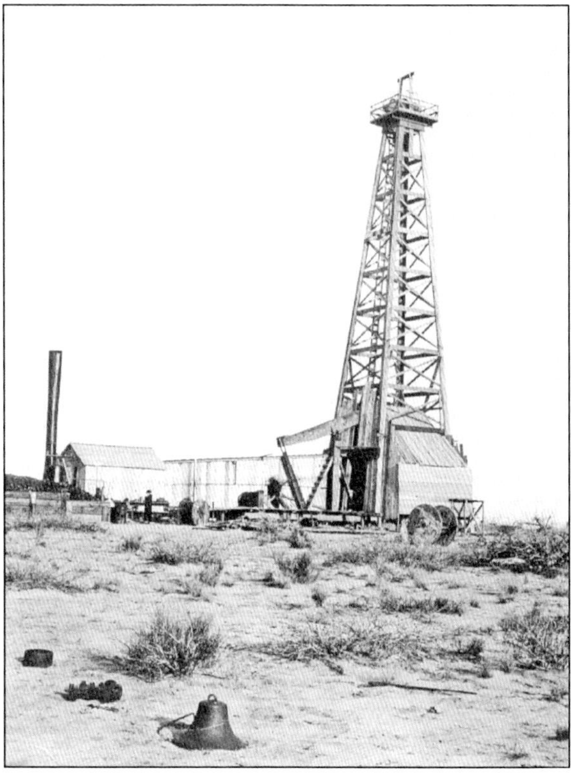

In November 1910, oil claims were filed on Mack Freeman's ranch east of Escala Station on the Arizona Eastern Railway. Experts predicted excellent oil production: "The most wonderful discovery in recent years will rival the oilfields of California." In 1920, US Oil Refining Company drilled to 4,000 feet. Oil was found, but they were not able to stop the flow of the artesian water. (Courtesy of Janice Grizzle.)

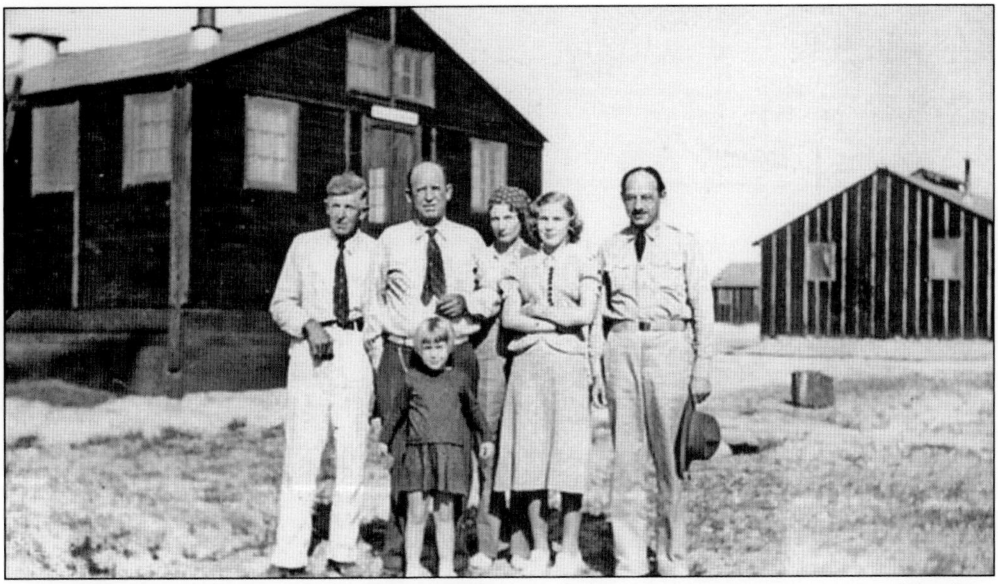

Of three Civilian Conservation Corps (CCC) camps, this one was in the mining area of Buckeye Canyon. Shown in 1938 are, from left to right, Ernest Harmon, Francis Marion Upham (who owned the lumber company in Bowie), his wife, daughter Frances, the director (unidentified), and Mary Anne Upham, in front. They lived in Army barracks and ate in mess halls. The focus was road building, land conservation, and reclamation projects. (Courtesy of Ed Crews.)

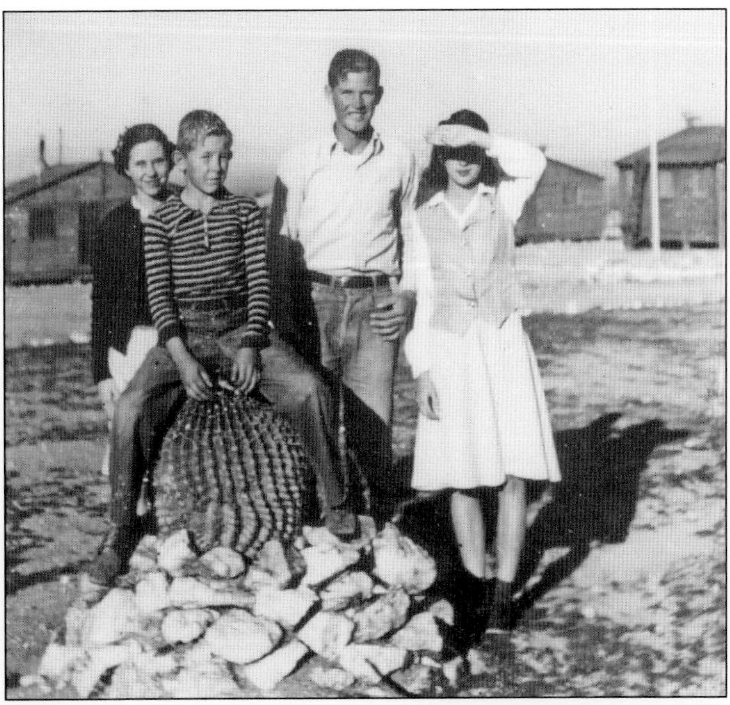

At the 12A CCC Camp in 1938 are, from left to right, Patricia Doyle, Charles Harmon, Bill Allen, and Neva Jane Connelly. The camp was torn down in about 1940. Patricia married Sam McKee in 1945. Bill married Wilma Bailey, from Bisbee. Their son Thad Allen became commandant of the US Coast Guard and was in charge during British Petroleum's 2010 Gulf of Mexico oil catastrophe. (Courtesy of Ed Crews.)

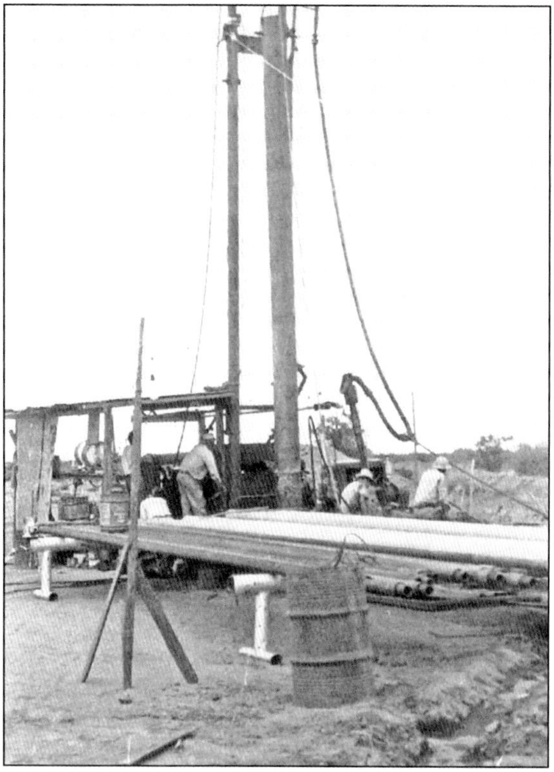

A drill is in operation at the Buckeye Apache Mine on October 23, 1949. A terrible accident here on February 16, 1903, claimed the lives of William Steel and Patrick O'Donnell. Steel dropped frozen dynamite into boiling water to thaw. The explosion threw him 25 feet and O'Donnell 150 yards, part of him landing in a tree. William Gravelle and Ezra Madison were not expected to survive. (Courtesy of the Cooke family.)

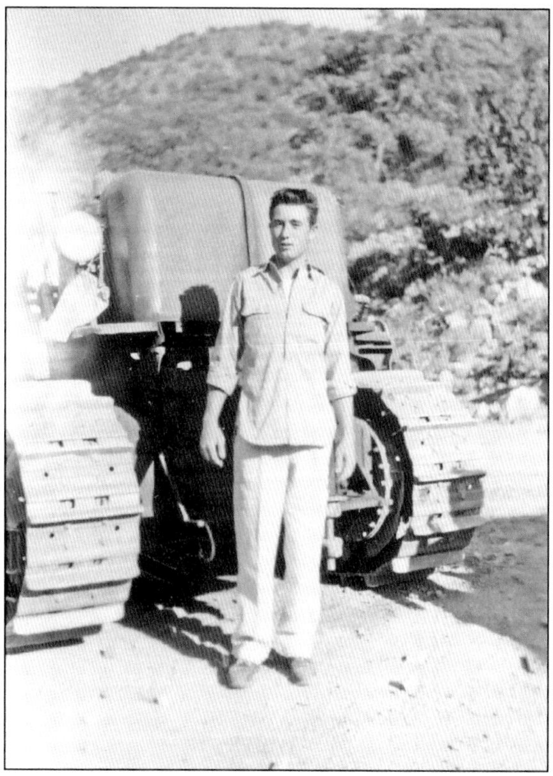

Tommy Cooke, pictured in 1950, now mines chabazite. The first to be marketed in the United States was from Bowie. This site contains the only deposit of any industrial size in North America. The lower quality upper bed is used for cementation and water filtration. The higher quality lower bed is used to absorb mercury and remove carbon dioxide and hydrogen sulfide from methane. (Courtesy of the Cooke family.)

Four

Early Families and Businesses

Joseph Jaque was a huge promoter of Bowie through the *Bowie Enterprise* newspaper and his real estate office. Other publishers were T.M. Winsor, W.E. Rood, LeRoy Lancaster, N. Sands, and Dr. William Gillespie. Estelle Jaque ran the new Bowie Hotel in 1916. Hotel Howle became the Natic Hotel, with owners Bud and Tennessee "Tiney" Roten Snow, Mary Jane Contraman, Shade Kelley, and Samuel Davis. H.R. Hindman was proprietor of the Annex Hotel, which he sold to Dana Milner. It was subleased to Mrs. R.E. Ballou, of Cochise, in 1918. In 1931, Mollie Smith was proprietor.

Other businessmen who made a tremendous difference in the promotion and growth of Bowie were Dana Milner, Albert Spikes, Larren Scott, and Douglas Welker. Bowie Water Company and Light Plant was organized by Joseph P. Schafer, F.L. Torrence, J.J. Hutchison, Dana Milner, and N.G. Richards. In 1917, Milner and Hempstead bought the Tevis block to build apartments, and the first subdivision of five-acre parcels was offered. The 1917 Red Light Abatement Act made it illegal to rent property for purposes of prostitution. The same year, the businessmen formed the Bowie Board of Trade, a forerunner of the chamber of commerce.

After Highway 86 was completed, motels replaced the hotels. Gasoline stations, garages, and cafés served the numerous travelers on the road. The business owners took pride in the facades of their buildings, creating some noticeably unique ones.

As Interstate 10 was being built, Bowie fought to have the Safford Interchange intersect the town and for an interchange that would bring the tourists into downtown. They lost both battles. Interchanges were put one mile out on each side, and the Safford Interchange ended up in the middle of nowhere.

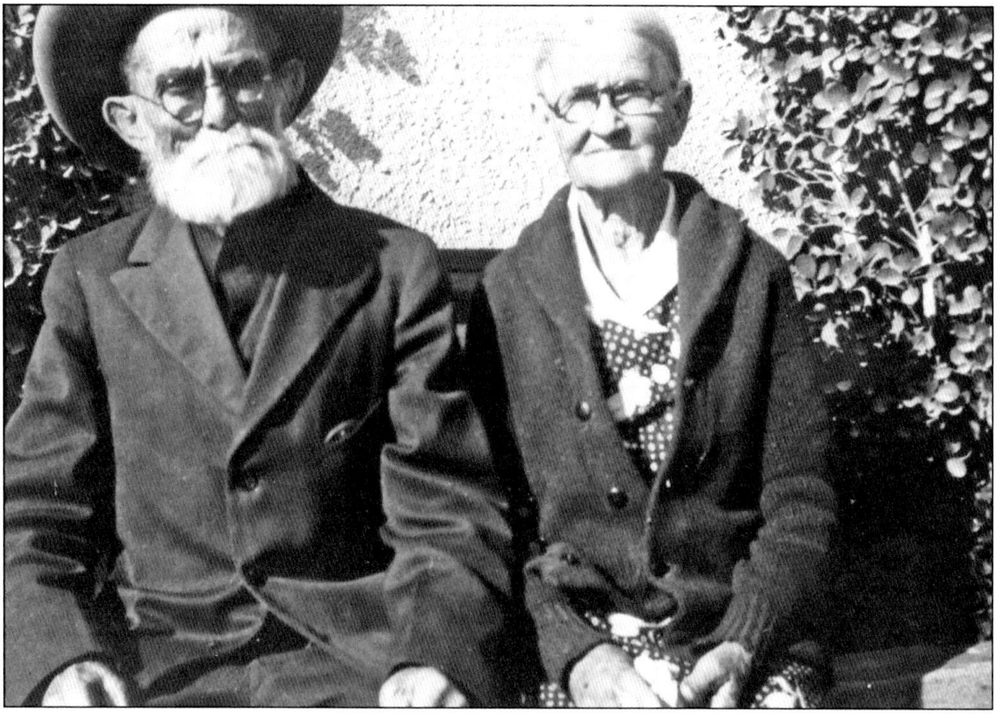

Xury White and Ann Eliza Hancock Pulliam came from Uvalde, Texas, filing for a homestead one mile north of town on January 18, 1912. Daughters May and Clara filed nearby homesteads. Daughter Thelma married William O'Connor, who worked for Southern Pacific. They also had a son, Roy. (Courtesy of Dewain Lockwood.)

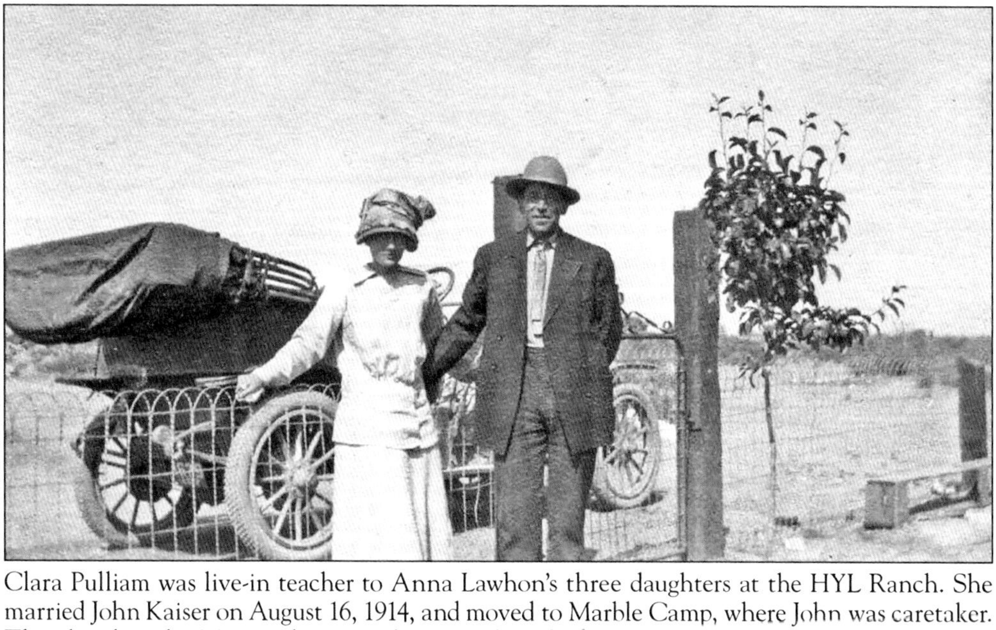

Clara Pulliam was live-in teacher to Anna Lawhon's three daughters at the HYL Ranch. She married John Kaiser on August 16, 1914, and moved to Marble Camp, where John was caretaker. They lived in the McNutt house. Whenever the telephone line broke, Clara would load the children on burros and go repair the line. They moved into town in 1922. Clara served as treasurer of the Yucca Garden Club. (Courtesy of Dewain Lockwood.)

Clara and John Kaiser's children were Velma Ann and Jack. Jack missed school because of illness, and they graduated together in 1935. Jack married Vida Ray Price and worked in Nogales. Velma Ann married Henry Dewain "Dutch" Lockwood. Dutch worked for Tanner Construction when paving Highway 86. He drilled the first deep irrigation well in 1948 and ginned the first bale of cotton in 1950. (Courtesy of Dewain Lockwood.)

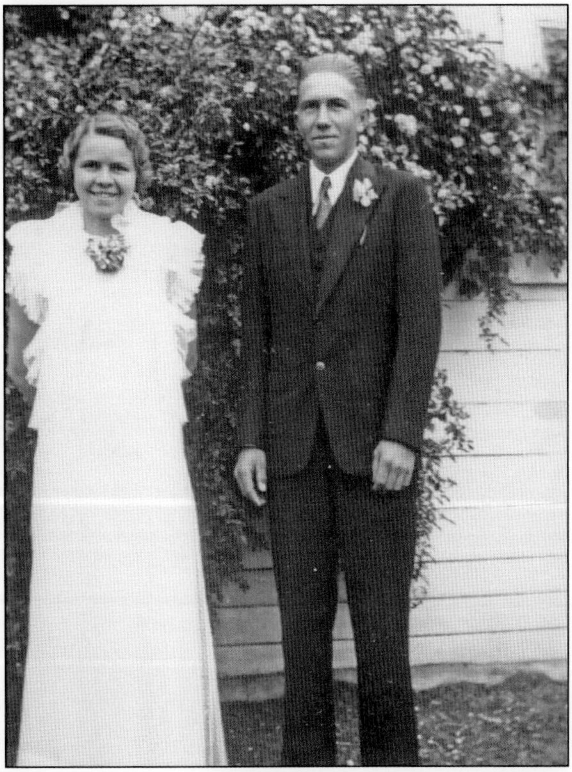

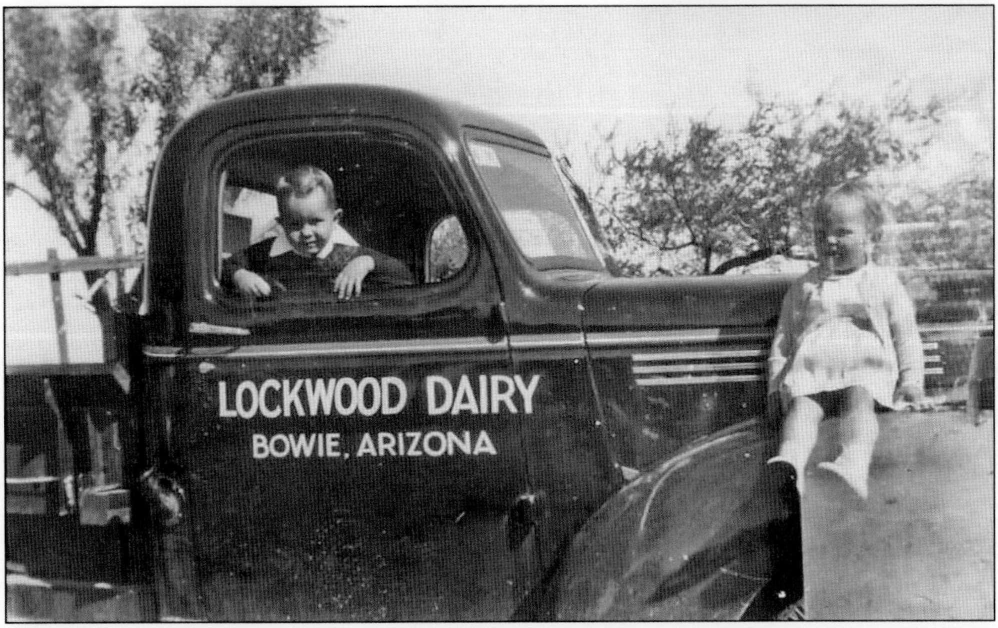

Velma Ann and Dutch started the Lockwood Dairy in 1943 on the old Xury and Anna Pulliam homestead, offering home delivery of milk, cream, and butter. Their son Dewain looks out the window as his sister Judith Ann sits on the bumper. After Dutch's death in 1954, the farm was leased to Leland Jones. Velma Ann worked at the Lone Star Café and as clerk for the justice of the peace. (Courtesy of Dewain Lockwood.)

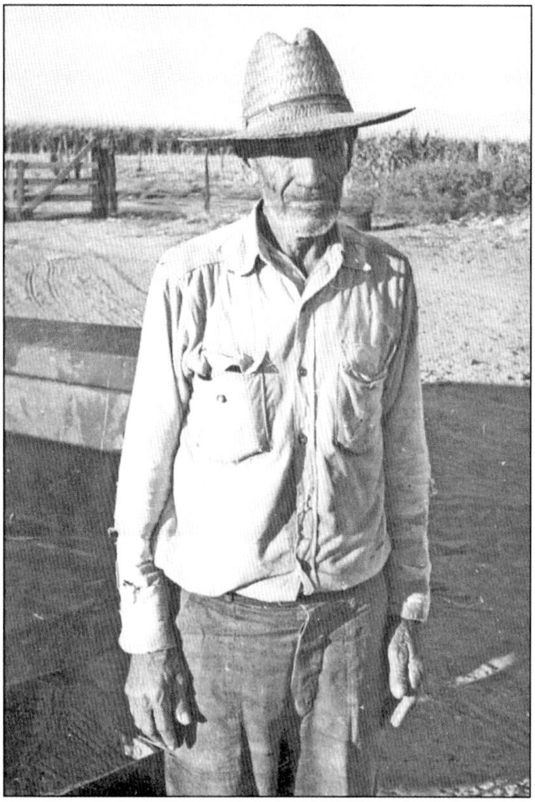

Alfonso "Tio" Jacques came to Bowie from San Andres, Mexico, in 1900. He worked for the railroad at Steins, New Mexico, at the rock crusher. Jacques was employed at the Mascot Mine, then as a cowboy for Anna Lawhon and Levy Knape. He worked at the goat ranch for the Gojkovich family and Albert Spikes. His wife was Gregoria Carrion. He died April 9, 1955. (Courtesy of Feliciano Jacques.)

Captain Burns, a Civil War veteran, had mining claims known as Gold Farm and Mineral Park. Large mining operations would send for him as an advisor. In April 1917, he went to the Soldiers Home in Sawtelle, California, where he ended his days. In September 1919, Bowie Garage was purchased by R.V. Misenhimer. In April 1924, George Cadman was proprietor. (Courtesy of Janice Grizzle.)

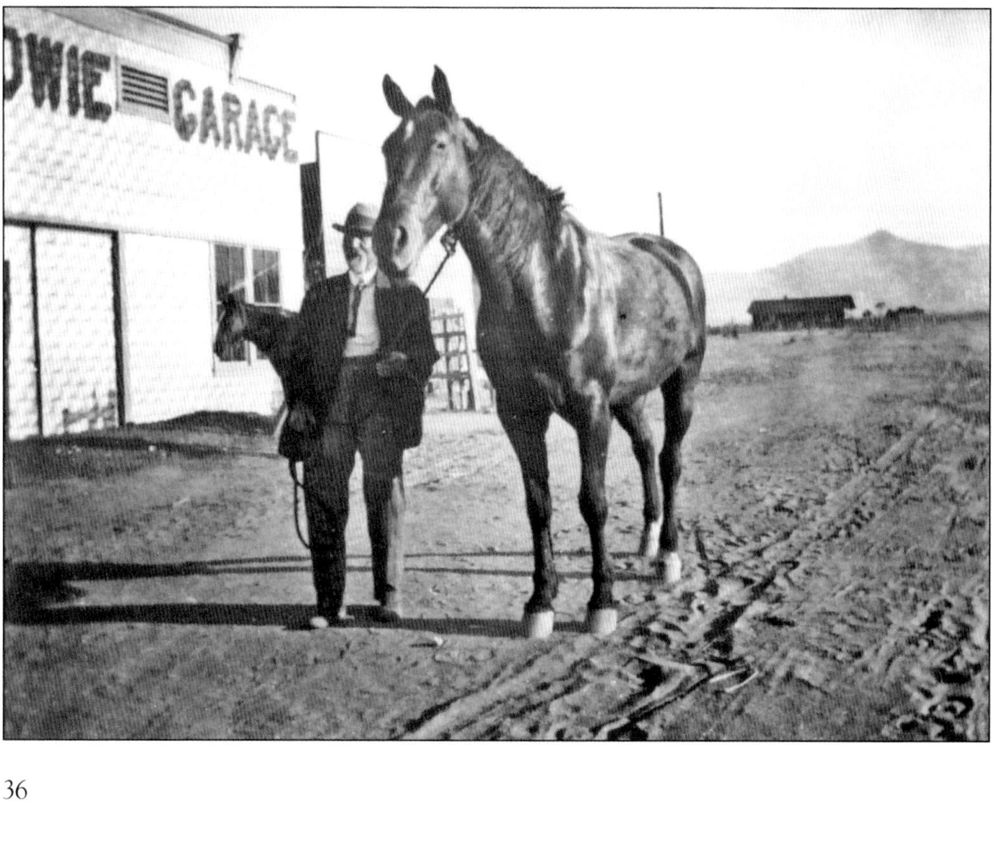

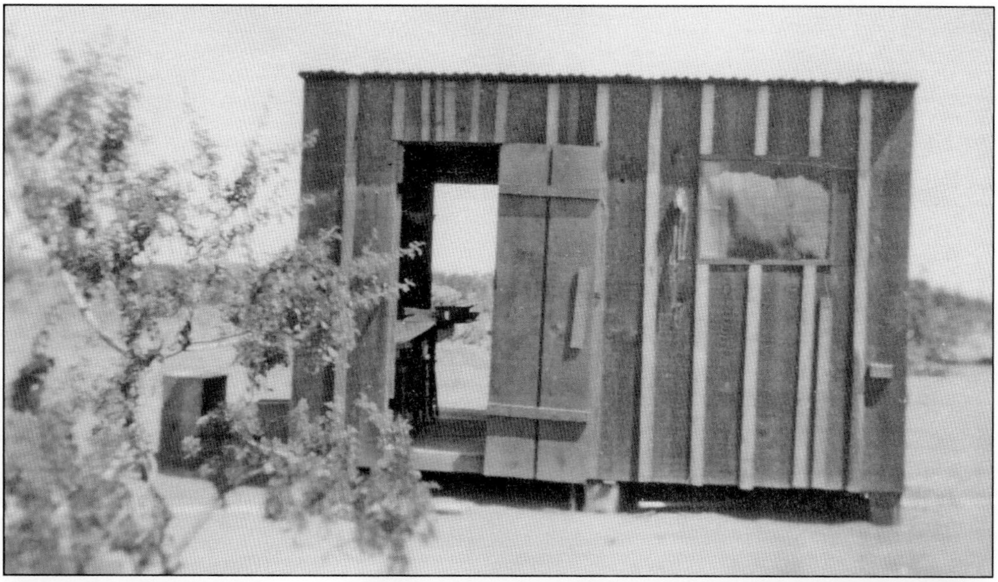

Larren O. and Welcome "Mimi" Scott arrived on August 2, 1915. Their first home was a railroad car with few, if any, amenities. Mimi wrote on the back, "This is how it looked when we got here." It was at Escala Station on the Arizona Eastern Railway, between Bowie and Safford. (Courtesy of Barbara Blandin.)

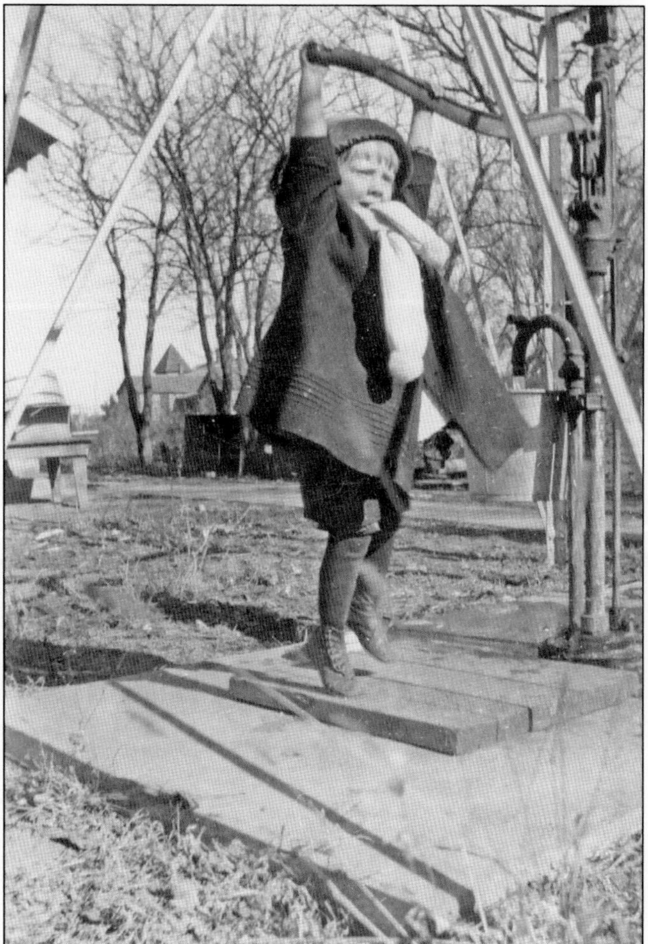

Welcome Scott, the daughter of Larren and Welcome "Mimi" Scott, born in 1919, swings from the water pump at the well in Bowie. She married William Yelton and had a son, Larren. Her sister Barbara Jean, born in 1921, married Doug Welker and was the first female justice of the peace, from 1982 to 1990. (Courtesy of Barbara Blandin.)

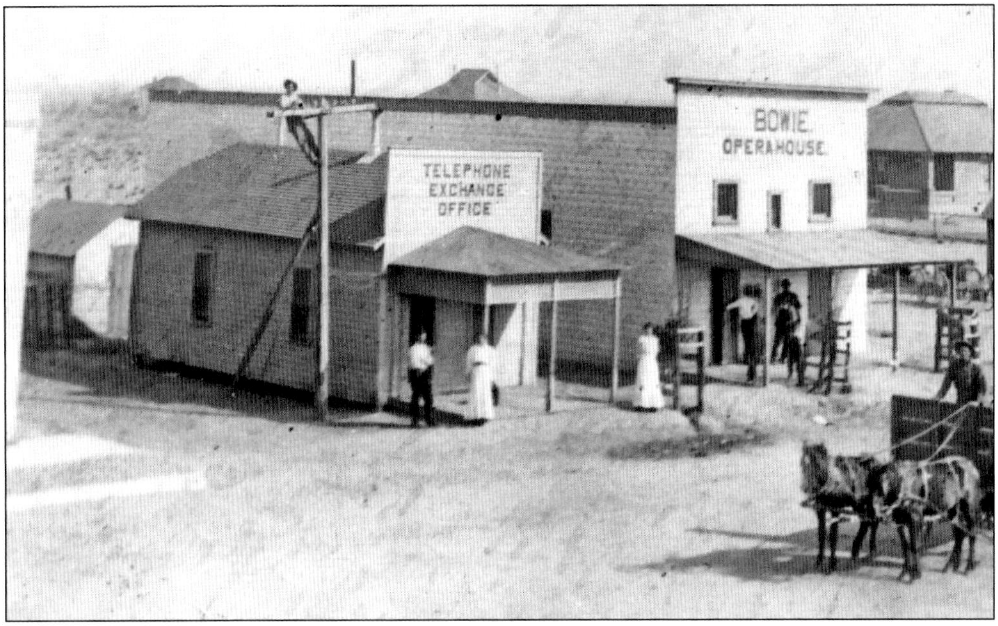

Minnie Plaster was in charge and answering calls since 1915 in the Mountain States Telephone Exchange office, owned by A.D. Adams. Next door, the opera house, owned by Thomas Riggs, provided space for town social events, guest performers, the Christian Church services, and school graduations. By 1917, moving pictures were being shown there and down the street in the Airdrome, owned by Virgil T. Howell. (Courtesy of Vic Boll.)

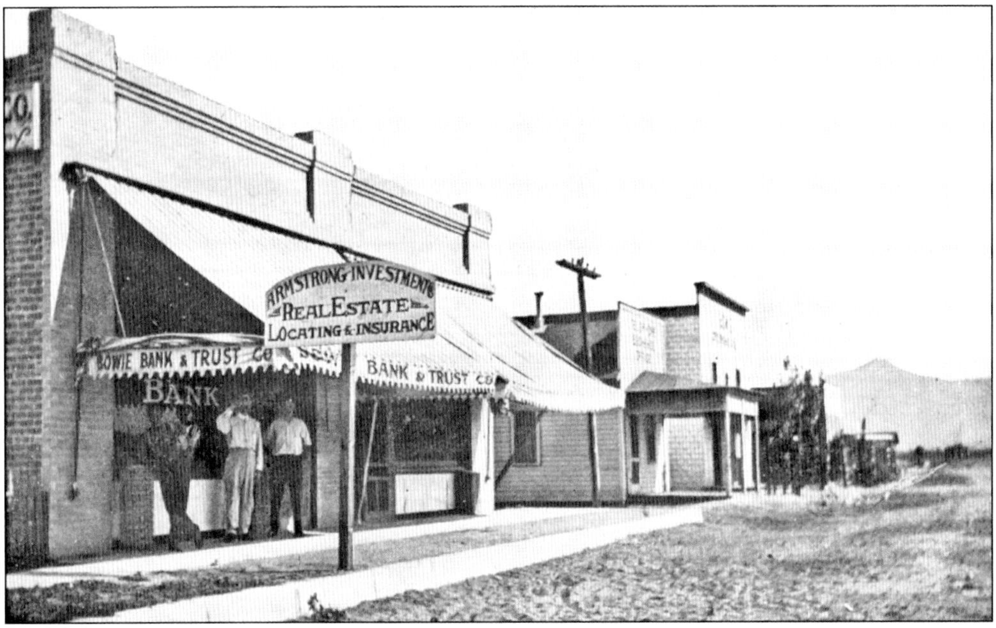

The Armstrong brothers opened the Bank and Trust with their real estate and insurance business. Built in 1912, it failed in 1915. The vault was found empty of its $3,500. Pres. Joseph Armstrong did not get far. He was apprehended in San Simon, on his way to Omaha. In August 1924, L.C. Riggs opened a meat market in the telephone exchange building next to the opera house. (Courtesy of Barbara Blandin.)

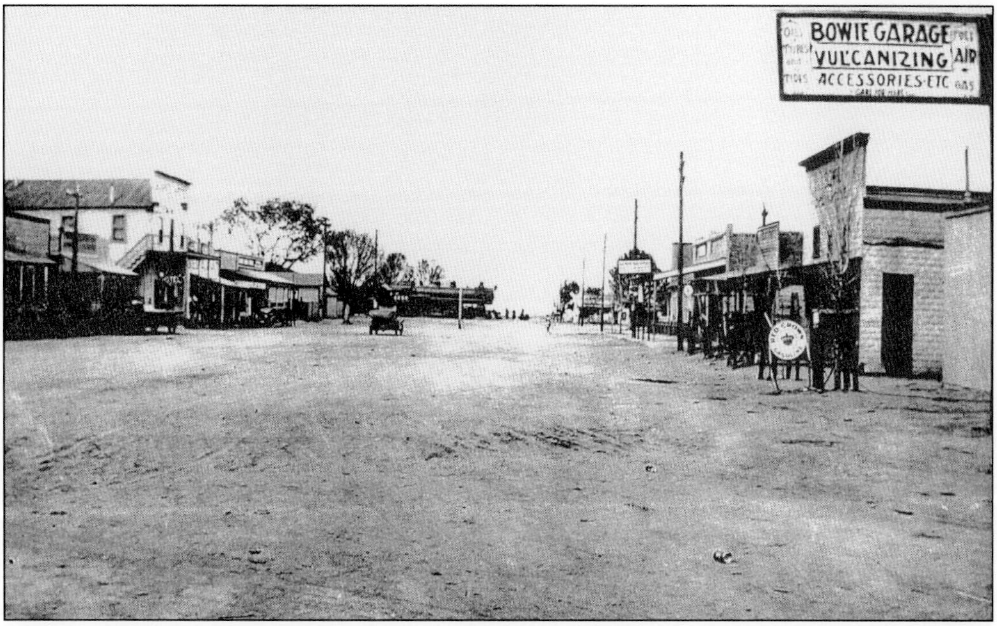

Above, looking north toward the tracks in 1915 shows the Bowie Garage, owned by Earl Boyd and sold to Antice Dickson. In 1919, Dickson Brothers installed a new gasoline station with Texas Company gasoline, considered "better than what Bowie has been getting." Below, businesses line Central Avenue in 1917. Looking south, on the left are the Hindman's Annex Hotel, Hagerty's drugstore and ice cream parlor, the bank (later Bowie Lumber and grocery store), post office, telephone exchange, opera house, and the Airdrome. On the right are Weinberger's mercantile, a barbershop/pool hall, Harry Henderson's pool hall, Bowie Hotel (operated by Estelle Jaque), the Kellum buildings with Rife's Sweet Shop and the justice of the peace's office, Jaque's real estate office, and the grammar school with bell tower. (Both, courtesy of SSVHS.)

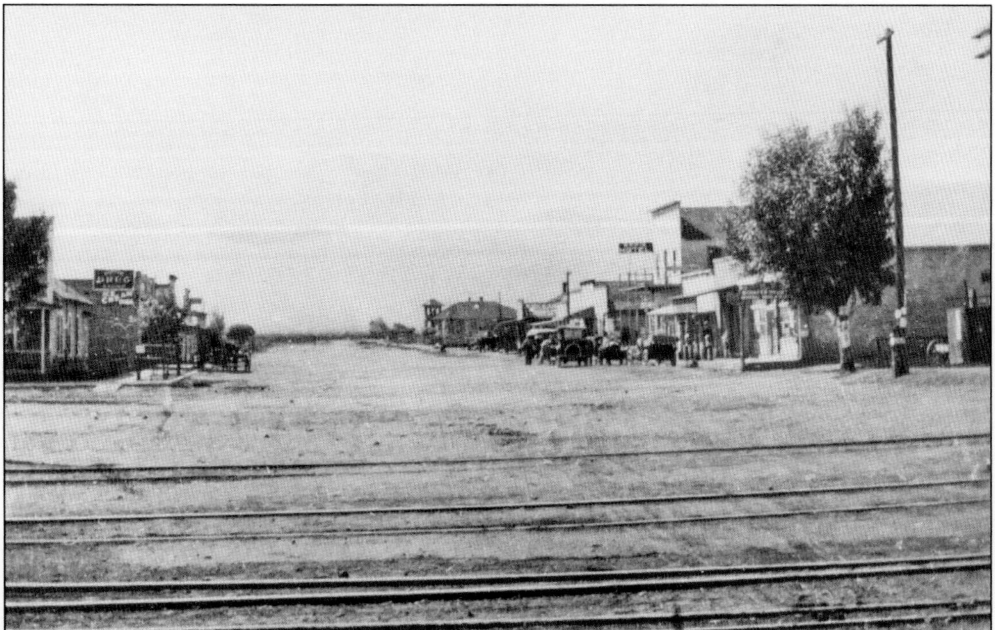

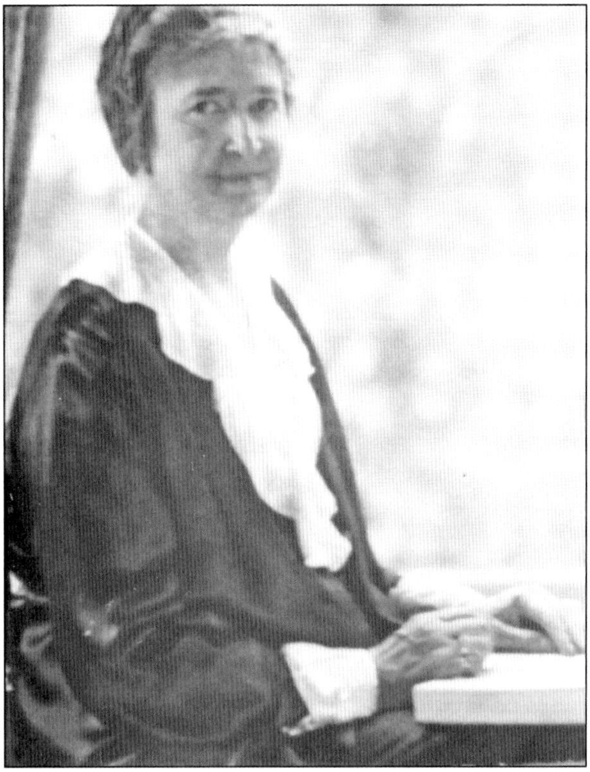

Lola Blake Tomlinson, a photographer and stenographer, had an office that included a rental library. Thanks to her, early town photographs exist. She filed for homestead in December 1914, was postmistress from 1914 to 1925, secretary for the Irrigation District Association, and matron of the Order of the Eastern Star. Preceding postmasters were William Martin, Adolph Solomon, David Wickersham, Edward Tevis, Lambert Frye, James Tevis, Joseph Prewitt, Homer Henrich, and Henry Henrich. (Courtesy of Janice Grizzle.)

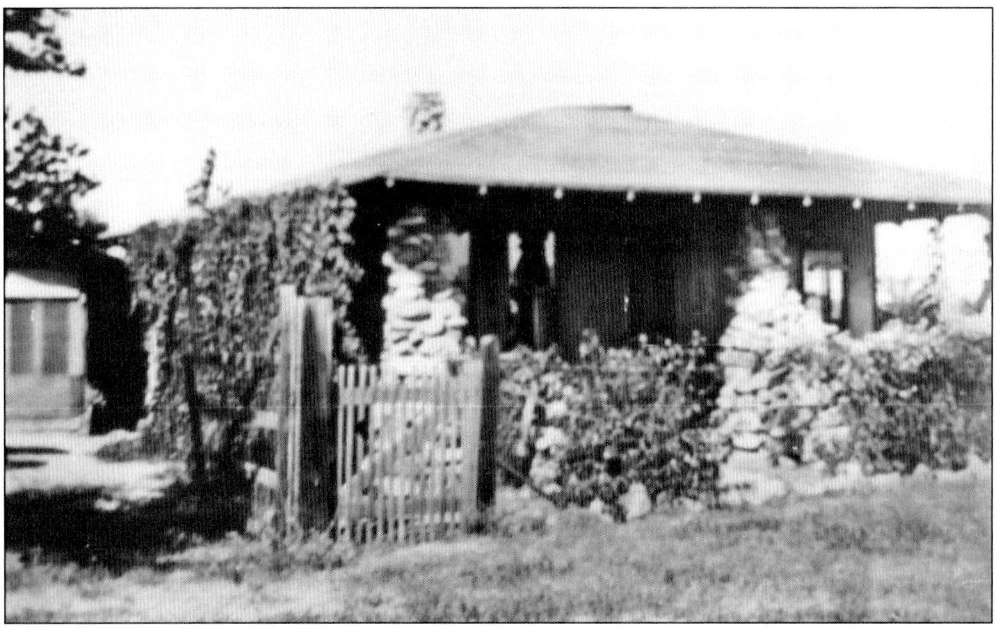

Frank and Lena Hempstead lived in the old Tevis home. He ran the drugstore, and she became postmistress in March 1925. The first Rural Free Delivery for the valley started on June 1, 1914, with J.J. Thompson as the first carrier. Lena was followed by postmasters William Ira Welker, Ethel Parkhurst, Jessie Mae Scott, John Grimes, Ruth Cox, Gilbert Alfaro, and Nasario Bedolla. (Courtesy of Janice Grizzle.)

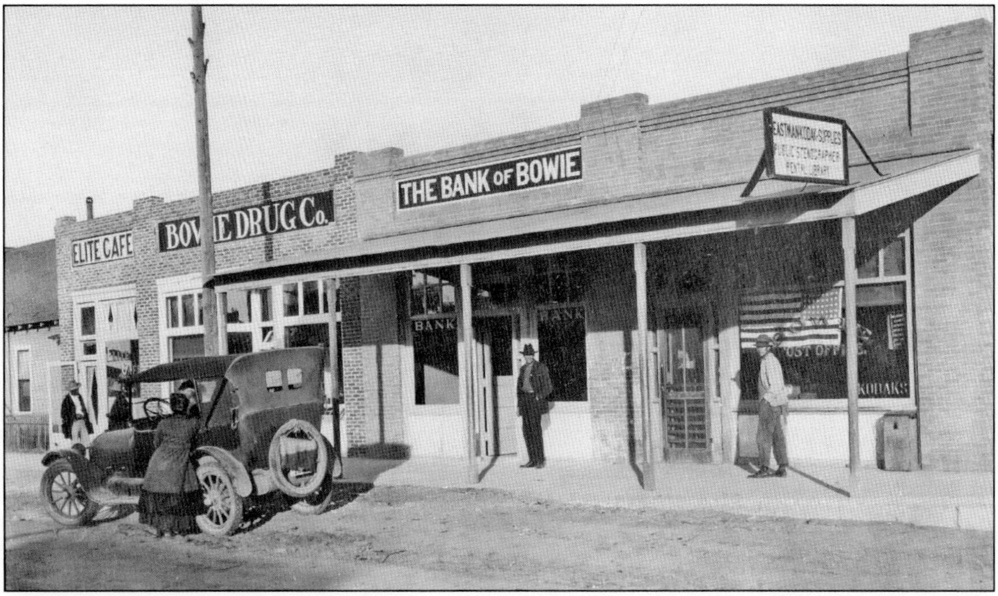

In 1917, Virgil Howell owned the Elite Café. In 1923, Frank Gonzales had his store here. H.D. Hagerty owned the drugstore and sold out to Frank Hempstead on April 14, 1923. The Bank of Bowie opened April 16, 1917, with Pres. Tom Riggs, Vice Pres. F.L. Torrence, and cashier Dana Milner. It became a branch of Riggs Bank in 1931. (Courtesy of Barbara Blandin.)

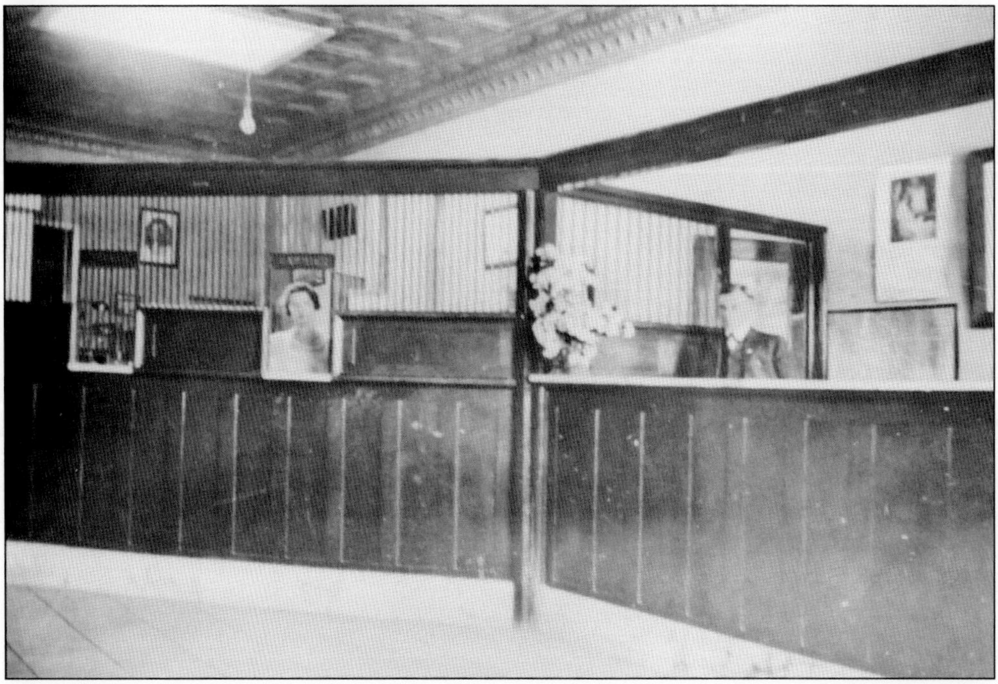

Bank receptionist Hattie Denniston left in November 1923 to take a position with the board of supervisors in Tombstone. She was replaced by Bessie York. Dana T. Milner had seven employees between the bank and his store. He was elected to the Arizona State Legislature in 1920. Business was so brisk that teams would be tied to hitching posts, extending one block on each side of the bank. (Courtesy of Janice Grizzle.)

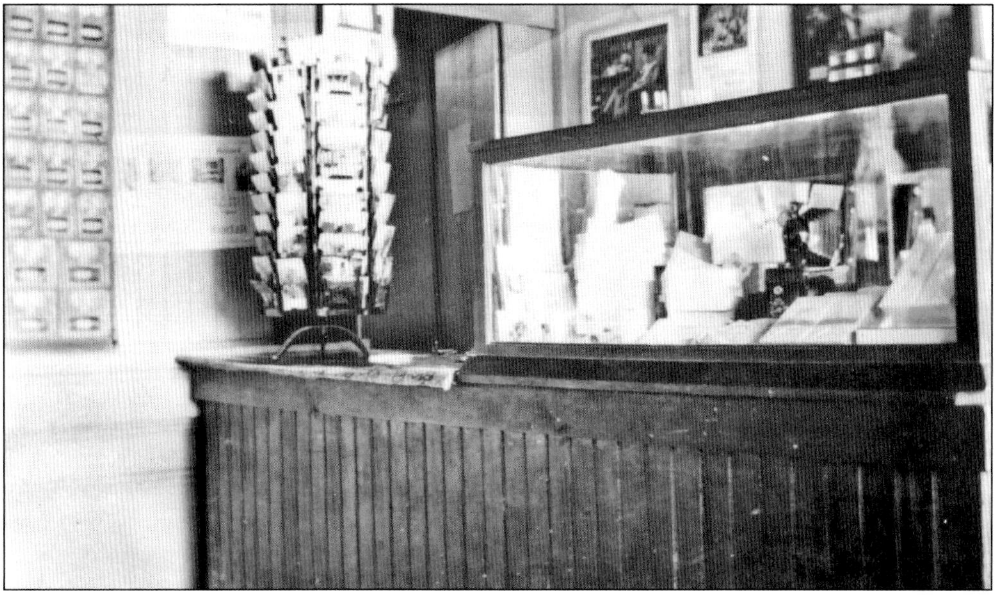

Lola B. Tomlinson photographed the inside of the post office. It was also the Eastman Kodak Agency, selling camera supplies, stationery, and a complete stock of postcards. Gladys Page was assistant postmistress in 1915. Her aunt was Mrs. C.M. Johnson, a former principal of Bowie School. In 1917, Carrie Chandler was post office assistant, followed by Delta Chandler in 1919. (Courtesy of Janice Grizzle.)

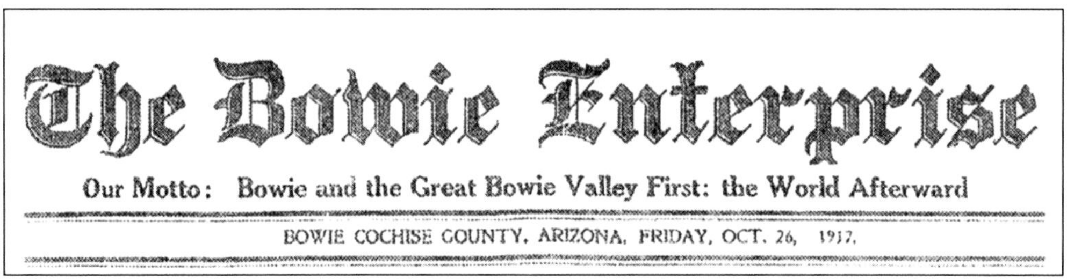

The Bowie Enterprise

Our Motto: Bowie and the Great Bowie Valley First: the World Afterward

BOWIE COCHISE COUNTY, ARIZONA, FRIDAY, OCT. 26, 1917.

Bowie Enterprise newspaper's first issue was published September 5, 1913. W.D. Riser and N.E. Miles, from Fort Davis, Texas, were editors and proprietors. Herman Freese published the *Arizonian* at the same time. In March 1917, the *Bowie News* was absorbed by the *Enterprise*, with new owner Joseph Jaque (pronounced *jake-way*). W.R. and Delta Townsend bought *Bowie Enterprise* and *San Simon Valley News* from Jaque in September 1920. (Courtesy of Evelyn Lathram.)

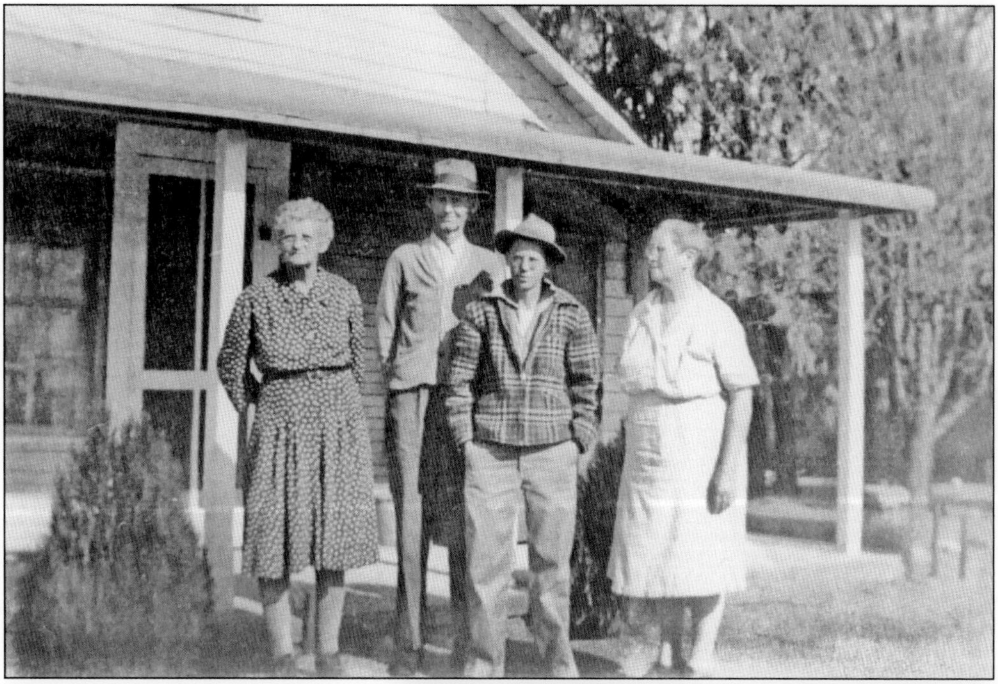

Dicie Dooley Parkhurst and her husband, Burt, who owned the shoe shop in 1923, are with their daughter Ethel "Parky" Parkhurst (third from left) and Frances "Biddy" Chamberlain (far right). Dicie was janitor at the school, stoked the fires, and rang the handheld school bell. Parky was postmistress from March 1949 to 1970. Parky's postal clerk assistants were Nathalie Grusendorf, who worked in the post office for 38 years, and Jessie Scott. (Courtesy of Evelyn Lathram.)

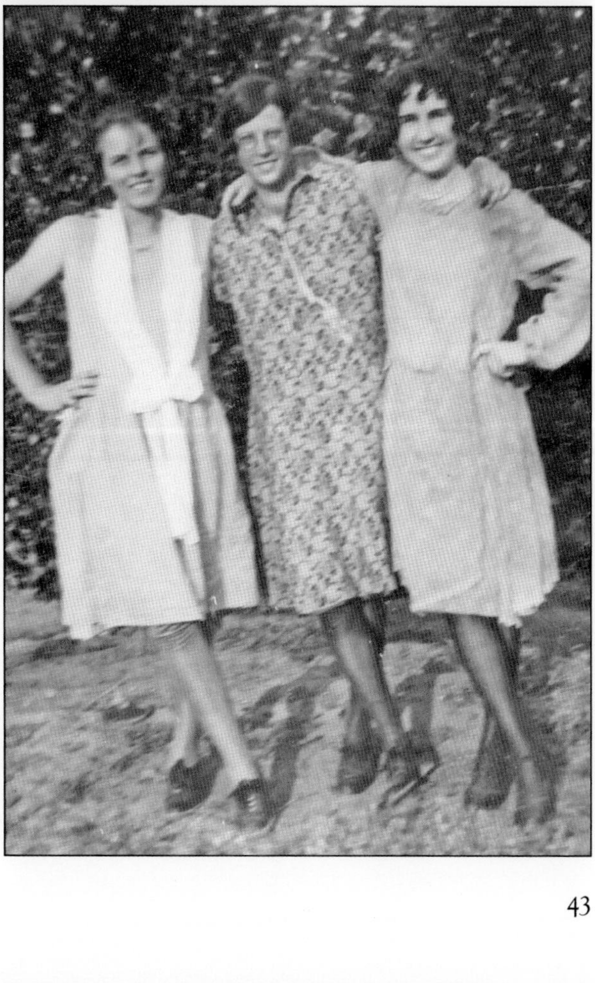

From left to right, Marion Boll, Ethel Parkhurst, and Goldie Mantooth were college classmates at the University of Arizona. Marion and her parents came to Bowie from Hope, Kansas, by way of Cochise, Arizona. A Bowie graduate in 1926, she married Howard Barbaree in 1944. She taught school in Bowie for 20 years, the last 14 in the first-grade room that was dedicated to her in 1999. (Courtesy of Barbara Blandin.)

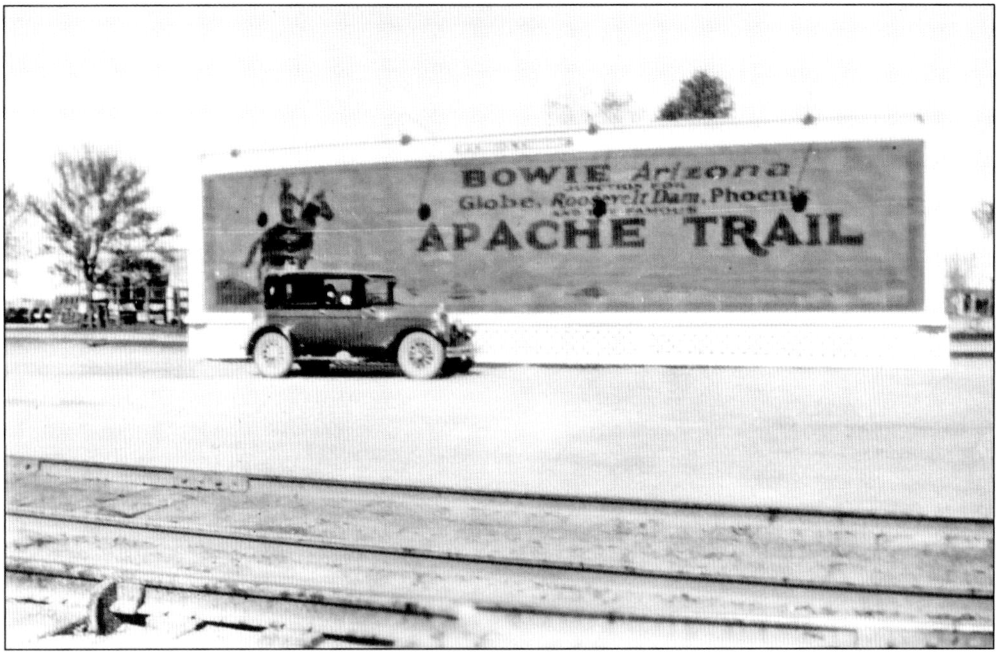

In August 1923, Southern Pacific built a huge sign, measuring 24 feet long by 12 feet high, to advertise the Apache Trail. It was placed where all travelers passing through town would notice. Electric lights on the sign were powered from the plant at the railroad station. Sightseeing tours to Globe included bus service to Roosevelt Dam and Phoenix. (Courtesy of Barbara Blandin.)

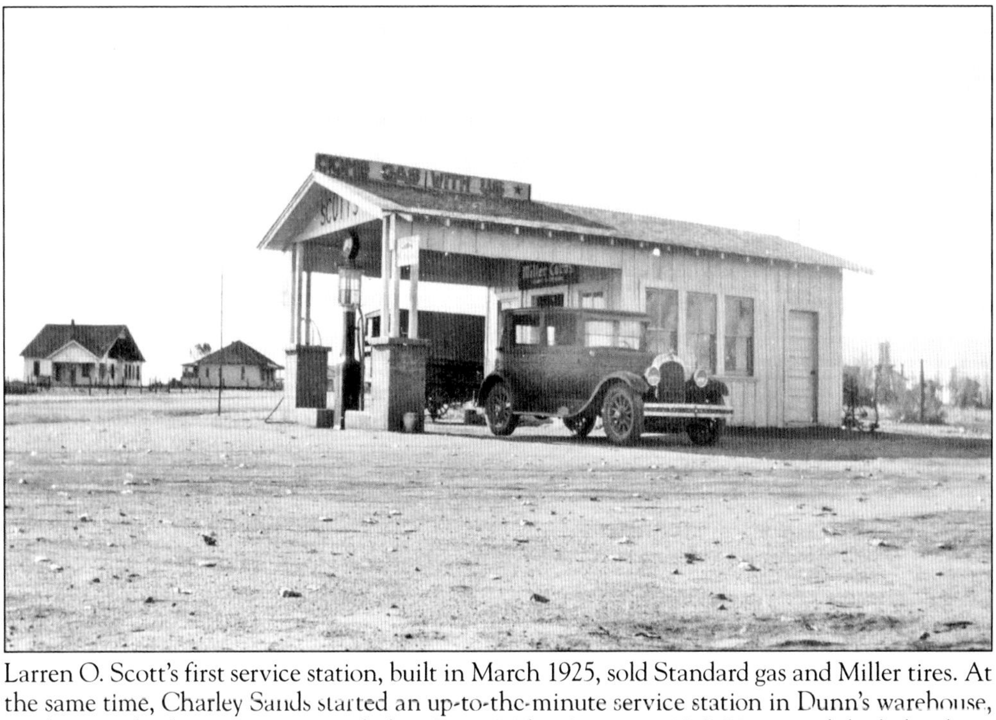

Larren O. Scott's first service station, built in March 1925, sold Standard gas and Miller tires. At the same time, Charley Sands started an up-to-the-minute service station in Dunn's warehouse, on the main highway. Scott was a clerk in Dana Milner's store in 1917. He started the light plant, which he sold to Arizona Public Service in 1930. (Courtesy of Barbara Blandin.)

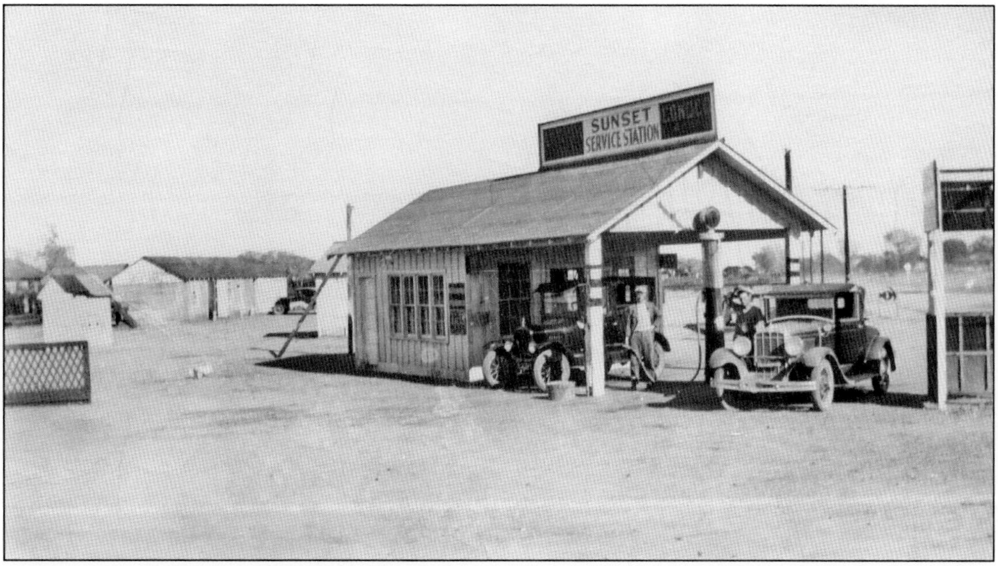

Sunset service station, in 1930, sold Sinclair gasoline. Tom Fousel, owner from 1928 to 1948, pumps gas by hand. Receiving power from a Kohler light plant, the Fousels were the first non-railroad family in town to have electric power. The 1927 Model T Ford was sold to Eva Hall. In 1939, the building was jacked up, turned, and moved back 100 feet to accommodate the new highway. (Courtesy of Raymond Fousel.)

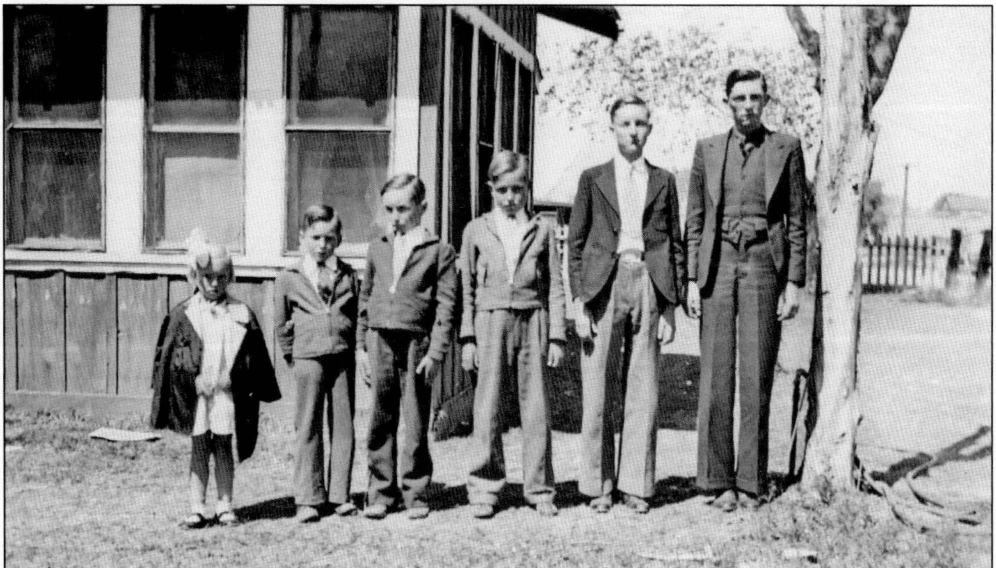

The Fousel children all graduated from Bowie High School. Photographed in 1937 are, from left to right, Mary Doreen, Kenneth, Victor, Raymond, Delbert, and Edward. Edward and Delbert attended aircraft-building school. Ray ran the service station, while his dad worked on a bridge-building gang for the railroad. They lived in an old schoolhouse, with blackboards still on the walls. Ray Fousel married Billie Jean Sheffield, daughter of a foreman for Southern Pacific. (Courtesy of Delbert Fousel.)

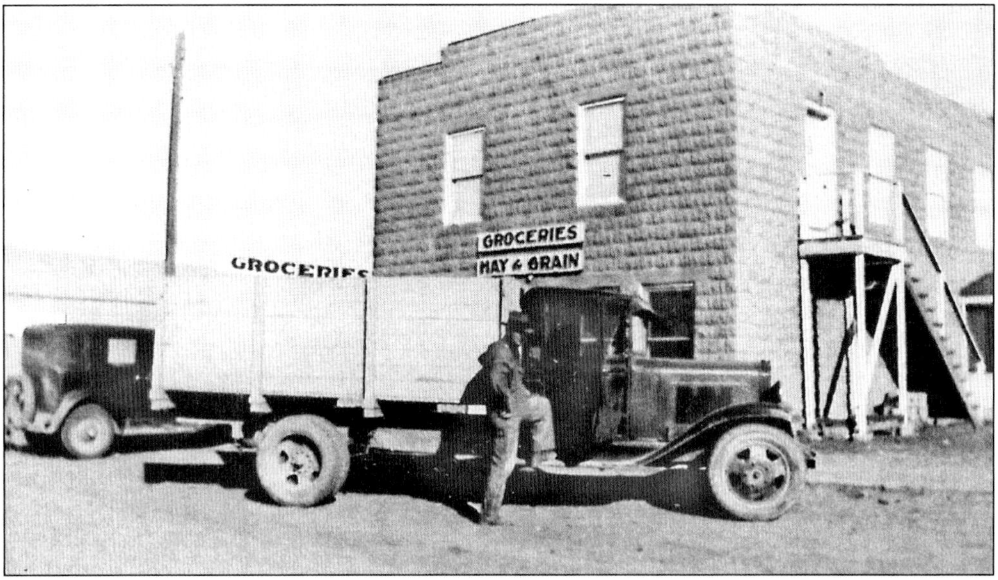

Charles and Stella Grusendorf's grocery store, hay and grain, and drayage business was located in the Solomon Wickersham building on the corner of Central and Seventh Streets. They purchased George Potter's Ford truck and opened for business on March 7, 1924. They moved to Jackson, Mississippi, in 1932. (Courtesy of Melvin Grusendorf.)

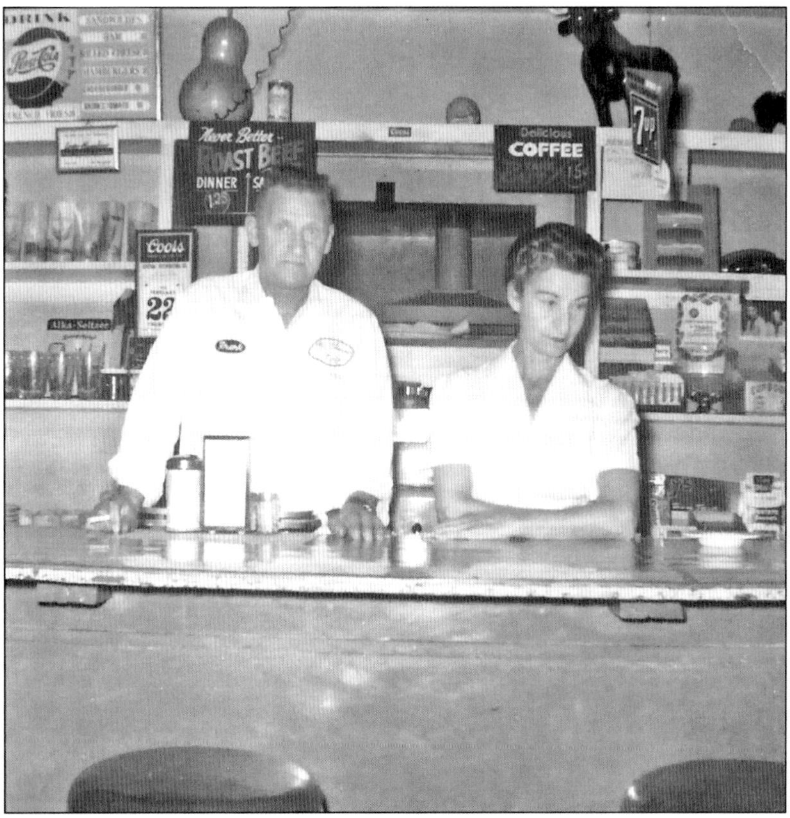

The Yucca Lodge was a popular motel after Highway 86 was paved through town. Frank and Margaret Nelson operated it from 1966 to 1978. Their son Bob is retired from the railroad. Their daughter Bunny married Chano Jacques. The Nelsons sold the lodge to Bill and Ollie Sensor. (Courtesy of Rachel Paul.)

Anna Sue Garrett is kneeling at the Yucca Lodge in 1950. During her senior year of high school, she rented the front room for $5 per week. Owners Earl and Thelma Bates later built apartments behind the coffee shop (on the current Dairy Burger site), which they sold to Bill and Jessie Scott. Anna Sue married Earl Mahan. (Courtesy of Anna Sue Mahan.)

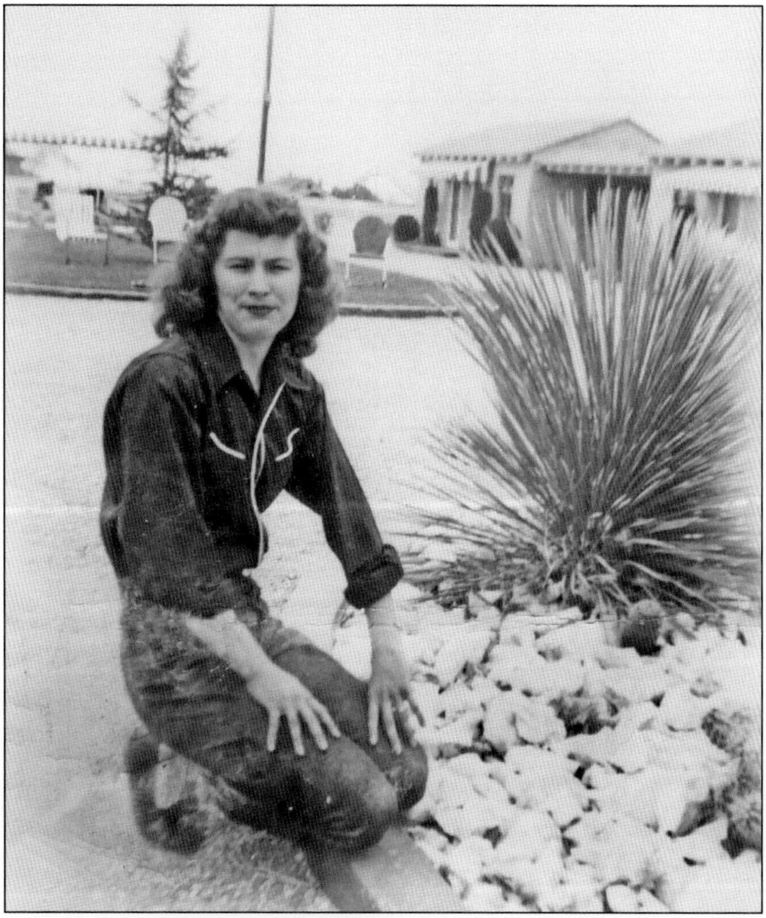

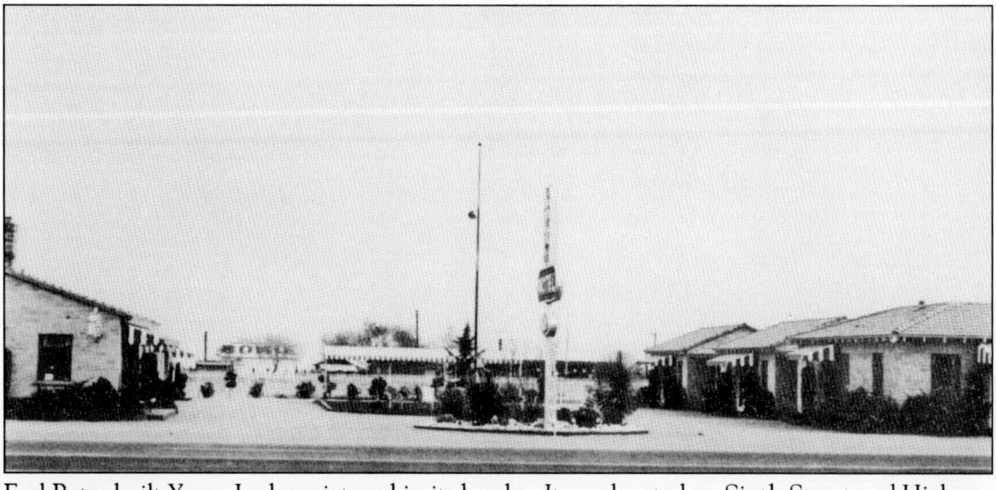

Earl Bates built Yucca Lodge, pictured in its heyday. It was located on Sixth Street and Highway 86. (Courtesy of Janice Grizzle.)

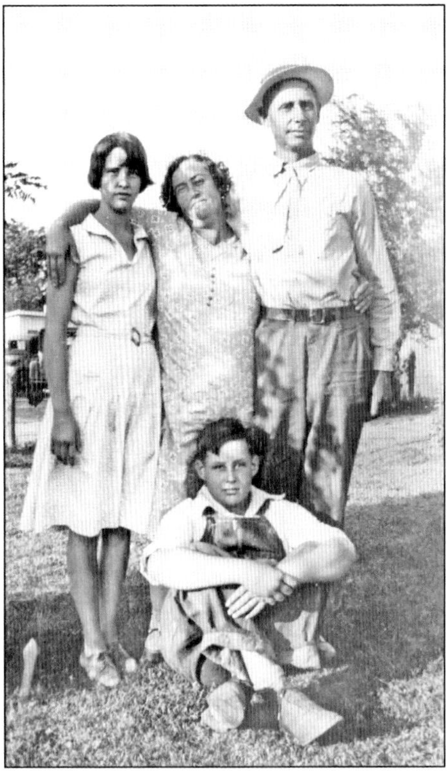

Marguerite, Sadie, Ben, and Bud Kratzberg are pictured, from left to right, about 1930. Ben was a professional baseball player, owned the Chevrolet Agency with Isham "Ike" Chastain, and was deputy sheriff, justice of the peace, and on the Irrigation District Association Board. Marguerite married Victor Boll. Henry and Pauline Kratzberg arrived from Greeley, Kansas, with homestead entry on December 13, 1913. Ben married Sarah "Sadie" Brown in Bowie, on January 25, 1914. (Courtesy of Vic Boll.)

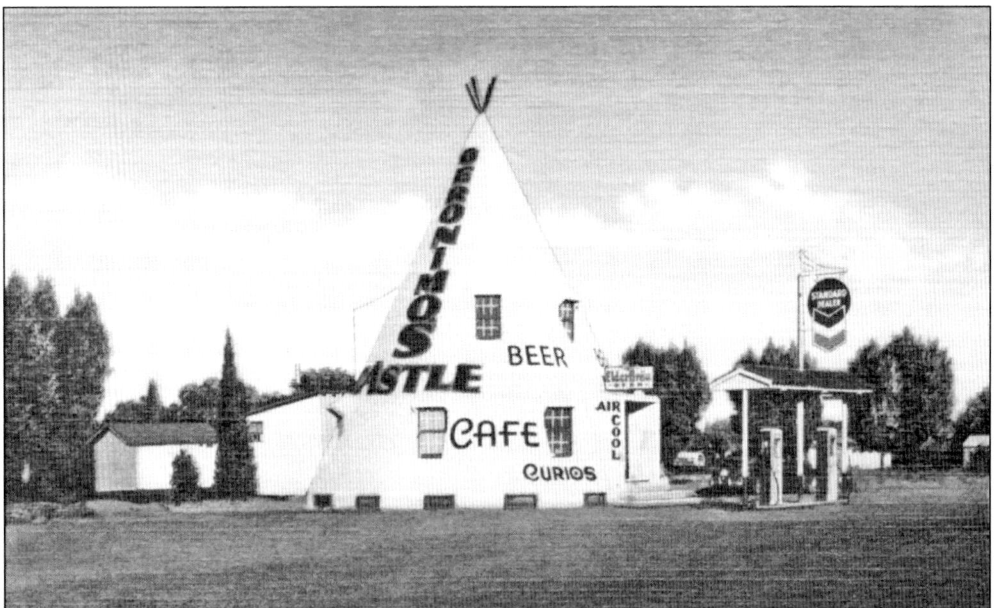

Geronimo's Castle, built by Clifford Head, opened for business in May 1940. A favorite hangout for teenagers, it stands 50 feet high and 36 feet in diameter, with the outside covered in asphalt shingles. There are a main-floor restaurant, curio shop, pool hall, basement living quarters, and a gas station outside. It was the Greyhound bus stop and located next door to Ben Barsk's Teepee Motel. (Courtesy of Marisela Gonzalez.)

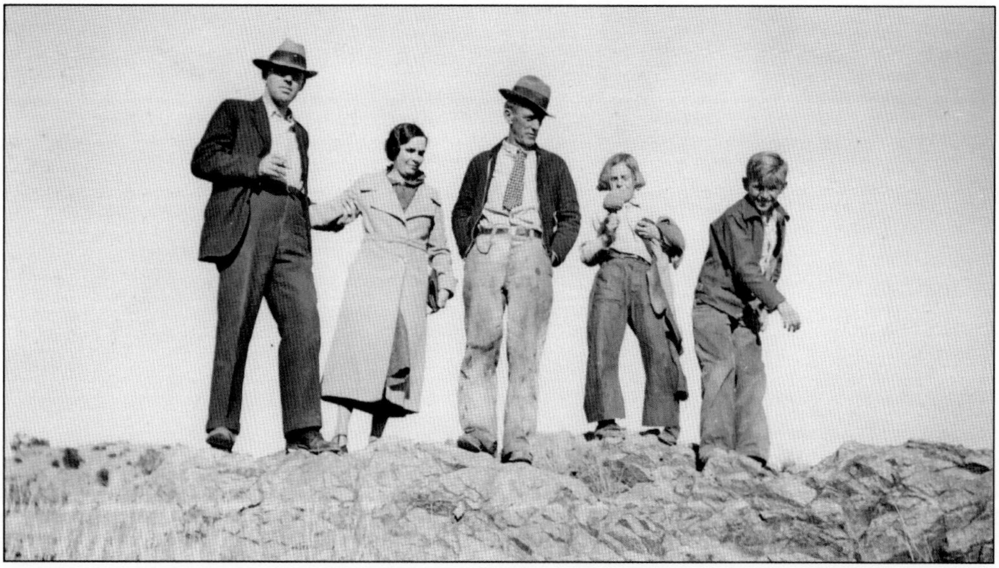

From left to right, Samuel and Emily Kidwell Holland McKee are on a family outing with Al Dillon, his daughter Shirley, and young Samuel "Buddy" McKee. Samuel McKee was a barber and electric appliance dealer. McKee's Pleasure Parlor advertisement was in the 1939 school yearbook. It was the first yearbook and had a wooden cover with original photographs. Only about 30 books were published. It was many years before there was another school yearbook. In 1941, Beulah's Café moved into the Pleasure Parlor, and McKee moved his barbershop across the street into the hotel building. (Both, courtesy of Sam McKee.)

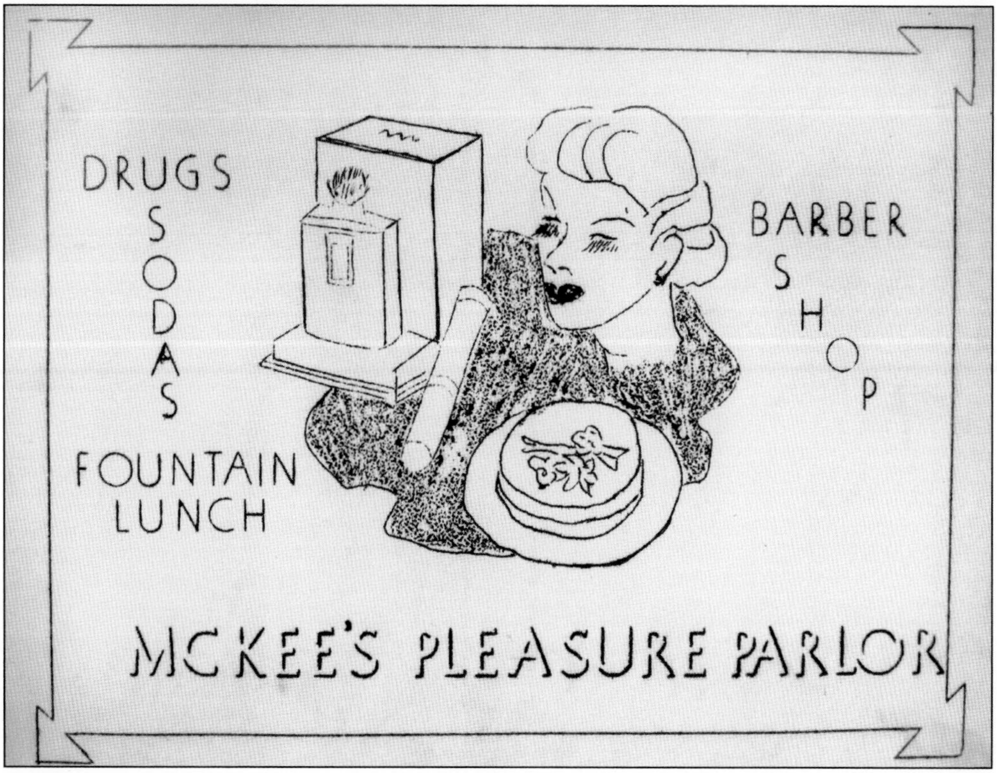

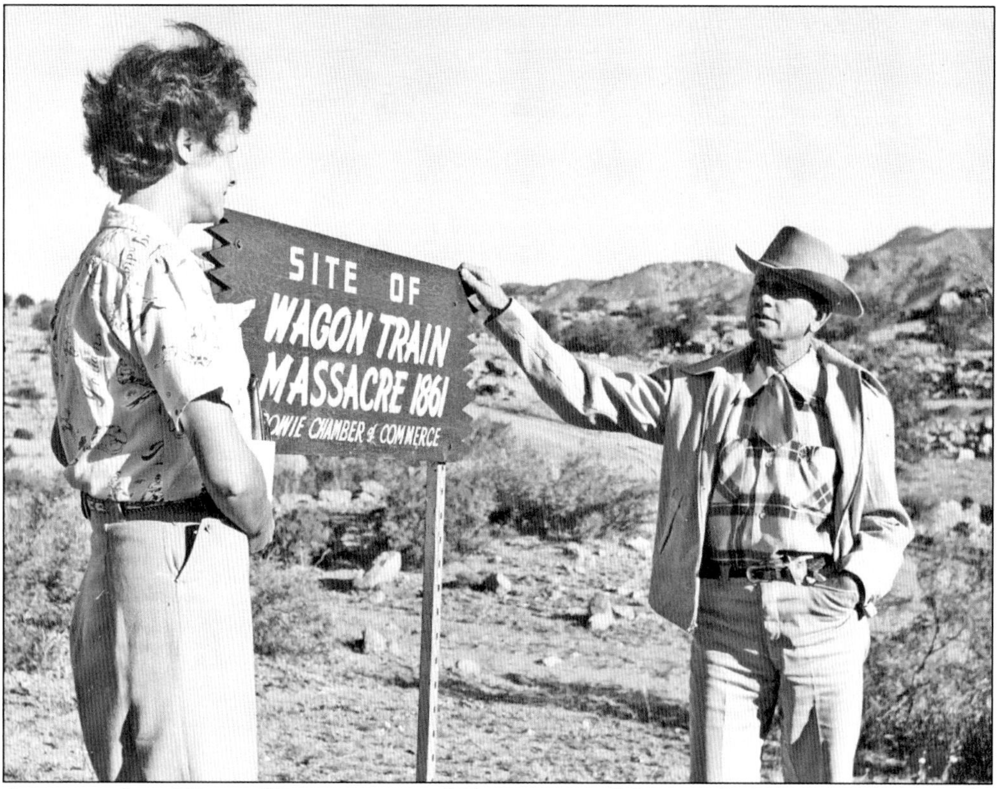

A reporter from *Western Ways* magazine, of Phoenix, is with Larren O. Scott in preparation for writing a story to promote Bowie. The sign marks the spot where Cochise's father, then chief of the Apaches, ordered the massacre of everyone in White's wagon train, who were on their way to California. (Courtesy of Barbara Blandin.)

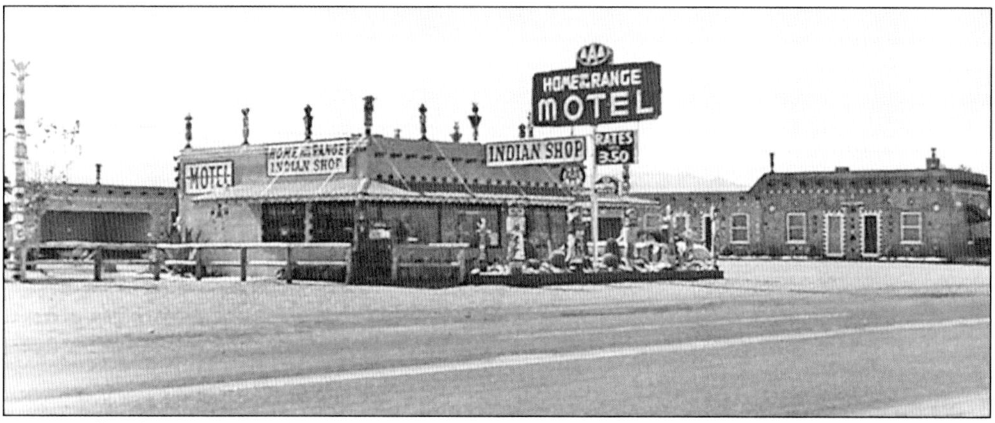

Louis Adler, from New York, built the Home on the Range Motel. He hand carved 125 totem poles of Kachina dolls from bridge timbers and sold them for $15 a linear foot. A 15-foot pole required 10 days of steady carving. Painted by Russell Brankley, local sign painter, some were up to 40 feet tall. Pauline Adler managed the motel after his death in January 1952. (Courtesy of the Cooke family.)

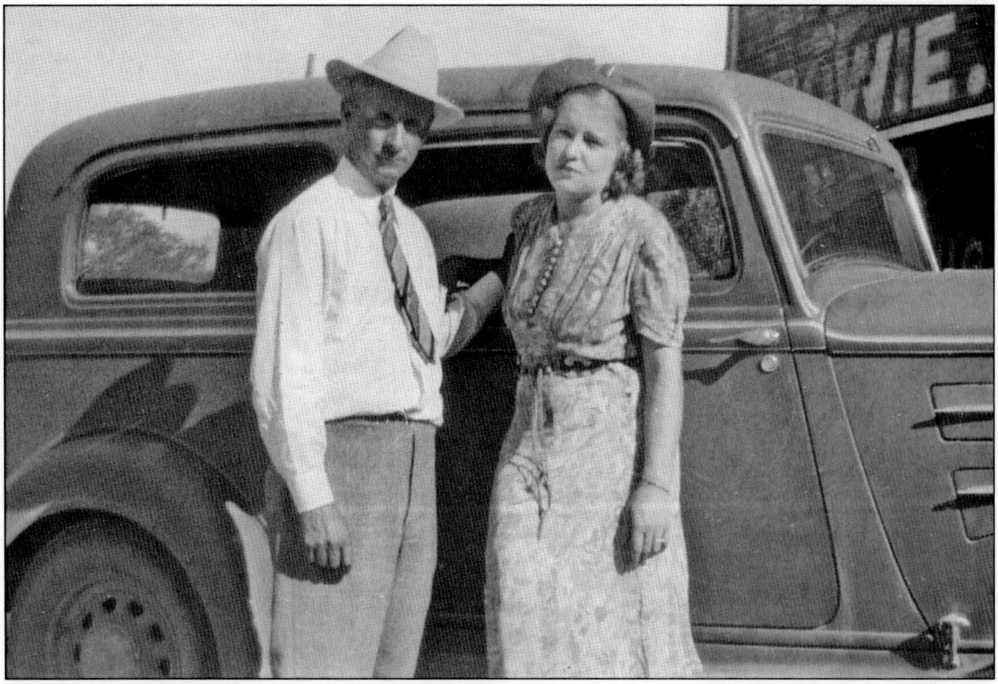

George Milton "Skeets" and Lois Burell Thomas stand by their car about 1938. He was so nicknamed because he was a 98-pound mosquito. His family came to the area by covered wagon in 1894. His mother was a waitress in the railroad hotel. Originally in the old bank building, the new Skeets Tavern was constructed by Skeets and Bob Bejar on Sixth Street and Highway 86. Thomas, still running the bar at age 89, said, "I don't mind telling you I'm one of the best bartenders there ever was." Wayne Cox also bartended. Shown about 1944, it also housed the Greyhound bus stop and a café. Located next door was Skeets's Mobile gas station. At various times, he owned a garage and lumberyard and worked as a rodeo promoter, owning three rodeo grounds. (Courtesy of George Ann Moore and Carisa Fulkerson.)

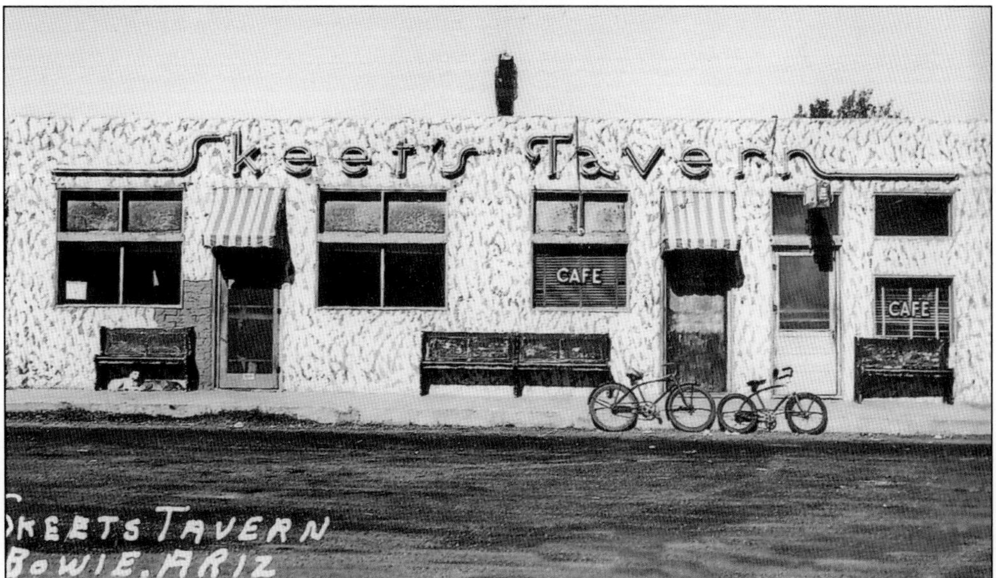

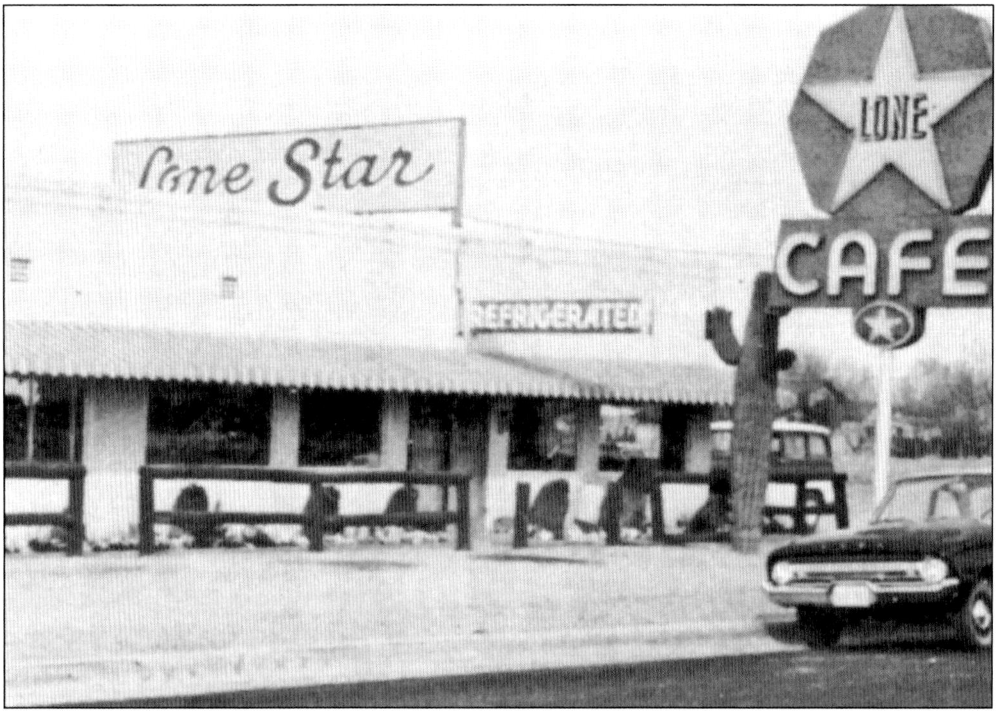

George Pepper built the Lone Star Café and made a beautiful restaurant out of it. He was operating it in 1954 but had transferred ownership to L.W. Tilton by 1958. Dewey Kissinger was the chef. Reva Lowe ran it at one time. Wherever Reva cooked, the customers followed because she had the best donuts and pies anyone ever ate. (Courtesy of Sam McKee.)

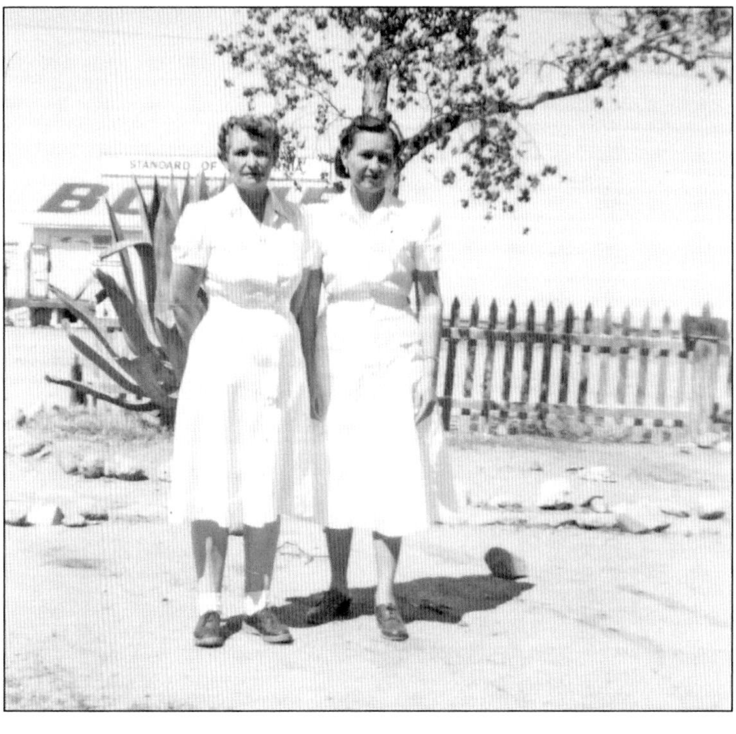

Frances Morris (left) and Euline Harmon are dressed in their waitress uniforms, on their way to work at the Lone Star Café in 1950. Frances's son Billy was a talented trombone player. He became a great bandleader in the Douglas and Benson Schools. (Courtesy of Ed Crews.)

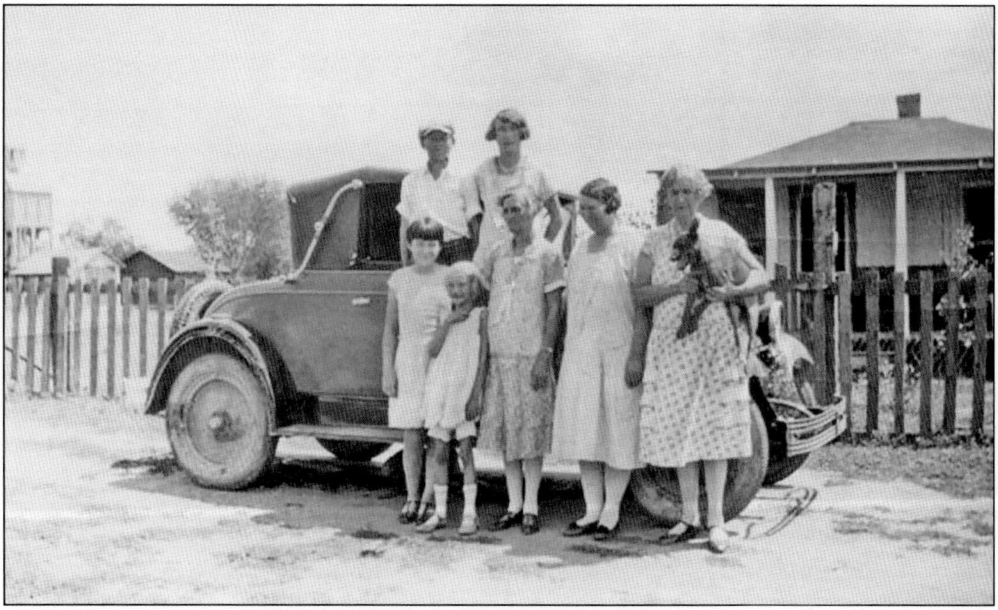

Pictured above around 1930 are (standing in front of car) Louise Holland, an unidentified girl, "Grandma" Summers, Mildred Summers (Hugh's mother), and "Grammie" (Marcia Ella Kimball) Harmon; (standing in car) Hugh Summers, a teacher, and Emily Holland, who later married Samuel McKee. The coal chute is at far left. (Courtesy of Ed Crews.)

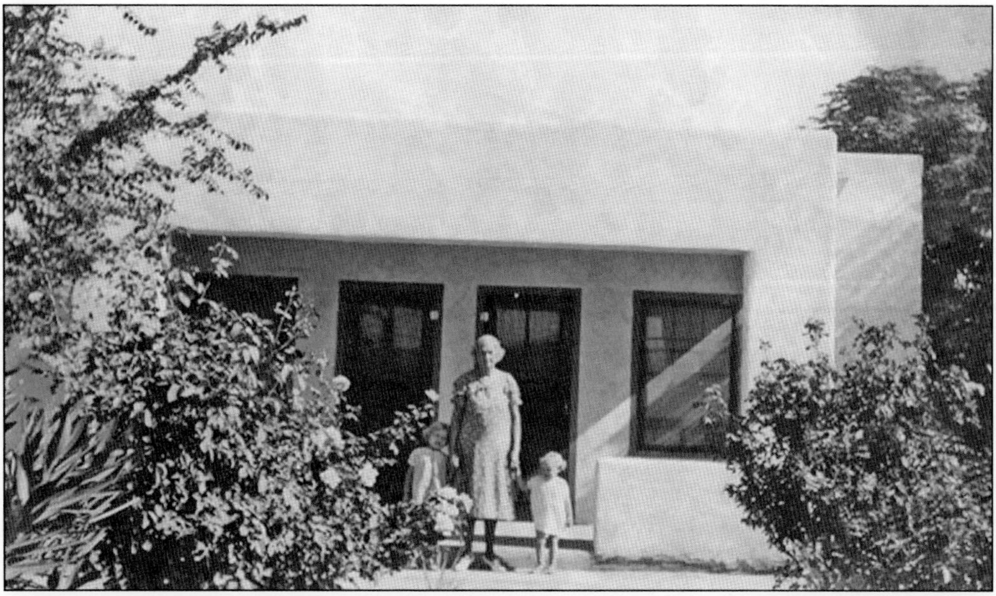

Standing in front of the Pendarvis house are Marcia Ella Harmon and her granddaughters Marcia and Ernestine. James. B. Pendarvis was the undertaker for 30 years. He came from Illinois in 1918 to benefit from the warm climate. He opened his funeral home in 1919. Before that, the nearest embalmer was in Tucson. (Courtesy of Ed Crews.)

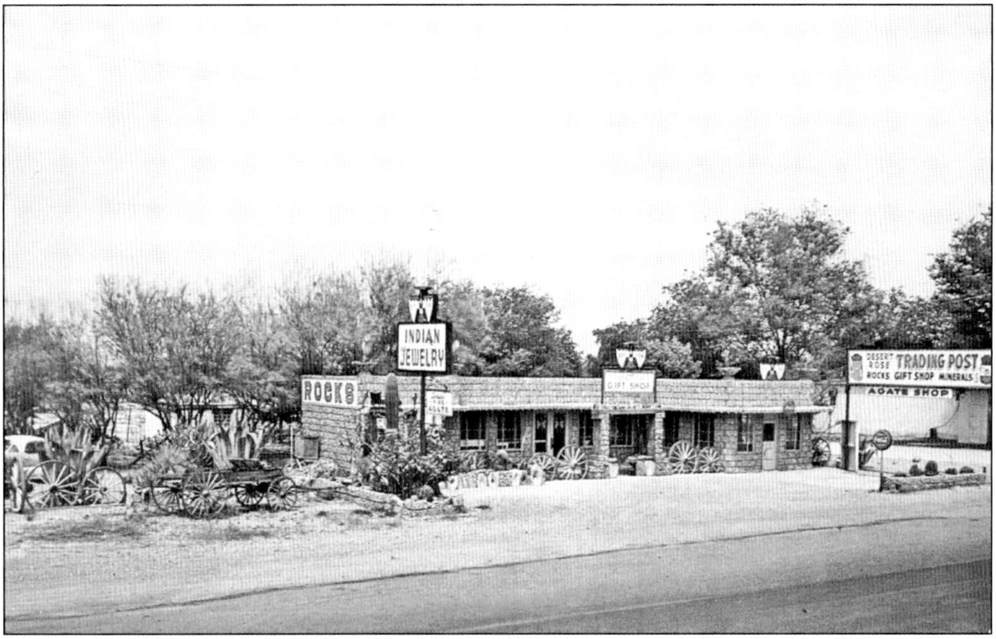

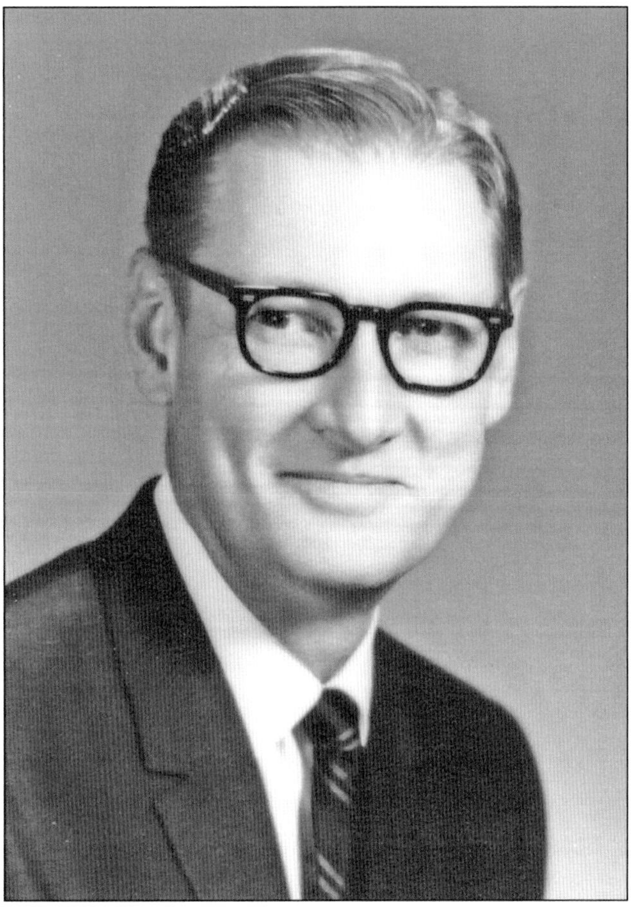

Oscar Connelly built the Desert Rose rock shop with wagon wheels in front. He collected rocks to cut and polish. His wife, Neva May Lyons, was clerk, selling curios and fire agate jewelry. He died in 1959, after living in Bowie for 26 years. In the 1980s, Larry Areingdale called this building the Ole Fort, where he displayed his lifetime collection of Old West memorabilia. (Courtesy of Brad Smith.)

Dr. George Spikes, son of Albert and Nellie, married Frances Odom, a navy nurse. In the 1960s, they would fly their airplane into Bowie each Thursday to tend to any medical needs. Through his father's legislative efforts of establishing a statewide junior college system, George was a principle organizer and board president of Cochise College. George and Frances had three daughters: Susan, Jane, and Mary. (Courtesy of Evelyn Lathram.)

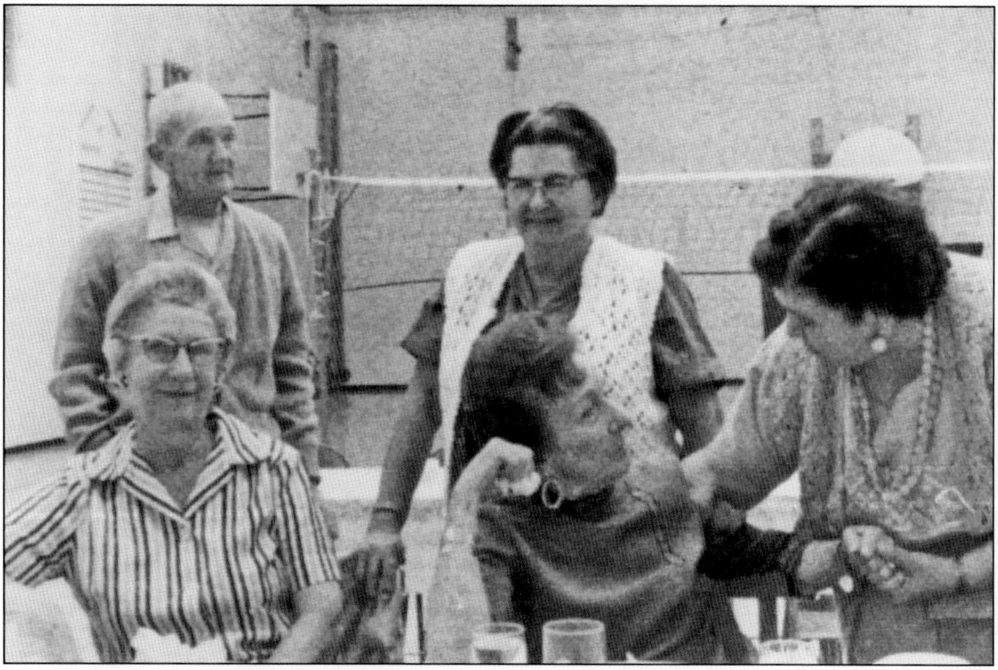

Pictured are, from left to right, (first row) Kathryn Orr, Welcome Scott, and unidentified; (second row) Johnny and Cornelia "Lila" Nash Gates. Kathryn Orr was a much-loved second-grade teacher who taught until 1970. In 1931, she married Paul Orr, who also taught in Bowie. Gates owned the Gulf Circle G service station and a secondhand store. (Above, courtesy of Barbara Blandin; below, courtesy of Janice Grizzle.)

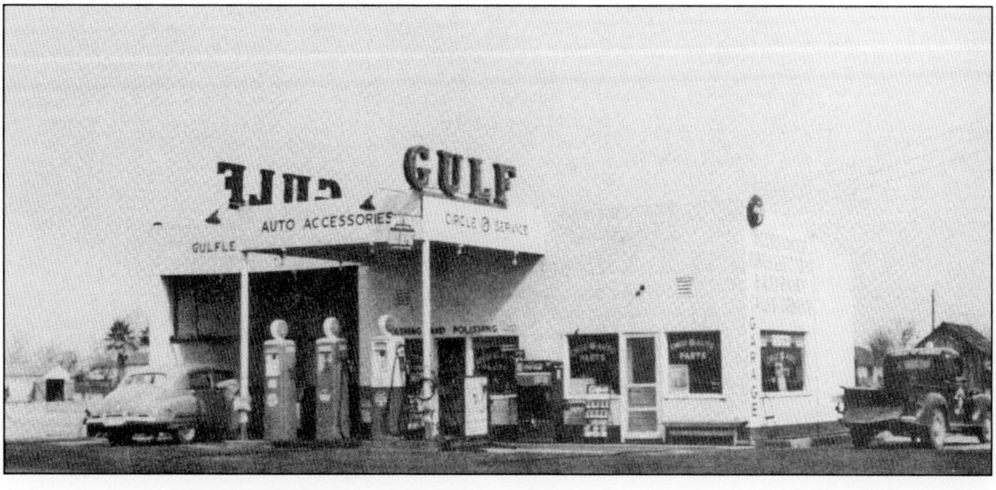

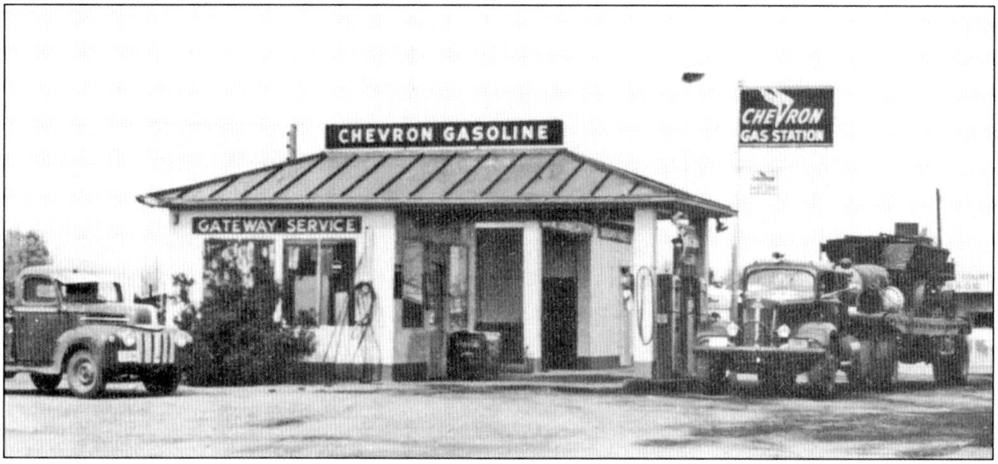

John H. and Edith Dunn Olney ran the Gateway Chevron service station on Seventh Street for Larren Scott. The Olneys were related to outlaw Joe Hill, who changed his name from Olney while running from the law. He was killed in 1884, when thrown by his horse, and is buried in the Bowie Cemetery. Ben Olney was an Arizona Ranger who later robbed the bank in Safford. (Courtesy of Janice Grizzle.)

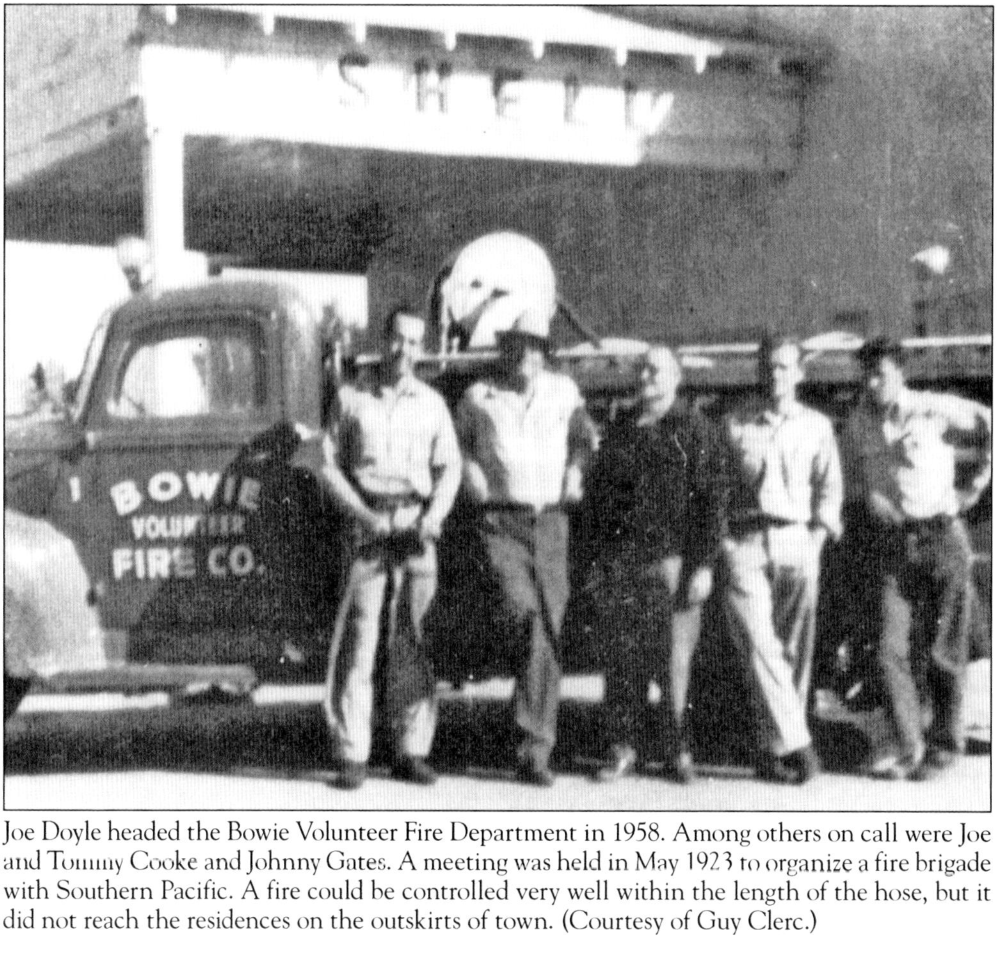

Joe Doyle headed the Bowie Volunteer Fire Department in 1958. Among others on call were Joe and Tommy Cooke and Johnny Gates. A meeting was held in May 1923 to organize a fire brigade with Southern Pacific. A fire could be controlled very well within the length of the hose, but it did not reach the residences on the outskirts of town. (Courtesy of Guy Clerc.)

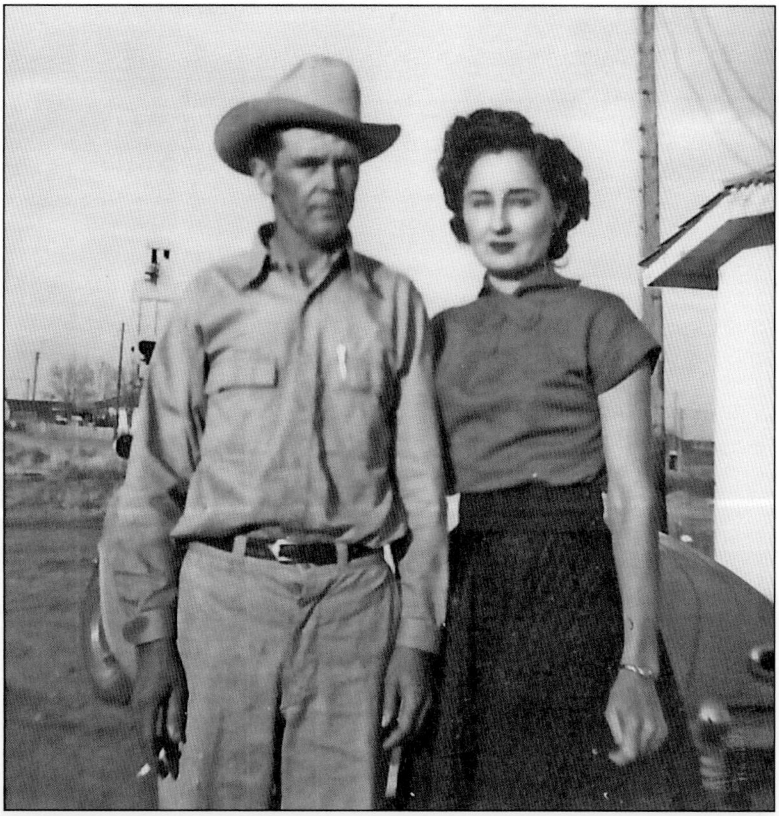

In 1949, Glenn and Nellie Royster arrived from Colorado. They owned Bowie Dixie Service Station and a real estate business, shown here in 1960. Their son Gary graduated in 1955. Their daughter Gail graduated in 1959 with Bowie School's highest grade average in history. The gas station closed in 1990 and the real estate office in 1996. Nellie was a member of Yucca Garden Club. (Courtesy of Gary Royster.)

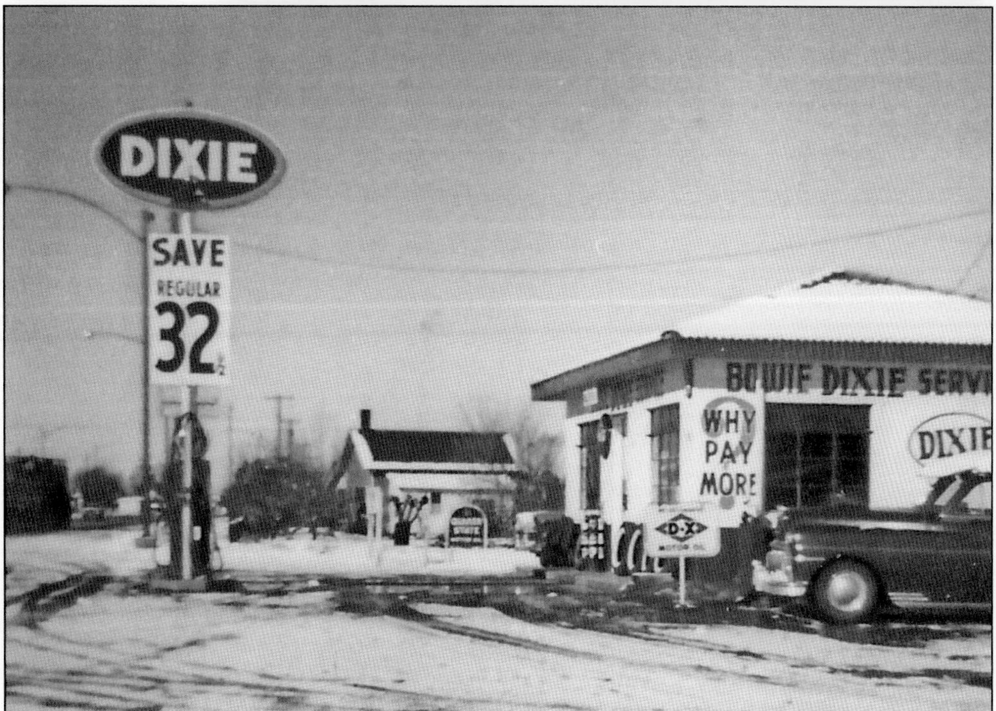

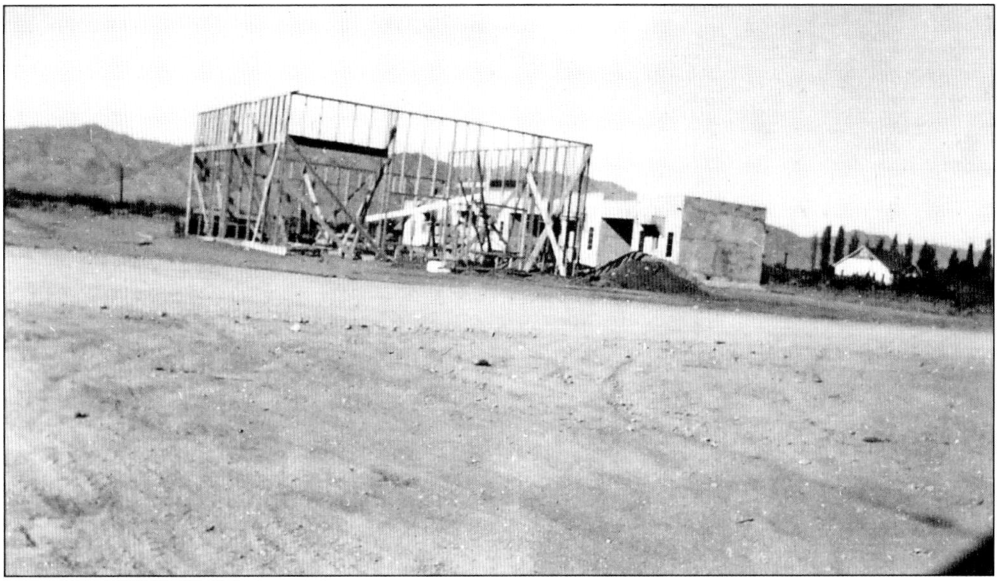

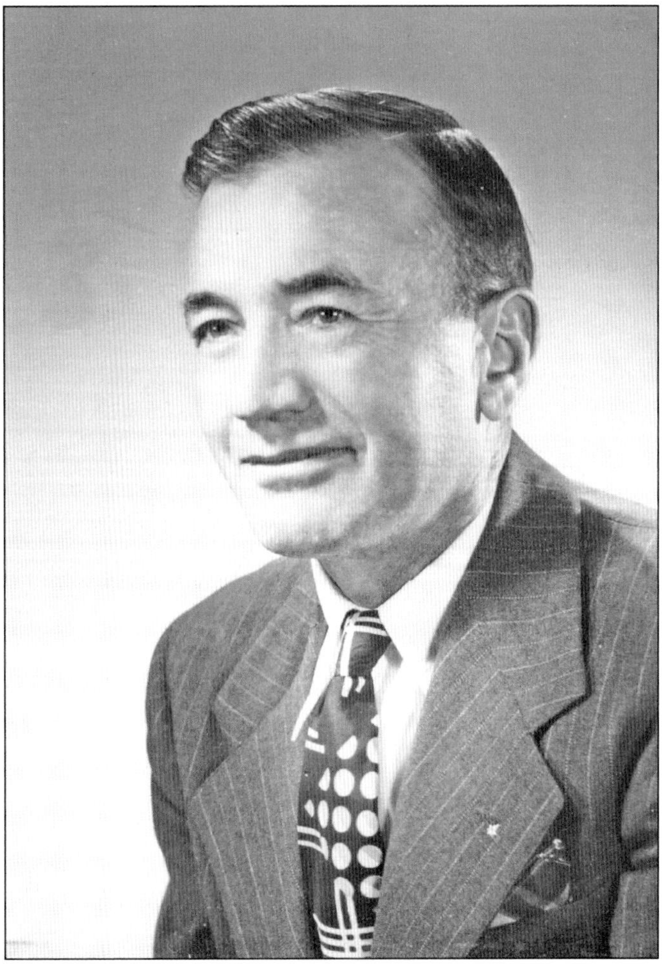

Victor Bertoglio was raised in Castellamonte, Italy. He and his wife, Mamie, arrived about 1928 and ran a gas station on one side of the road and a garage on the other side. After the highway was rerouted, he built Vic's Super Service in 1940. They were owners and managers until 1959. Bill Scott and Joe Doyle were the mechanics with Irene Doyle as bookkeeper. (Courtesy of Luiza Amodeo.)

Victor Bertoglio, in 1951, was a member of the board of education and belonged to the Masons. His wife, Mamie, was an Eastern Star. Their daughters were Lois and Pearl. Lois married Thomas Collins, whose family came to Bowie with the Tunnells, from Alton, Illinois, in 1947 and bought the grocery store across from Geronimo's Castle. Lois earned her doctorate in educational psychology and Southwest history. (Courtesy of Luiza Amodeo.)

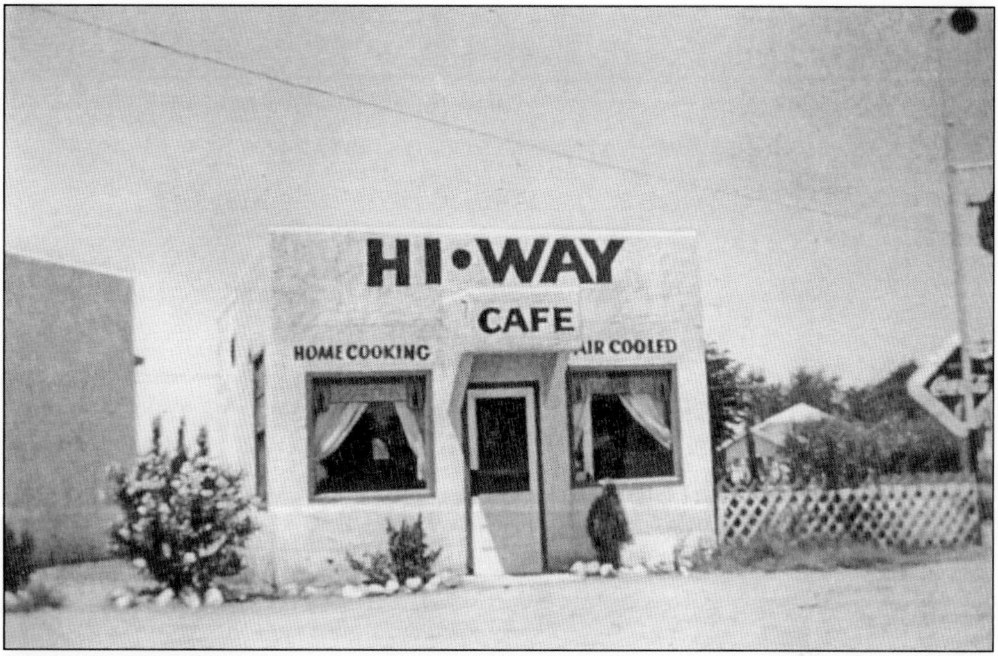

The Hi-Way Café appears as it was originally. Welcome Yelton operated it during the war years. It was managed by Joseph Figlewecz and his wife in 1954. Local women who worked there included Emily McKee, Cassie Cawood, Doris Briscoe, and Frances Morris. Frances's children were Gayle, Donella, and Billy. (Courtesy of Evelyn Lathram.)

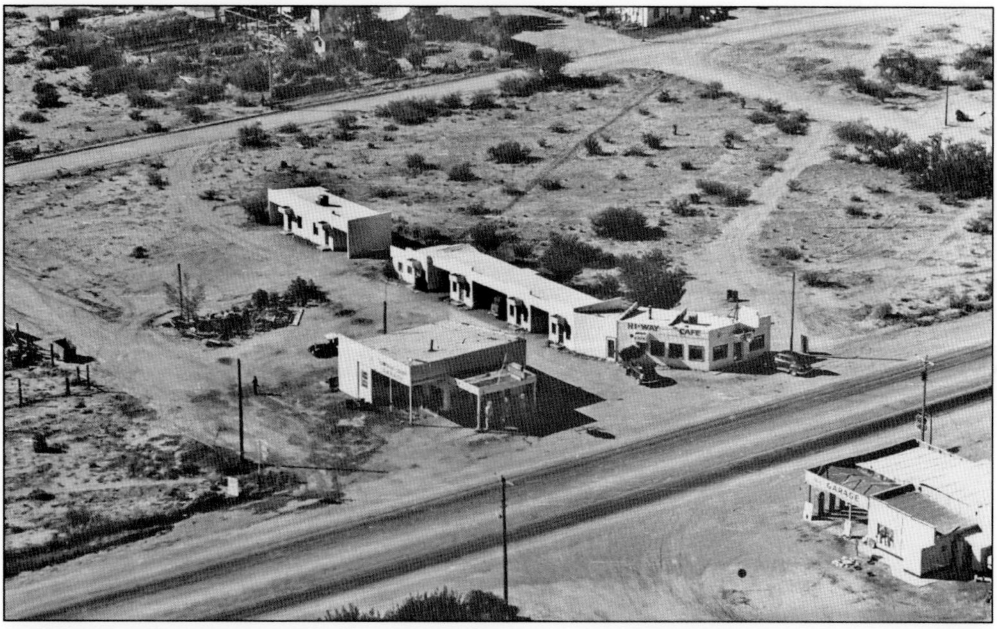

In 1951, Vic's Super Service Shell station and motor court included an expanded café building and two cabins added to the south. The café burned about 1959. The site is now an empty lot across from Liberty Café. During World War II, the business boomed. The Bertoglios were able to realize their dream to buy a ranch in New Mexico. Joe Doyle bought the business. (Courtesy of Luiza Amodeo.)

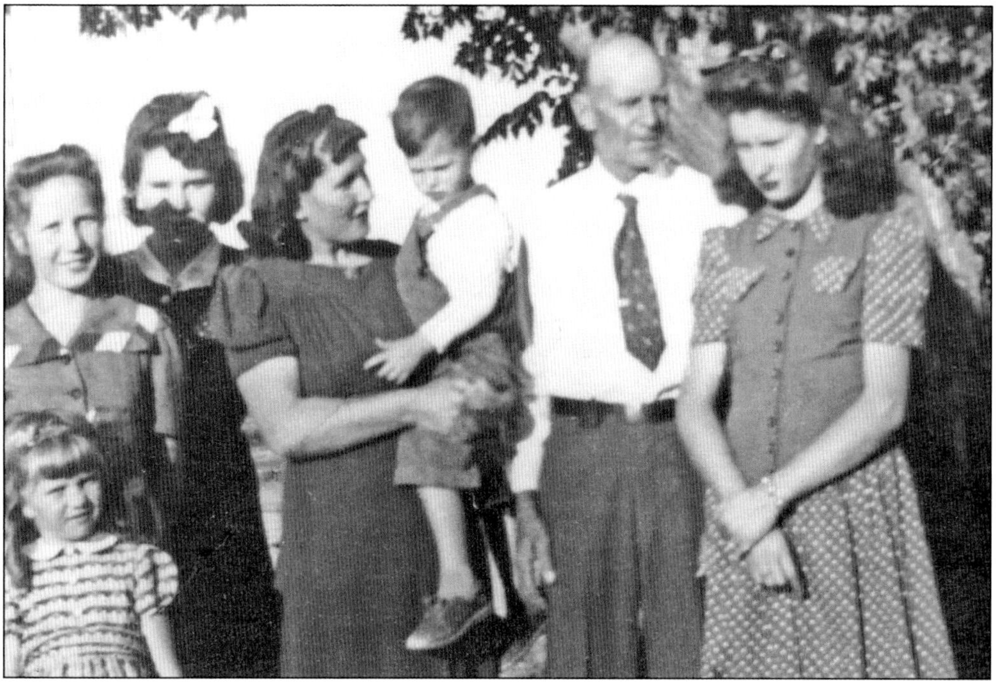

The Garey family, around 1943, included, from left to right, Twila, Pat, Doralie, mother Hilda holding Roger, father Lee, and Eunice. Lee Garey owned a service station and automobile court at the east end of town and drove the school bus. The family moved to Willcox in 1951. (Courtesy of Twila Shelton.)

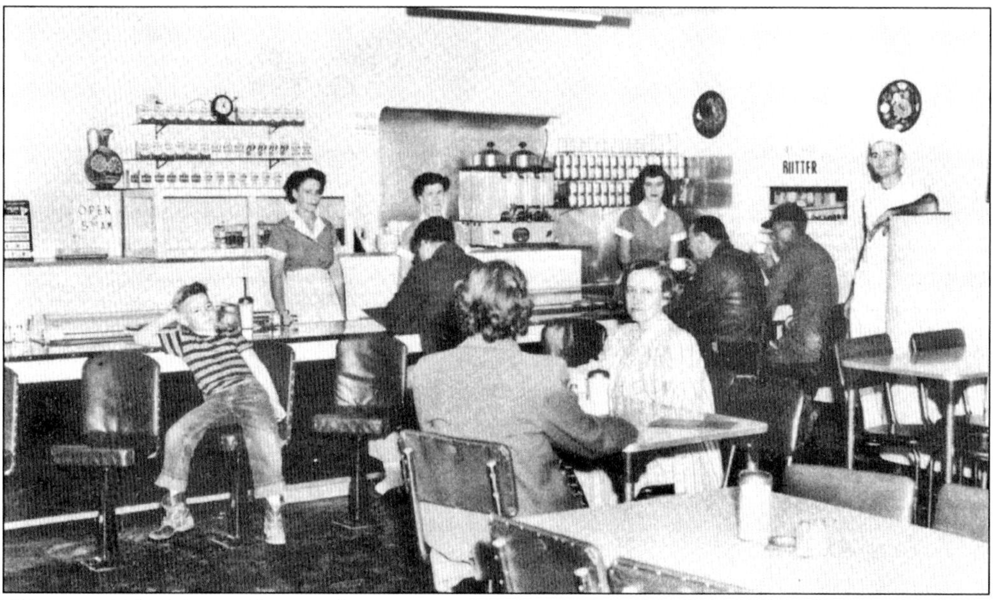

Taken in 1951, Martin Scott is leaning on the counter inside The Coffee Shop. Behind the counter are Leona Bartlett Haire, Jessie Scott (Martin's mother), and Anna Sue Garrett. Bill Scott is at far right. Sitting at the table are Kathryn Orr and Midge Enloe. Marion Areingdale was a waitress and Marion's husband, Dick, was the cook. Ruby Kiel worked sometimes as a dishwasher and cook. (Courtesy of Guy Clerc.)

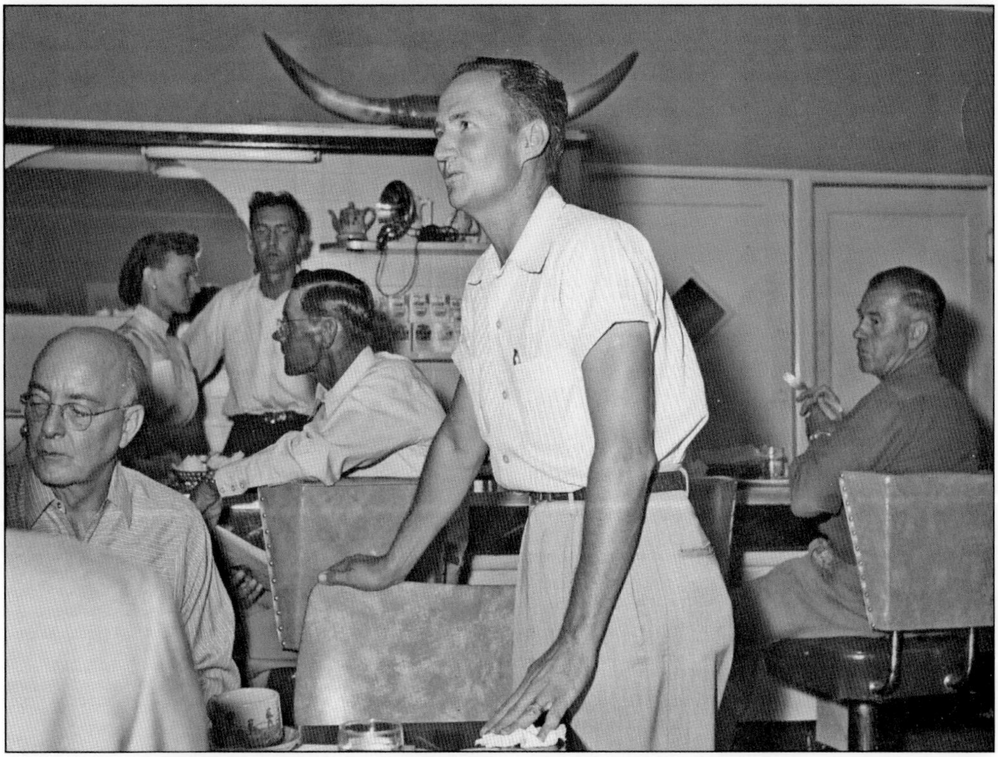

Pres. Douglas Welker is leading a meeting of the chamber of commerce in the Lone Star Café. Others pictured are, from left to right, Frank Tunnell (notary public and insurance salesman), Mr. & Mrs. L.W. Tilton (owners from 1958 to 1961), Tom Shown (farmer), and Sam Moseley (rancher). Other owners of the café were George and Bebe Pepper and Dewey Kissinger. Ray Thatcher, in the 1970s, called it the Bowie Stage Stop. (Courtesy of Barbara Blandin.)

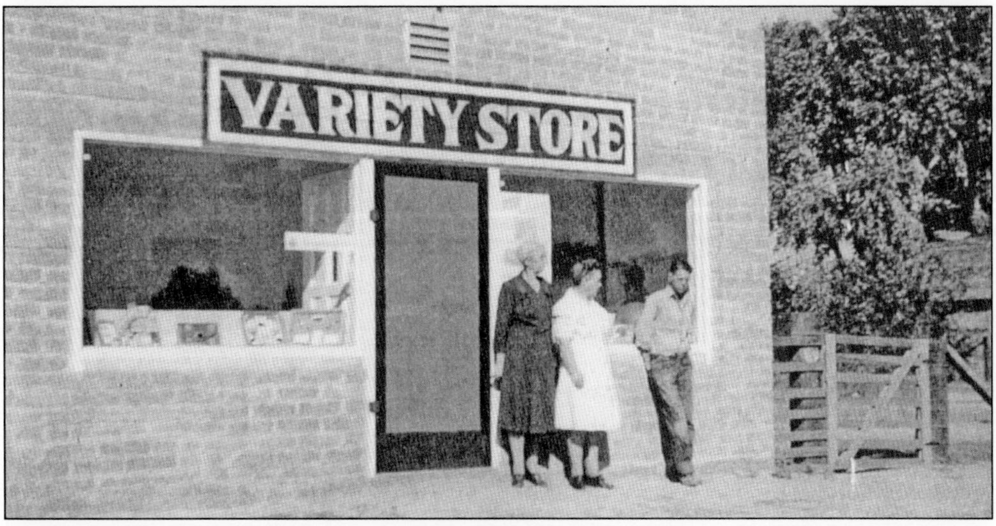

Standing in front of the Variety Store in the 1940s are, from left to right, Josie Lawhon (owner of the building), Frances "Biddy" Chamberlain (who operated a gift and hobby shop there), and Ethel "Parky" Parkhurst. Parky, the postmistress, always dressed like a man and even worked on the railroad bridge-building crew. (Courtesy of Evelyn Lathram.)

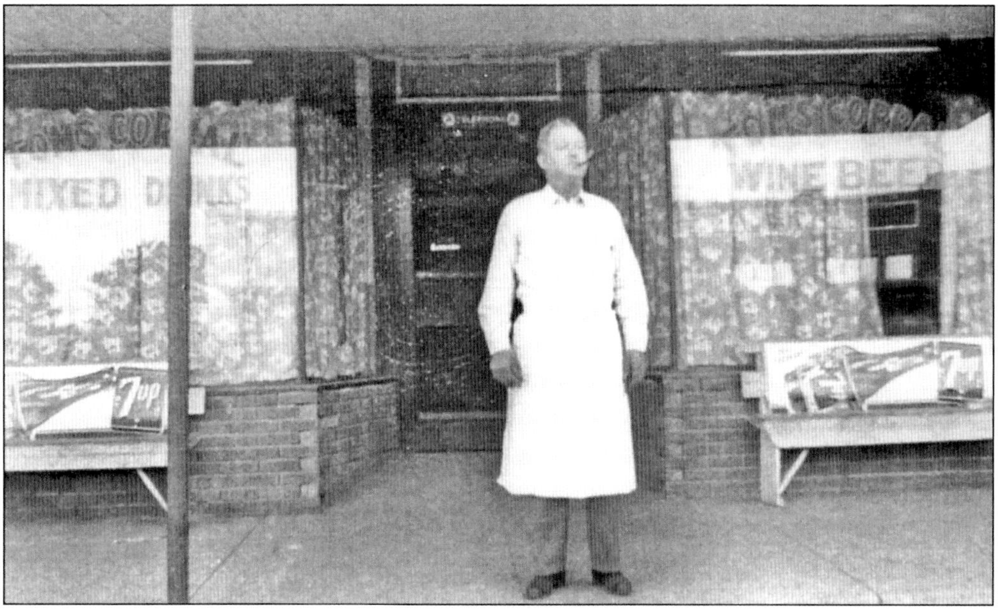

In 1949, C.E. Tombaugh served mixed drinks, wine, and beer in Tom's Corral, located in an old saloon building on Central Avenue. By 1954, the name was Tom's Corral and Chuck Wagon, owned and managed by Thomas DeLong. Violet Moyer was the café operator with Frances Morris as cook. (Courtesy of Evelyn Lathram.)

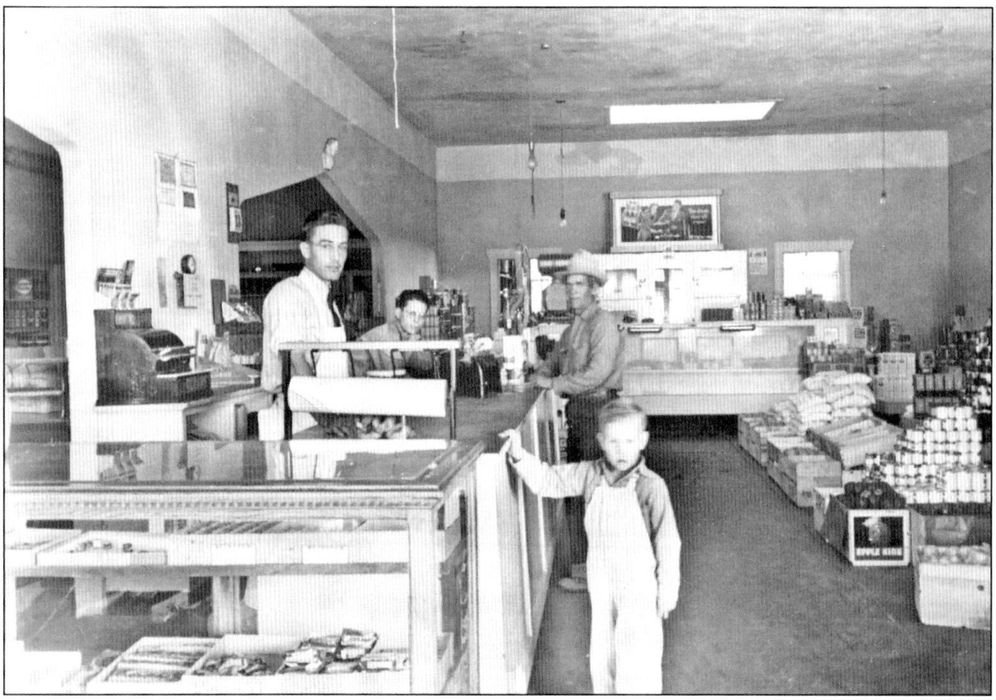

Owner Victor M. Boll and clerk Ethel "Parky" Parkhurst are behind the counter in the Bowie Market in the 1940s. Customers are Julius Dahlgren and his son. M.S. Robertson was butcher, and May Lenzner was another clerk. Victor was president of the Lions Club, past master of the Masons, on the board of education, and a chamber of commerce member. (Courtesy of Vic Boll.)

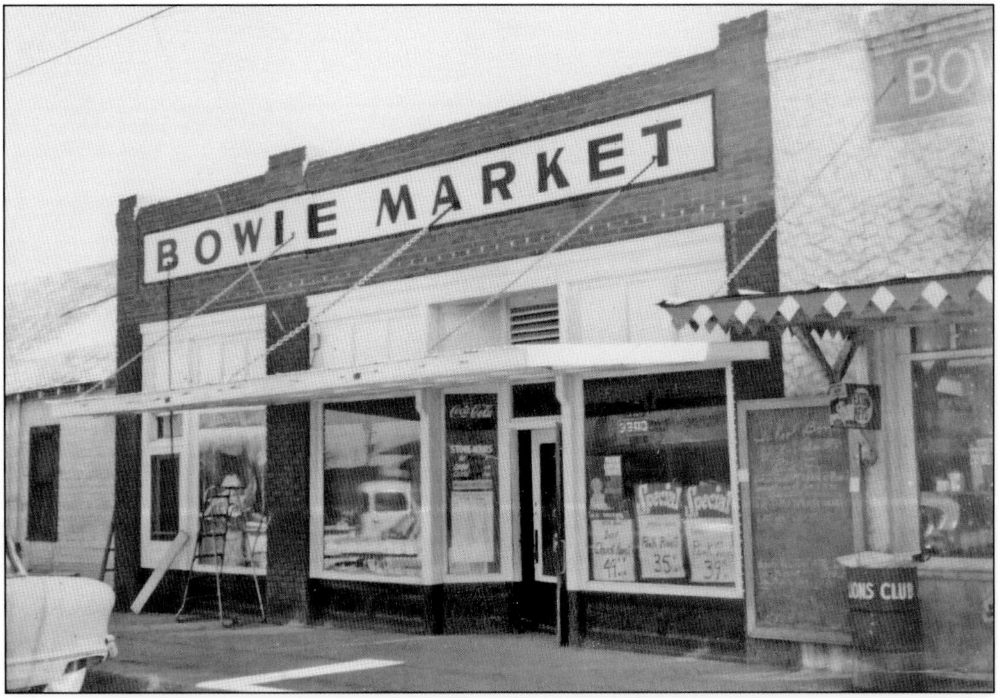

The Bowie Market, on Central Avenue, is pictured in 1958 after Doug and Barbara Welker bought it from Victor and Marguerite Boll. They sold it in 1965 to the Tom Hum family. Chuck roast is 49¢ a pound. There is an outside blackboard for community notices and a trash can put out by the Lions Club in an attempt to keep the town clean. Shown below, inside the store, are, from left to right, Tom and Josie Hum, their son Peter, Marguerite Boll, and John Gates. The building burned in June 1977. (Above, courtesy of Barbara Blandin; below, courtesy of Evelyn Lathram.)

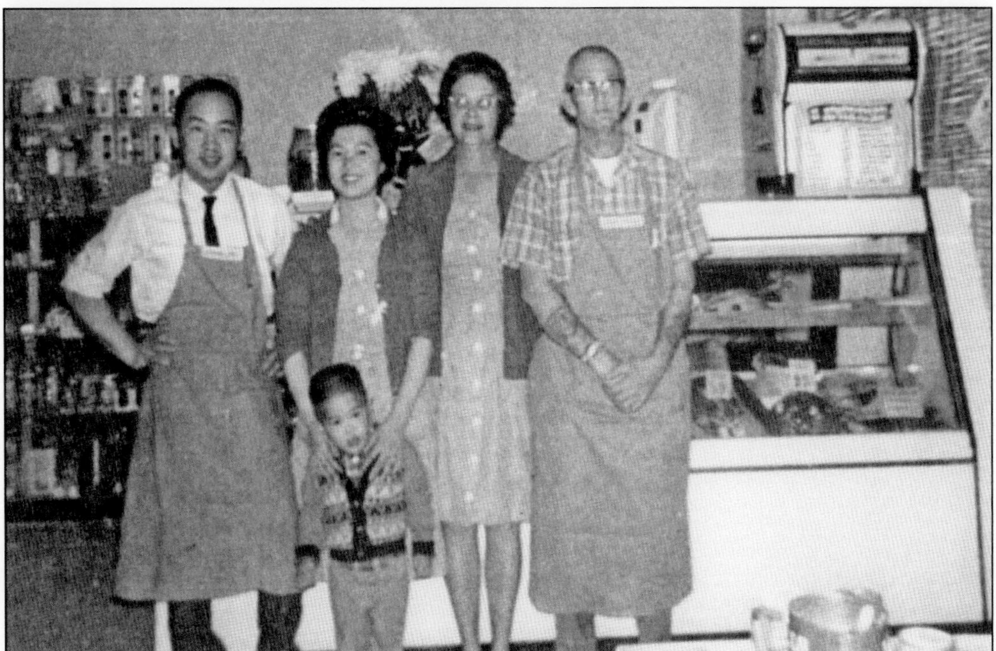

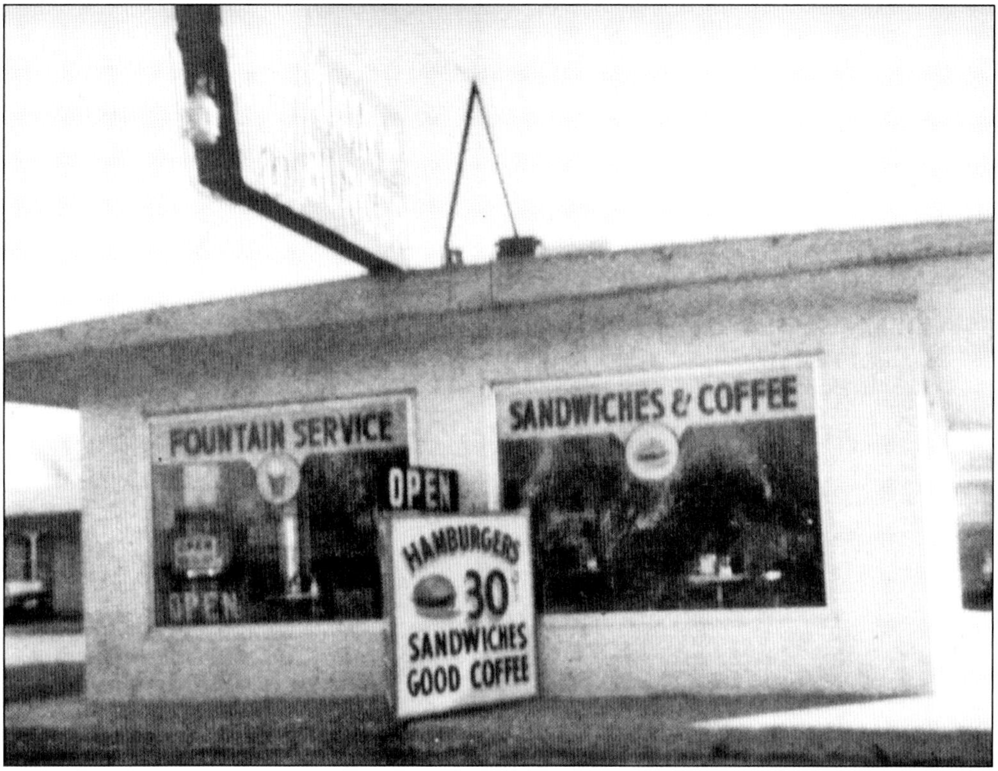

The Dairy Burger was built by W.B. and Mary Wilkins in the 1950s. In 1961, it was owned by Ted Krigbaum and in 1963 by John, Mildred, and Pat Medeke. Chan and Reva Lowe ran it in 1968. Claude Fortenberry called it the Desert Garden Oasis when he owned it, and the Candelaria family named it El Jacarita. In 1969, it was the scene of the shooting of Deputy Sheriff Leroy Brown, the result of a grudge held by a man he had once arrested. (Above, courtesy of Guy Clerc; below, courtesy of Jim Spikes.)

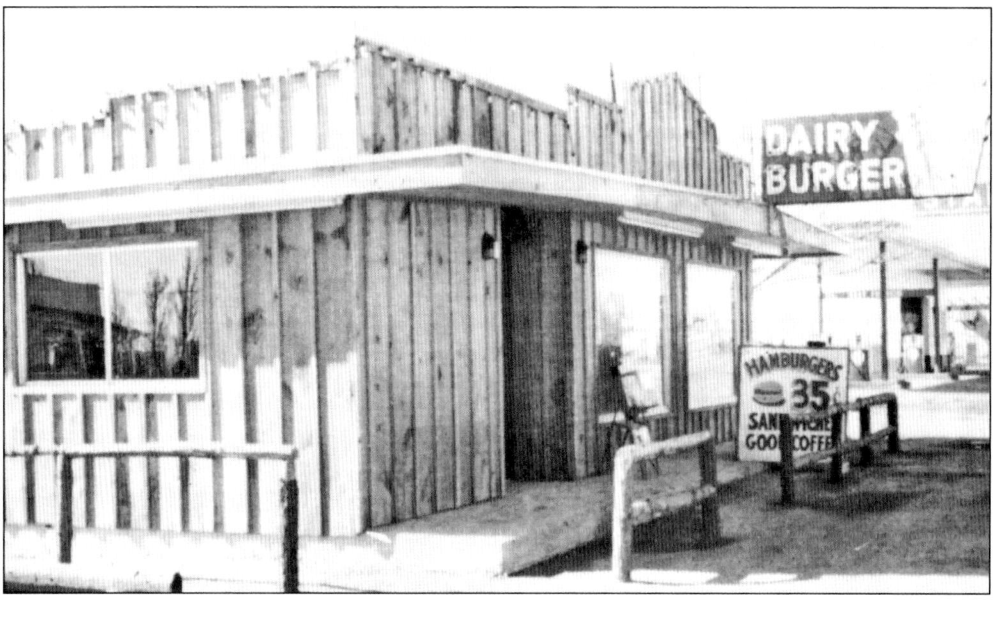

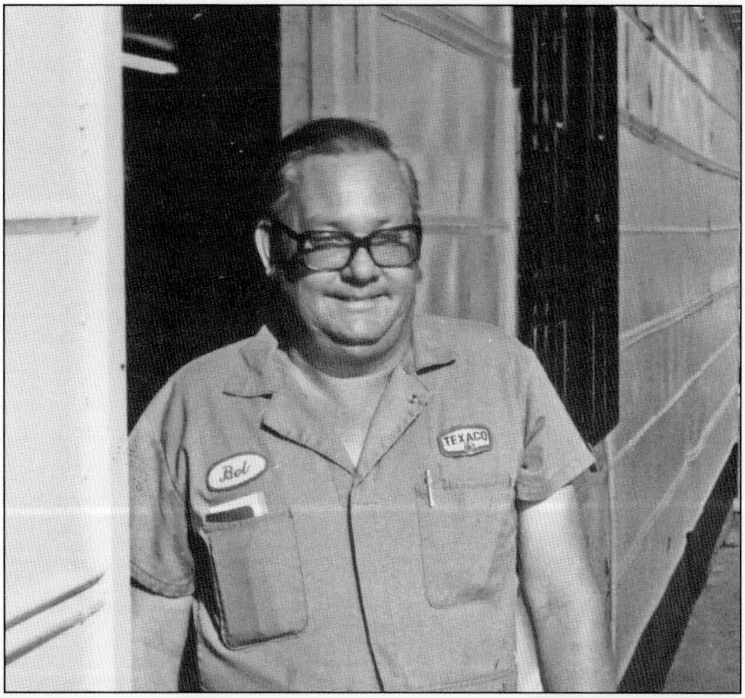

Robert Mefford, the "unofficial mayor," owned a service station and delicatessen that burned July 5, 2009. His father, Thomas Mefford, bought the Sunset service station from Tom Fousel in 1951. All traffic was stopped during a Bowie snowstorm when the family arrived from New Jersey. Thomas said, "I found a place where only six inches of snow stops everything, so this is where I want to live." (Courtesy of Barbara Blandin.)

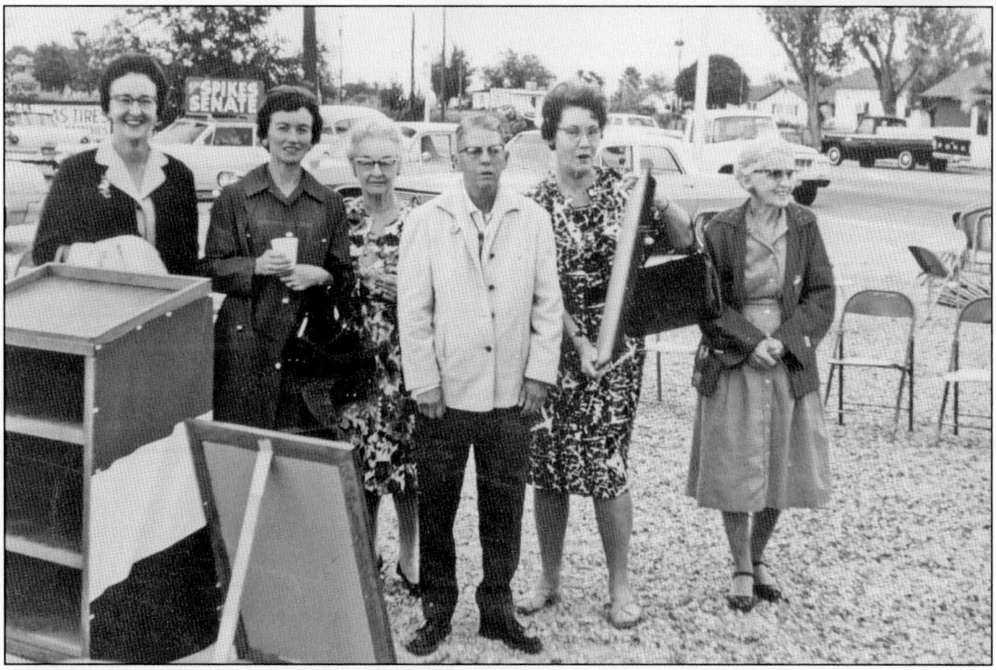

Dedication for the new post office was held on October 18, 1964. Master of ceremonies was Jack Spikes with music provided by Martin Scott and a dedication by William Murphy, of the Post Office Department in Denver, Colorado. Congressman Morris Udall presented the flag. Sen. Albert Spikes gave the address. Pictured are, from left to right, Mary Wertenberger Doyle, Barbara Welker, Nellie Spikes, postmistress Ethel Parkhurst, unidentified, and Nora Dickson. (Courtesy of Barbara Blandin.)

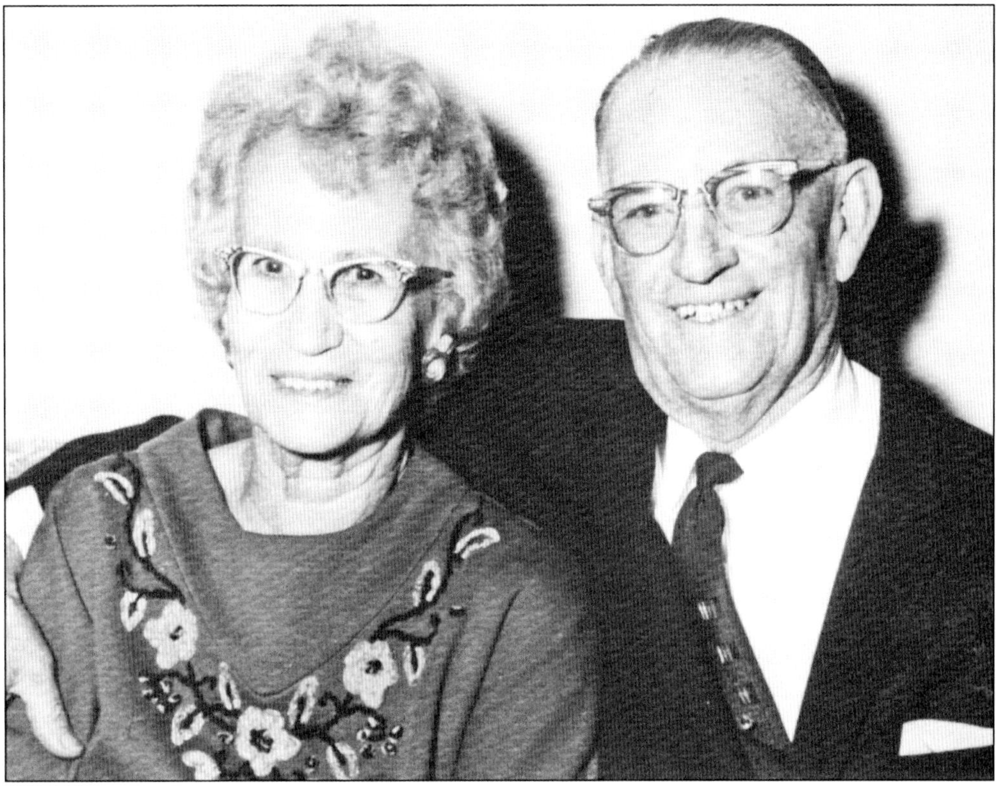

William Ira and Pauline Hall Welker had four children: Donald, Lorraine, Douglas, and Lamar. He was postmaster from 1932 to 1949 and an insurance broker. Welker's father was William Bamsley Welker, who came to Arizona in 1883, cut and hauled grama grass to Fort Bowie, and ran a freight line from Globe to Willcox. His mother was Mary Ella Wanslee. (Courtesy of the Welker family.)

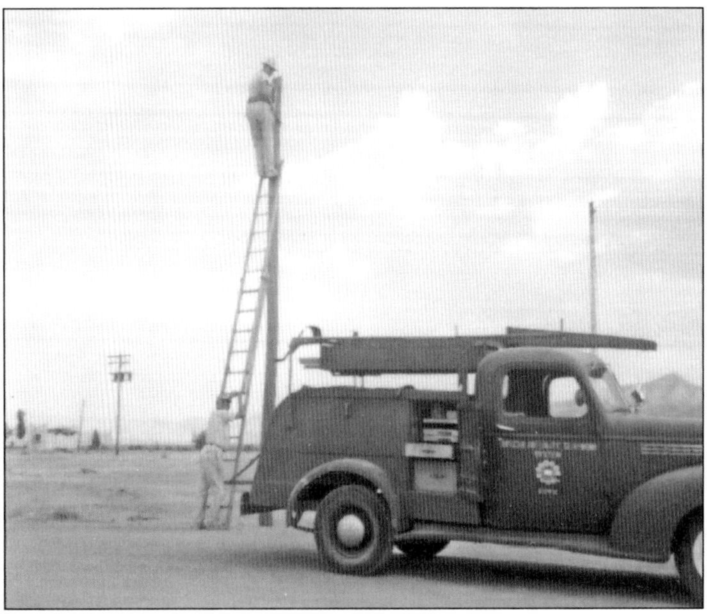

The telephone crew is putting up the poles and wires in 1956 for the first automatic-dial telephone system. Doug Welker (at top of ladder) and his father-in-law Larren Scott (on bottom rung) were the owners of Apache Automatic Telephone System. Work began in 1948 with underground lines. It was the first underground dial system in northern Cochise County. (Courtesy of the Welker family.)

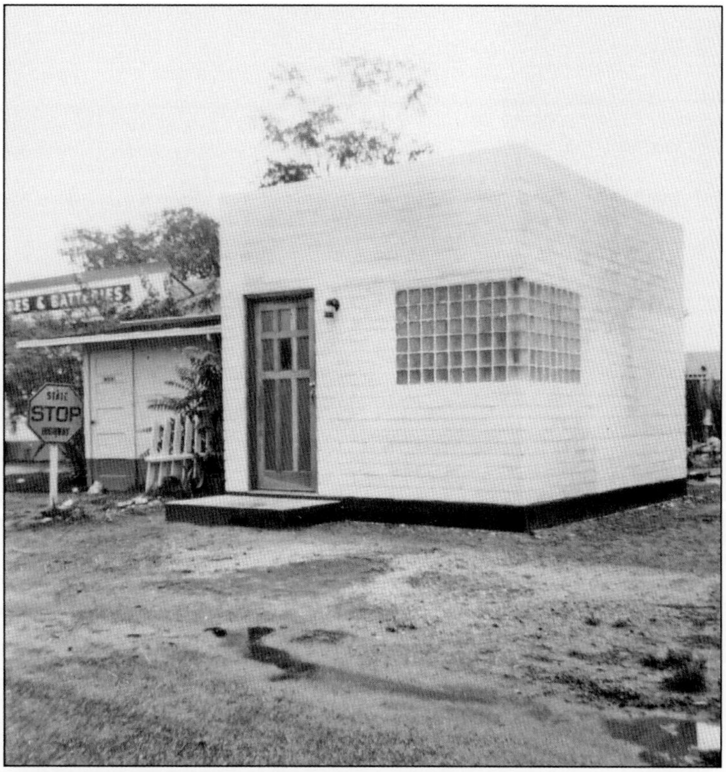

Apache Automatic Telephone System office was located at the rear of Welker's Standard service station on Central Avenue and Business Loop 10. It became operational on April 1, 1950, and was in service until 1964, when it was sold to Valley Telephone Cooperative, based in Willcox. (Courtesy of the Welker family.)

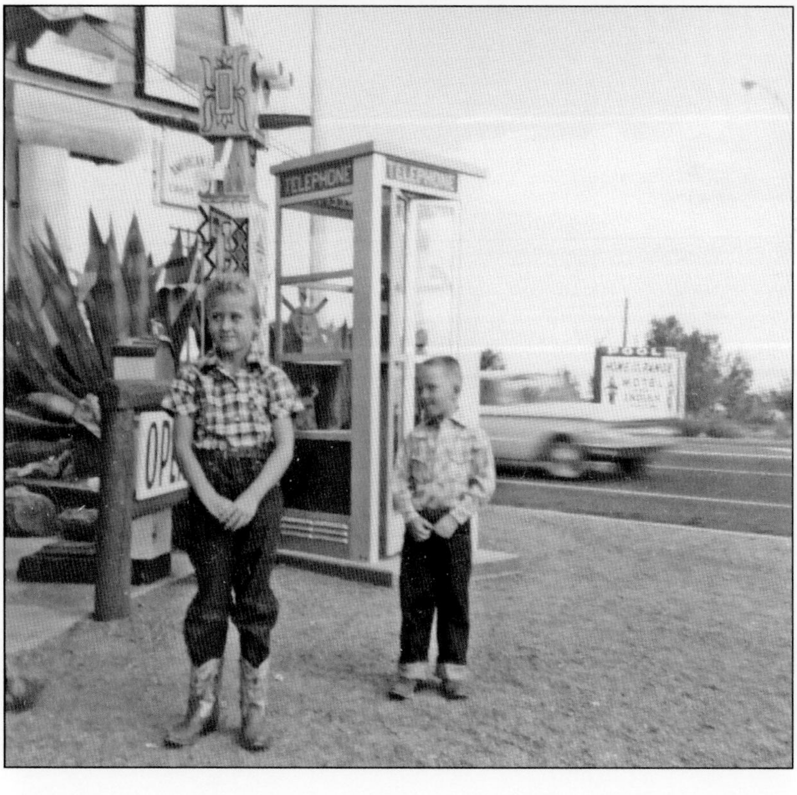

Nancy-Jean Welker and Tommy Cooke stand in front of the very first telephone booth in town in 1961. It was located in front of the Home on the Range Motel. Other booths were put up at Yucca Lodge and Skeets Tavern. The telephone prefix was Victor 7. (Courtesy of the Welker family.)

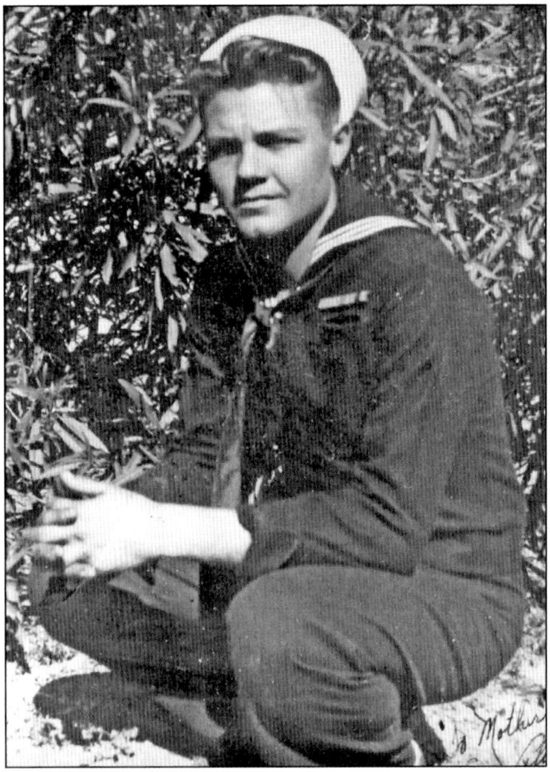

At age 31, Oscar Phillip "Dogie" Olander became the youngest sheriff ever in Arizona and served two terms as Cochise County sheriff. The 1960s television series *The Sheriff of Cochise County* was based on actual case files. Olander later became chief of security for Phelps Dodge Mining Company. His parents, Anton and Sallie Olander, made homestead entry on November 7, 1919, in Heaton Canyon. (Courtesy of Betty Dugie.)

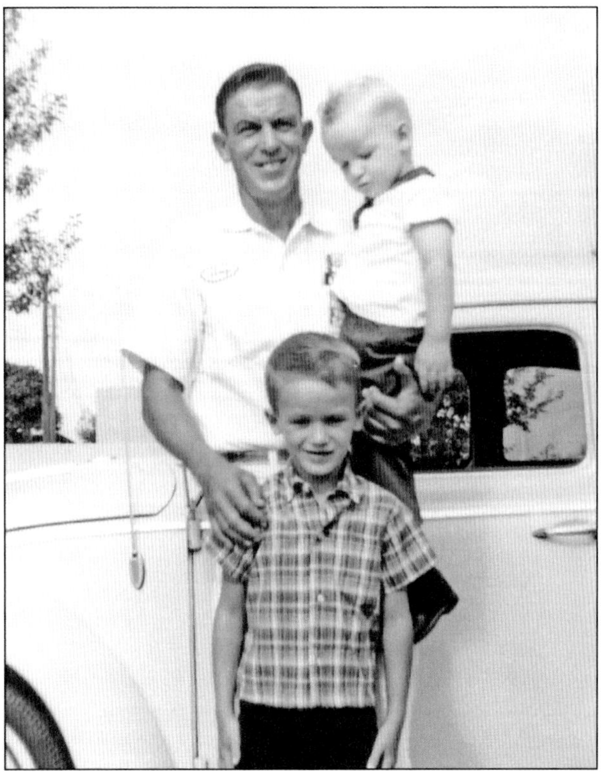

Deputy Sheriff Leroy Brown is holding son Todd with son Jeff in front. Brown was killed in the line of duty on December 6, 1969, in the Dairy Burger. Andres Griego threw hot coffee in Brown's face and shot him in the head. Griego ran to the high school, where he shot and killed himself. Brown's wife, Jackie, was presented his Medal of Valor. (Courtesy of Todd Brown.)

Thomas Cooke, born in England, learned the blacksmith trade. In 1928, he married Opal Wheeler, a Bowie schoolteacher, in Cortaro, Arizona, where he ran a store and post office. He served as Bowie justice of the peace from 1945 to 1962. His home was his office until he constructed the original court building in 1953. Their children are Doris, Tommy, Joe, Phyllis, and Joyce. (Courtesy of Bowie Justice Court.)

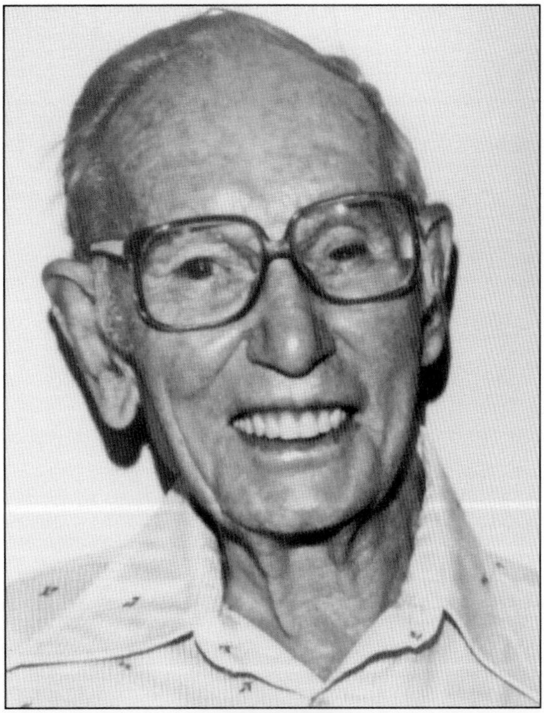

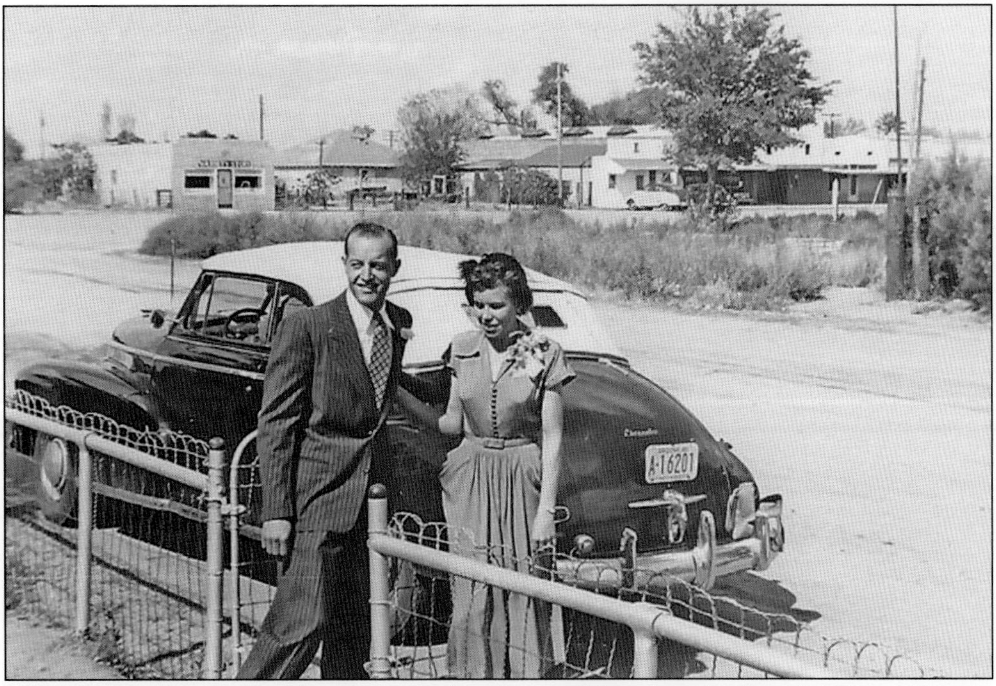

Doris Cook and Eugene Engler are pictured on their wedding day, October 23, 1949, with Bowie buildings in the background. Their children are Jeanette and Don. Doris was recognized for outstanding service while secretary at Bowie School. She worked at the school from 1964 to 1995, serving eight different school superintendents. Former students attest how her encouragement created a great positive influence in their lives. (Courtesy of Jeanette Burcham.)

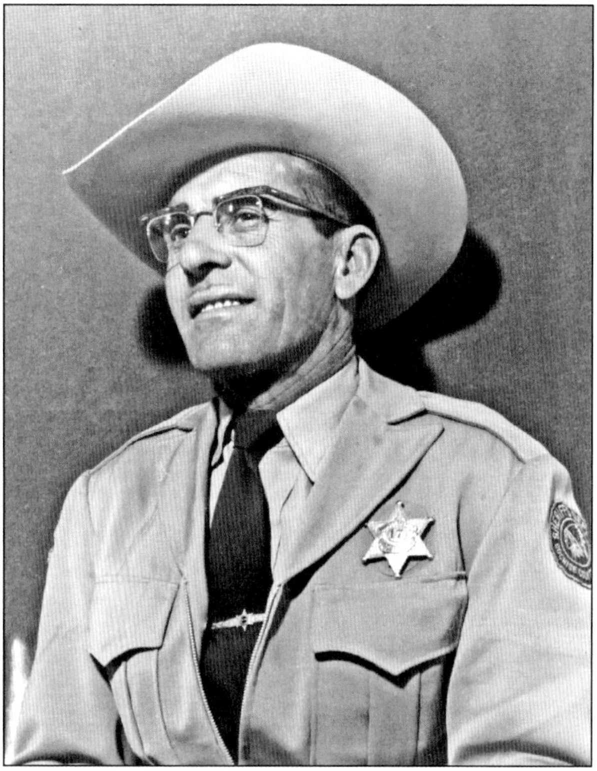

Cliff Dickson, local barber, was born in 1915 at Bear Springs and married Edra Frame. He was deputy sheriff and then justice of the peace, from 1963 to 1966. Escorted by his friend and fellow deputy Claude Fortenberry to the state prison in Florence, he served 18 months for mismanagement of court funds. He liked showing his customers his collection of photographs of highway accidents. (Courtesy of Bowie Justice Court.)

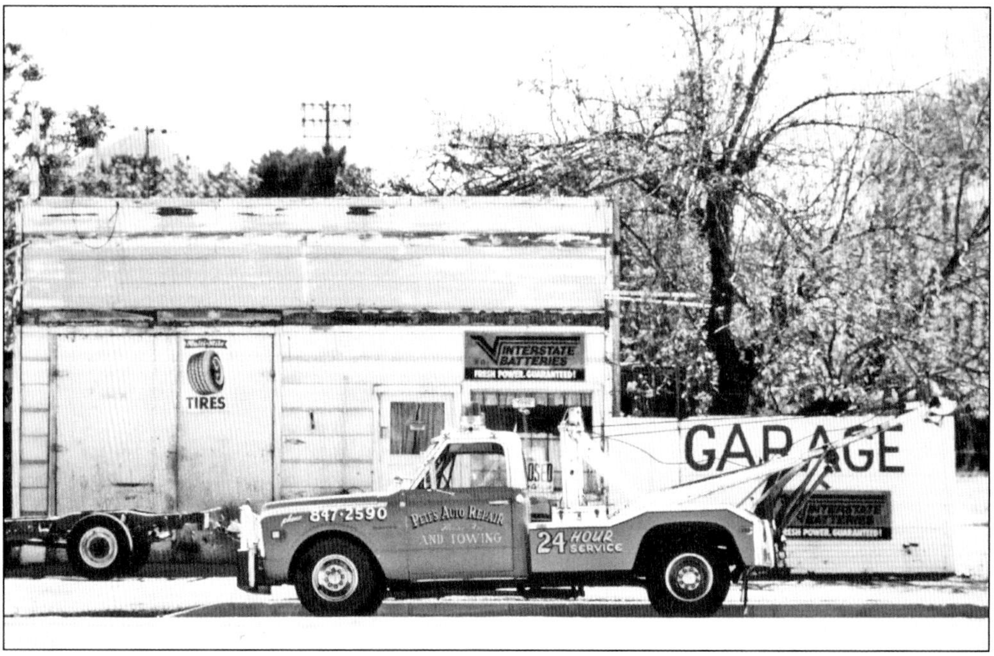

Pete's Garage was owned by Pete Hernandez. It was the old Dixie Dickson's Union 76 service station, owned by Cliff's brother Warren H. Dickson. Their parents were Antice and Nora Reed Dickson. Pete built stock cars for racing. He is married to Treva McConnell. (Courtesy of Barbara Blandin.)

Billie B. Cawood served as justice of the peace from 1967 to 1970. His wife is Rose. His parents were Henry and Cassie Blair Cawood. Their other children were Donald, Richard, and Pauline. Morris Cawood was his cousin. (Courtesy of Bowie Justice Court.)

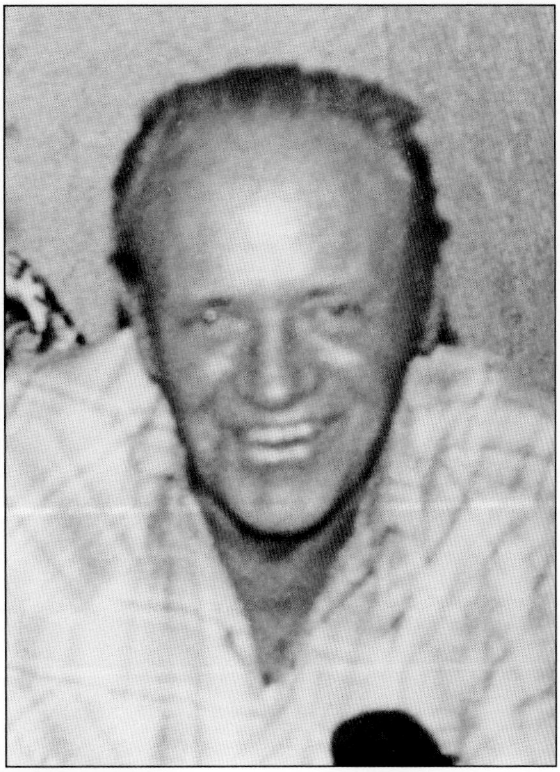

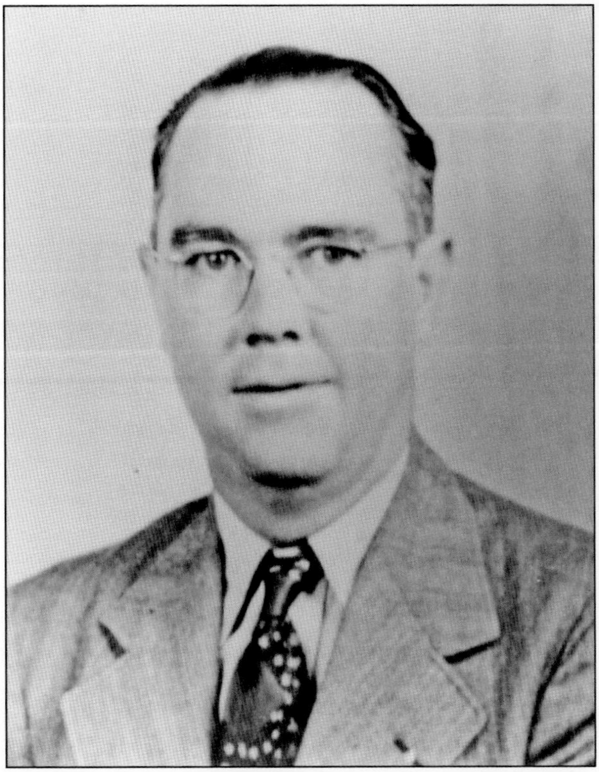

Wallace Lundquist was elected justice of the peace from 1971 to 1974. His father worked for Southern Pacific Railroad and moved the family to many different towns. He was a deputy sheriff and the first city manager of Willcox, Arizona. A street was named after him but later changed to Rex Allen Drive. He and wife, Vera Wooten, had two daughters, Phyllis and Laura. (Courtesy of Bowie Justice Court.)

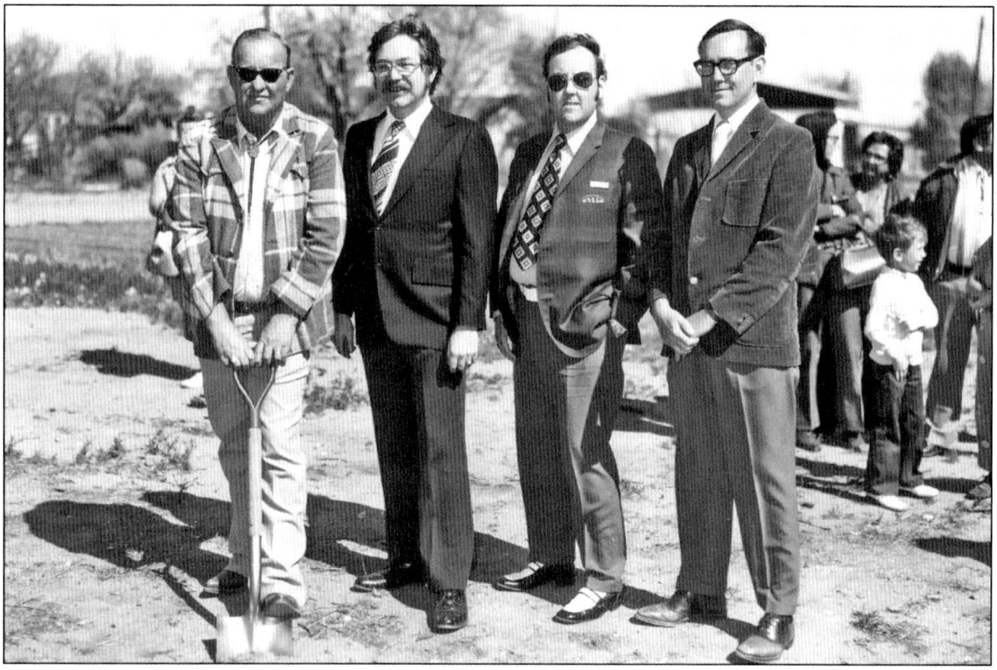

County supervisor Tommy Thompson, with a special golden shovel, digs the first shovelful of dirt in the groundbreaking ceremonies for the new medical clinic on March 17, 1975. From left to right are Thompson, Dr. Marvin Combs, of Willcox, was the doctor in charge; Russell Cullison was a full-time physician's associate, and Vernon Baker was chairman of the board of directors. Not pictured is Josie Lawhon, member of the board and great promoter of the clinic. (Courtesy of SSVHS.)

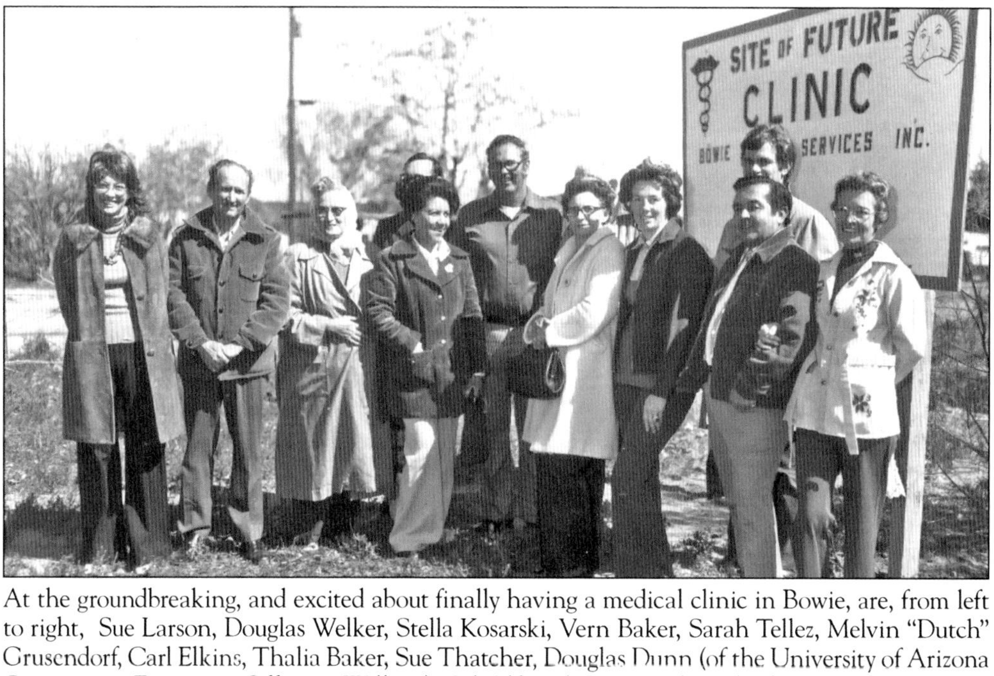

At the groundbreaking, and excited about finally having a medical clinic in Bowie, are, from left to right, Sue Larson, Douglas Welker, Stella Kosarski, Vern Baker, Sarah Tellez, Melvin "Dutch" Grusendorf, Carl Elkins, Thalia Baker, Sue Thatcher, Douglas Dunn (of the University of Arizona Cooperative Extension Office in Willcox), Gil Alfaro (postmaster), and Edna Weber. (Courtesy of SSVHS.)

Five

EDUCATION AND ATHLETICS

Bowie has been proud of its schools since the very first one in 1885. The school is the heart and soul of the town. Students received an excellent education from many fine teachers but especially from Albert and Nellie Spikes, Eva Hall, Mary Wertenberger Doyle, and Lendon and Mildred Enloe.

Albert R. Spikes was superintendent until 1942. During that time, the high school, gymnasium, swimming pool, and tennis courts were constructed. As a member of the State House of Representatives and the State Senate, from 1942 to 1968, he devoted his life to teachers' rights and the right of everyone to the best education possible. He pioneered the movement to create junior colleges, using county financing, through which Cochise College was founded. Bowie High School was dedicated to him in November 2010.

Spikes also recognized the importance of sports and athletics. He was secretary of the Rifle Club, organized October 24, 1916, with J.F. Ryan, T.D. Downey, J.B. Nash, A.C. Ward, C.F. Sensner, Dana Milner, Jack Hardy, and Pres. J.E. Frank. He played first base and was coach on the town's baseball team. He coached and played center on the 1916 basketball team. He was president of the Tennis Club, which had two teams, the Fords and the Cadillacs. The very first football team used old uniforms donated by the University of Arizona.

Lendon Enloe became superintendent from 1941 to 1964, during which time a new elementary school was built. He was responsible for forming the wonderful music program and the marching band. Sam Ambrose became superintendent in 1964 and added homemaking, business, agriculture departments with a new agriculture-shop building, and a new library. He was followed by Curtis Green, Daniel Forrest, and Vern Baker. On January 29, 2009, the gymnasium was named in honor of Supt. Bruce Brown.

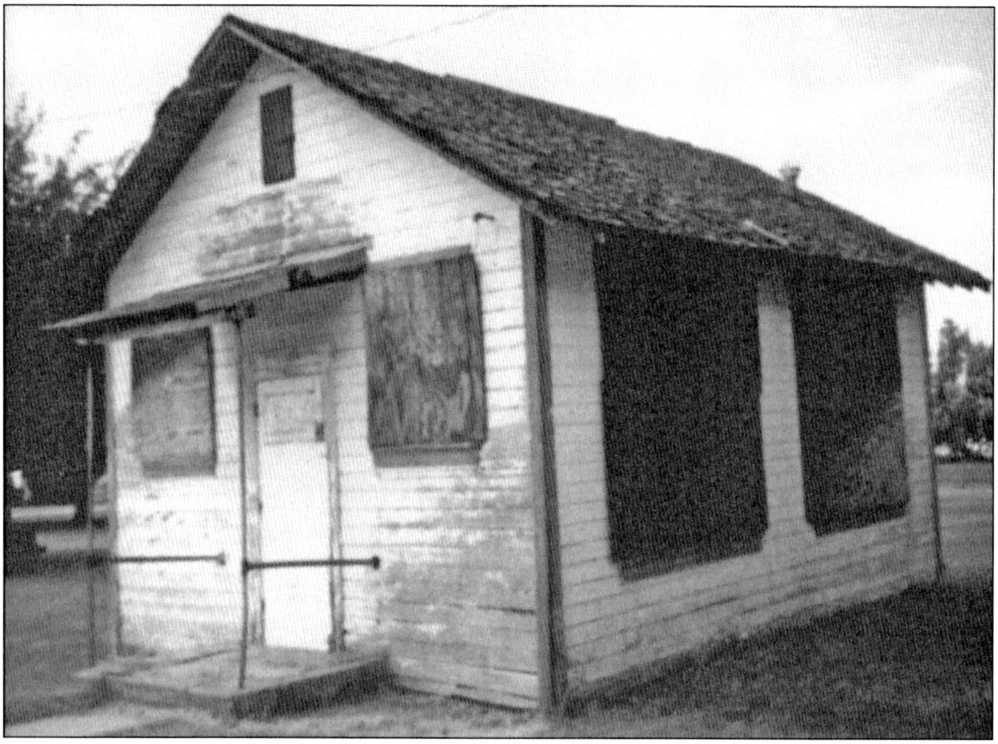

Captain Tevis donated the land, and Southern Pacific donated a portable building for the first school in May 1885. This one-room schoolhouse, measuring 18 feet by 24 feet, was used as a kindergarten from August 1920 until 1980. In December 1999, as a millennium project, a group called Global Volunteers worked with community members to renovate the old building. (Courtesy of Barbara Blandin.)

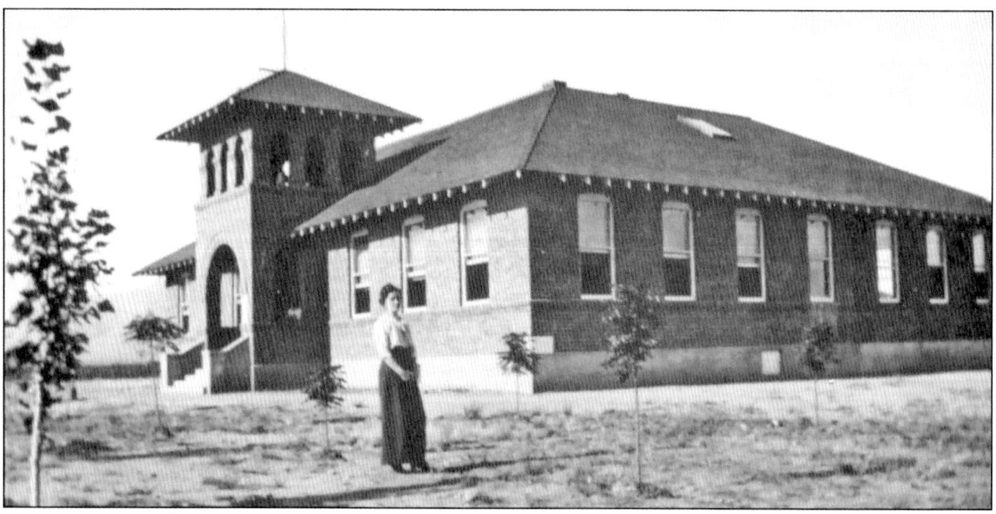

The grammar school, with principal Mrs. C.P. Dawson, was completed in March 1913 on property donated by Cuthbert S. Kellum. Cawood brothers excavated, and Angle & Bush provided the lumber. Ora Lee was the teacher. In 1914, another room was added. New teachers were Carey Fields, Stella Baker, and Bertha Erickson. It was named in honor of Eva Hall on February 22, 1999. (Courtesy of Janice Grizzle.)

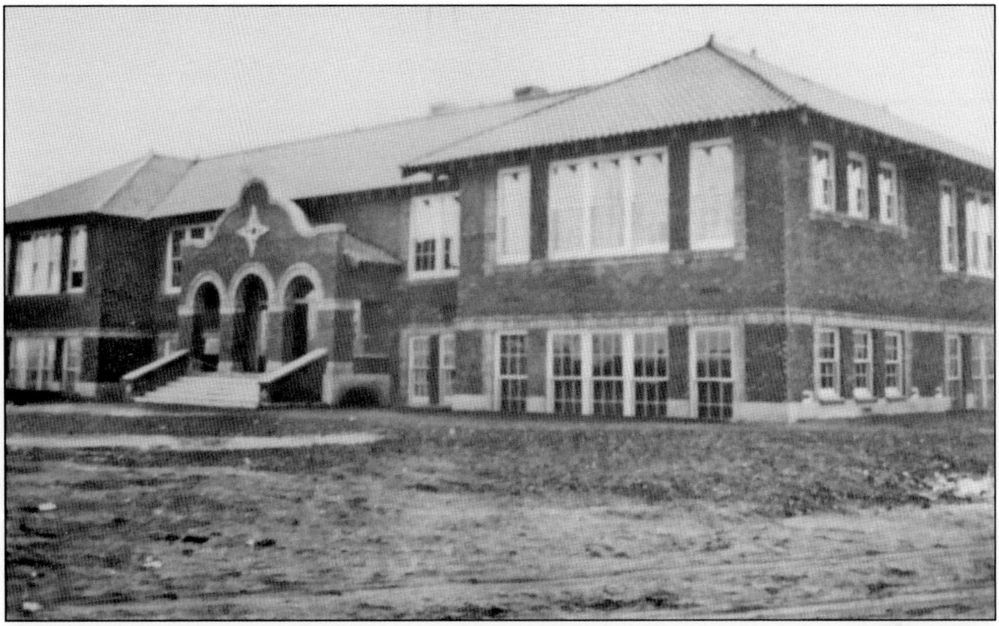

Only two years of high school were offered in 1920. Women were not allowed to vote in the 1921 school bond election unless they owned property in their name. The high school was built in 1922 with the first graduation on June 14, 1923, in the auditorium. The graduates were Nathalie Aldrich and Katherine Richards, who sang a duet. The school board president was W.M. Aldrich with members W.G. Richards and Joe Chambers. Henry O. Jaastad was the architect for the grammar school, high school, and gymnasium. Below, the teachers and students gather in front of the high school in 1923. Teachers were Jennie Lynn Lenox (mathematics and science), Frances Bowles (English and history), and principal and teacher Albert R. Spikes. (Both, courtesy of Janice Grizzle.)

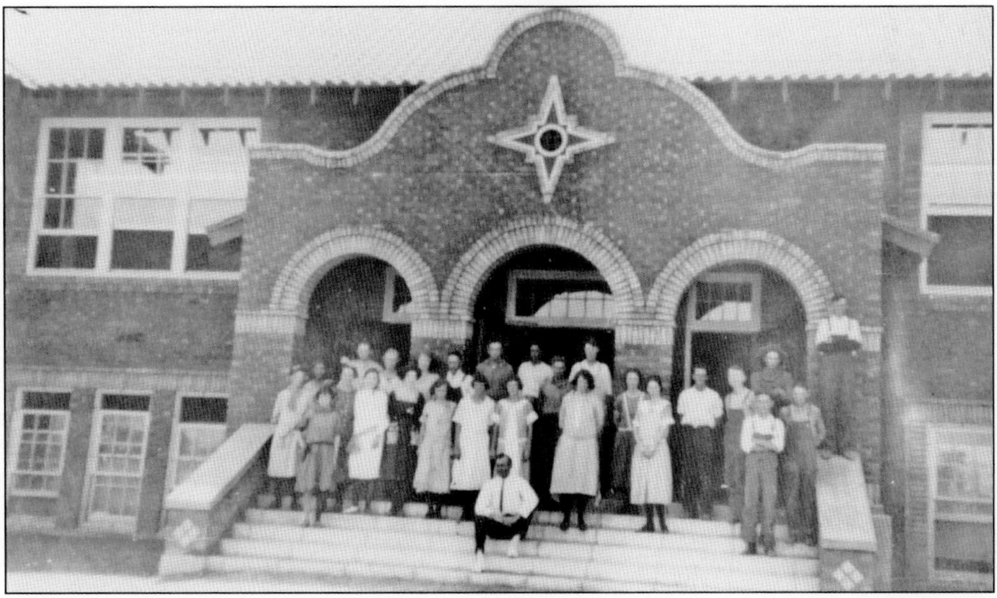

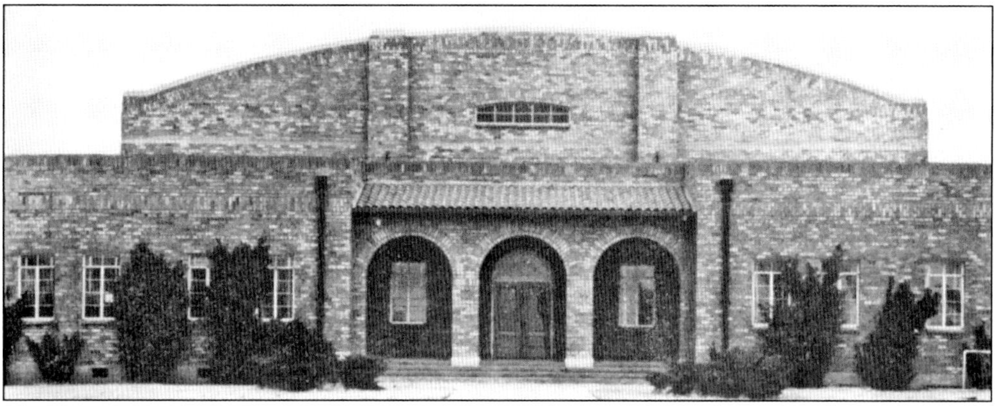

Womack Construction Company built one of the finest gymnasiums in the state in 1940 at a cost of $45,000. It was designed to accommodate 350 people for all school and town events. The 94-by-64-feet spring floor had one inch of spun glass under the wood floor for dancing, basketball, and volleyball. It included a kitchen, dining room, and lounge. (Courtesy of Evelyn Lathram.)

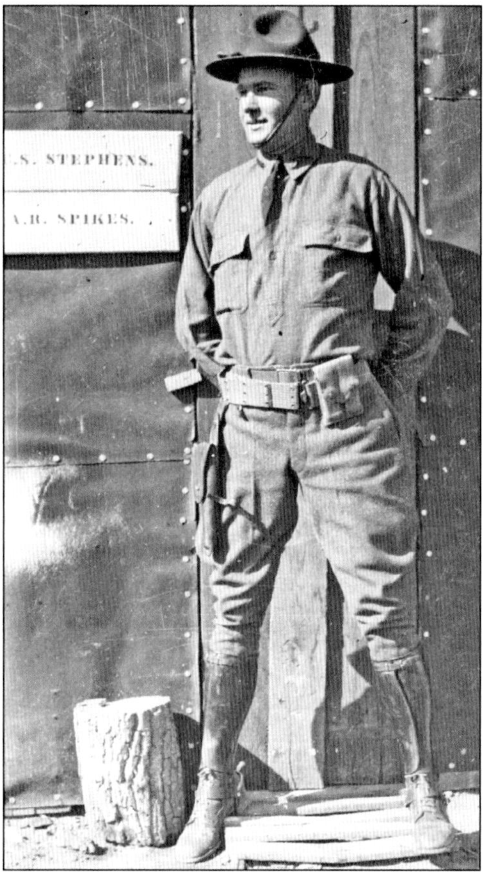

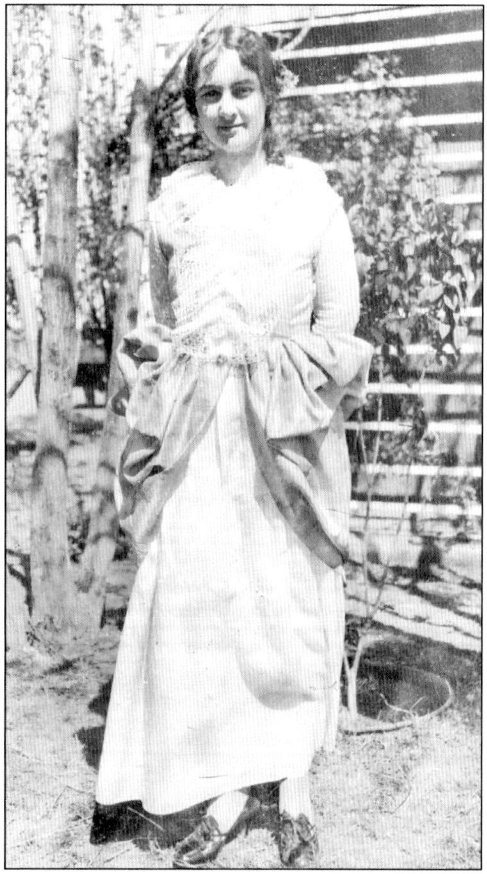

Albert R. Spikes became principal of schools in September 1915. He left for World War I and was cited for bravery in the Army occupation on the Rhine. G.L. Downs and later Mrs. Stansbury filled his position. When he returned as principal in 1919, Nellie Dechard, the new grammar school and music teacher, caught his eye. She supervised all plays and entertainment. They were married in May 1920. (Courtesy of Evelyn Lathram.)

Wanda Browning came to teach English, history, girls' athletics, and be school librarian in 1923. She accompanied the students when they competed in inter–high school debate contests in Phoenix. She was chosen by the State University to judge the debates between Safford and Tucson. Her parents were Jack and Hettie Browning. She and Clarence Falk were married on June 23, 1925, in Bowie. (Courtesy of Peta-Anne Tenney.)

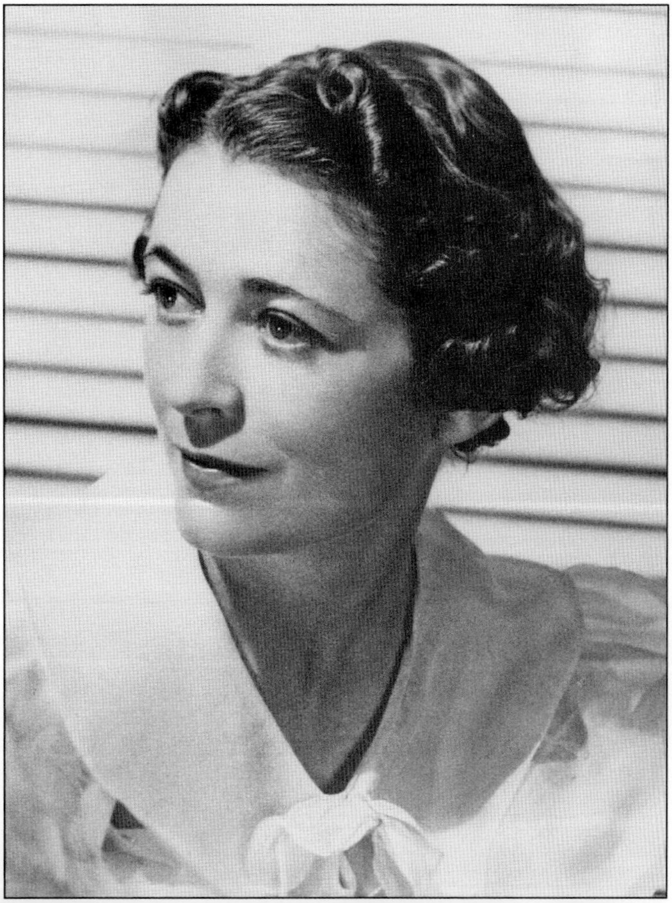

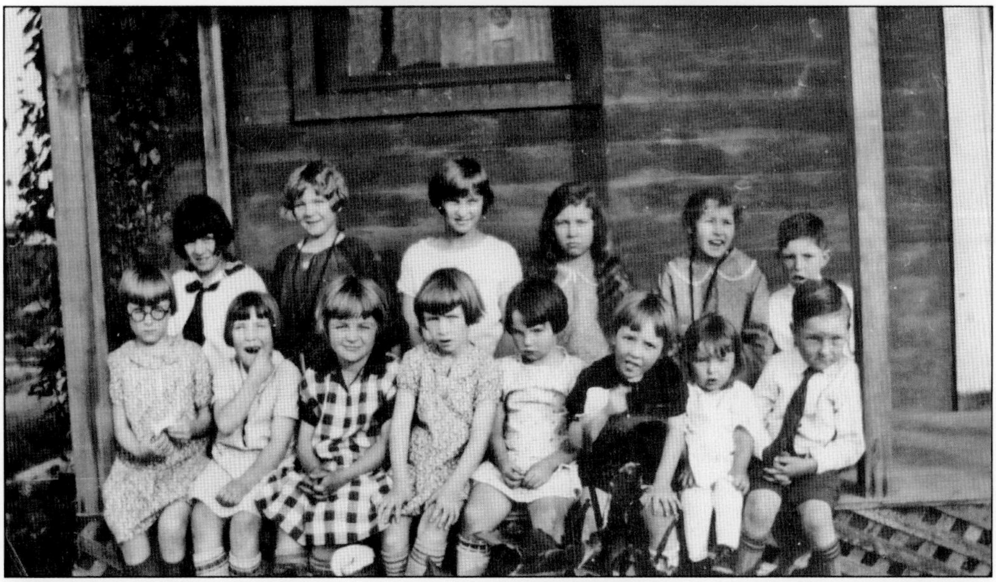

The second- and third-grade classes in 1929 included Delbert Fousel (first row, far right) and Edward Fousel (second row, far right). (Courtesy of Delbert Fousel.)

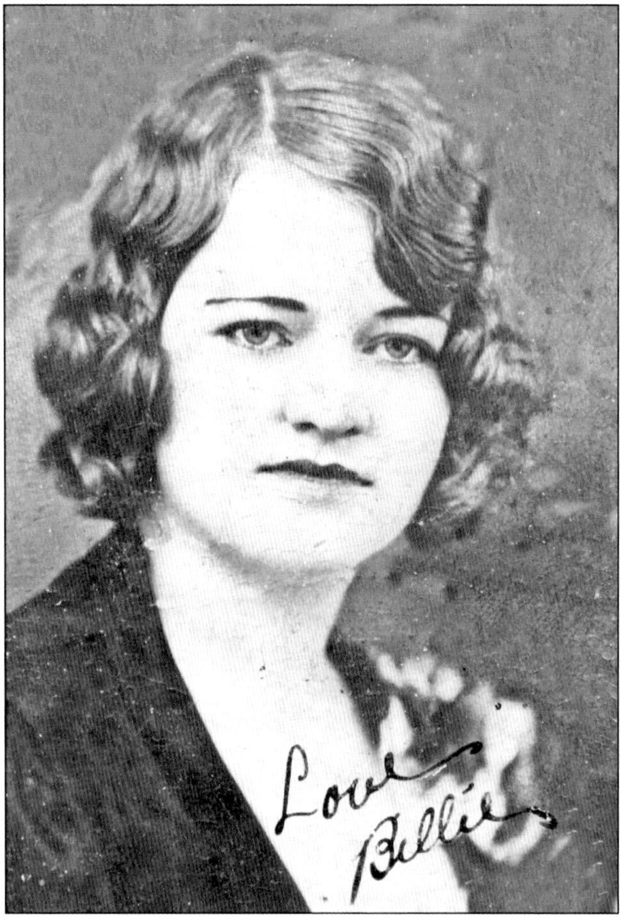

At left, Billie Driscoll was the kindergarten teacher hired in 1929. Her father was the section foreman for Southern Pacific Railroad. Below, students of 1935 are, from left to right, (first row) Leo Gertice, Gordon Gojkovich, Tommy Bartlett, Joe Allen, Jose Gonzales, Roman Hernandez, Jack Saner, Pete Guzman, Sam McKee, and Eddie LaFoe; (second row) Josephine Klump, Amelia Hernandez, Frances Upham, Mary Hunter, Tomasa ?, Opal Thompson, unidentified, Foncie Gillespie, Irma Hunter, Victoria Lopez, unidentified, Dit Gojkovich, and Dorothy Tuttle; (third row) Arthur Navarette, Henry Gonzales, John Thompson, two unidentified, Raymond Thompson, Bill Allen, Albert Olander, Raymond Irvin, Aurora Navarette, Patsy Gurtz, Frances Moore, and Shirley Dillan. (Left, courtesy of Marisela Gonzales; below, courtesy of Clyde W. Allen.)

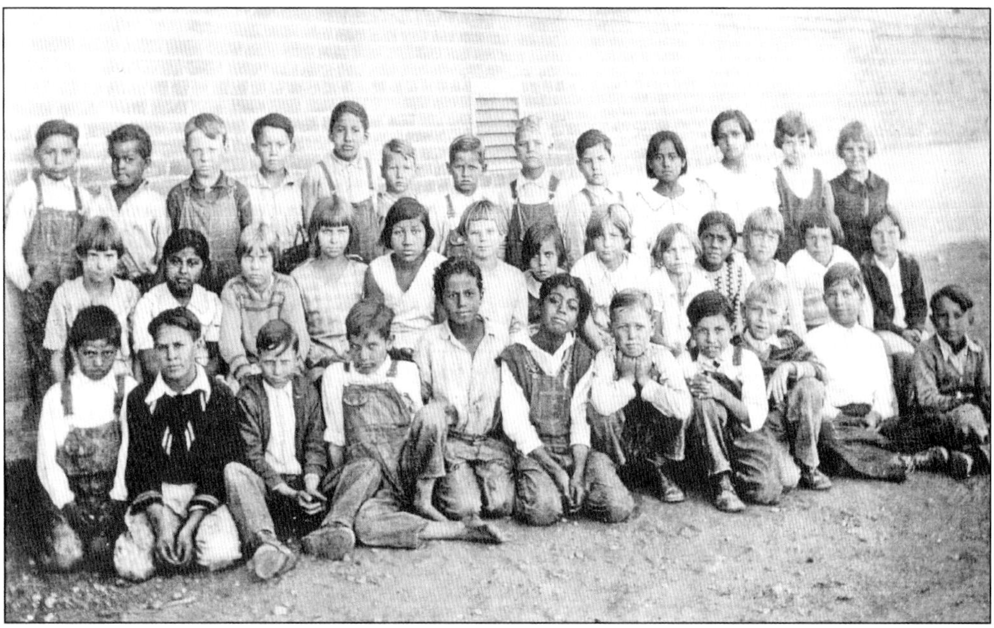

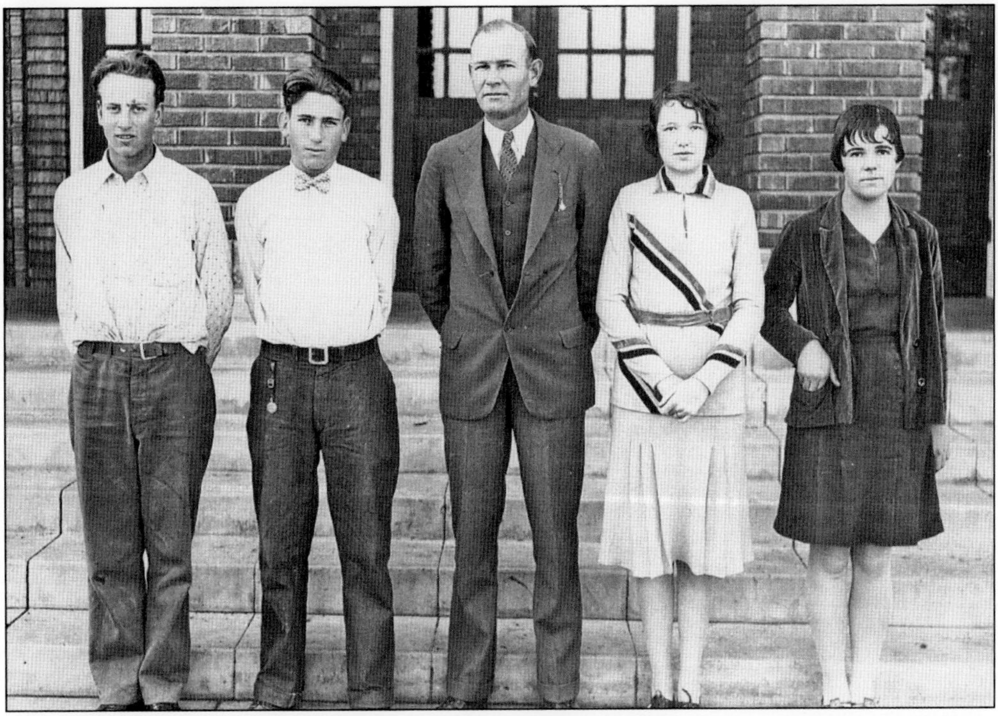

School faculty members around 1940 are, from left to right, Elmer Nelson, unidentified, Supt. Albert R. Spikes, Nannie Mae Pannell (whose father, Guy, worshipful master of the Masons and an agent for Southern Pacific Railroad, was killed in an automobile accident near Bowie in 1936), and Lillie Mae Riggs, daughter of Thomas and Anna Mae Riggs. (Courtesy of Bobby Montana.)

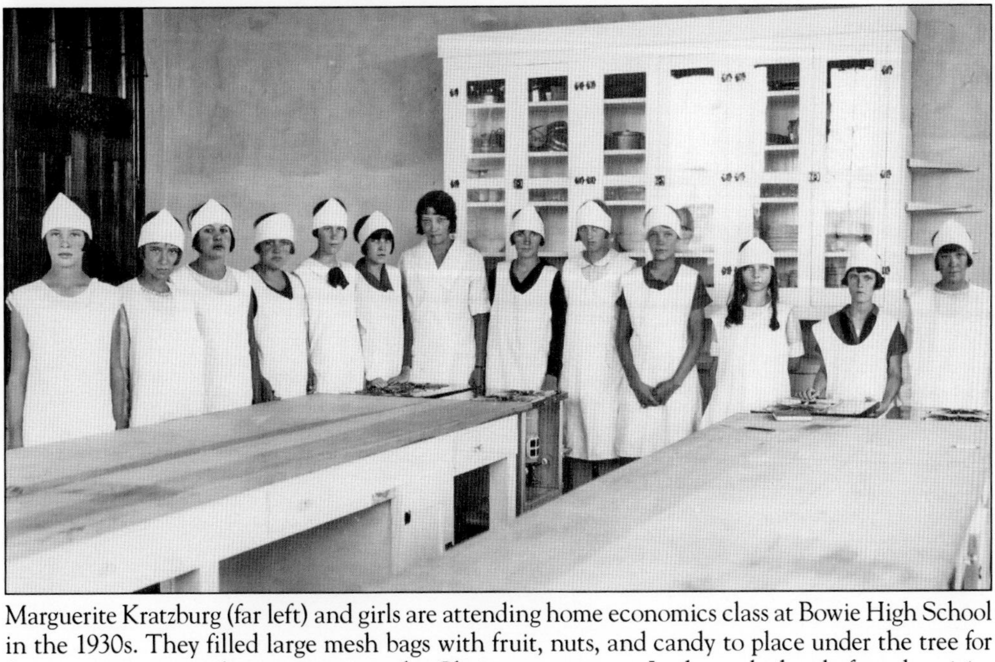

Marguerite Kratzburg (far left) and girls are attending home economics class at Bowie High School in the 1930s. They filled large mesh bags with fruit, nuts, and candy to place under the tree for Santa to give out to the youngsters at the Christmas program. In the early days before electricity or gas, the girls took turns carrying wood inside for the stove. (Courtesy of Vic Boll.)

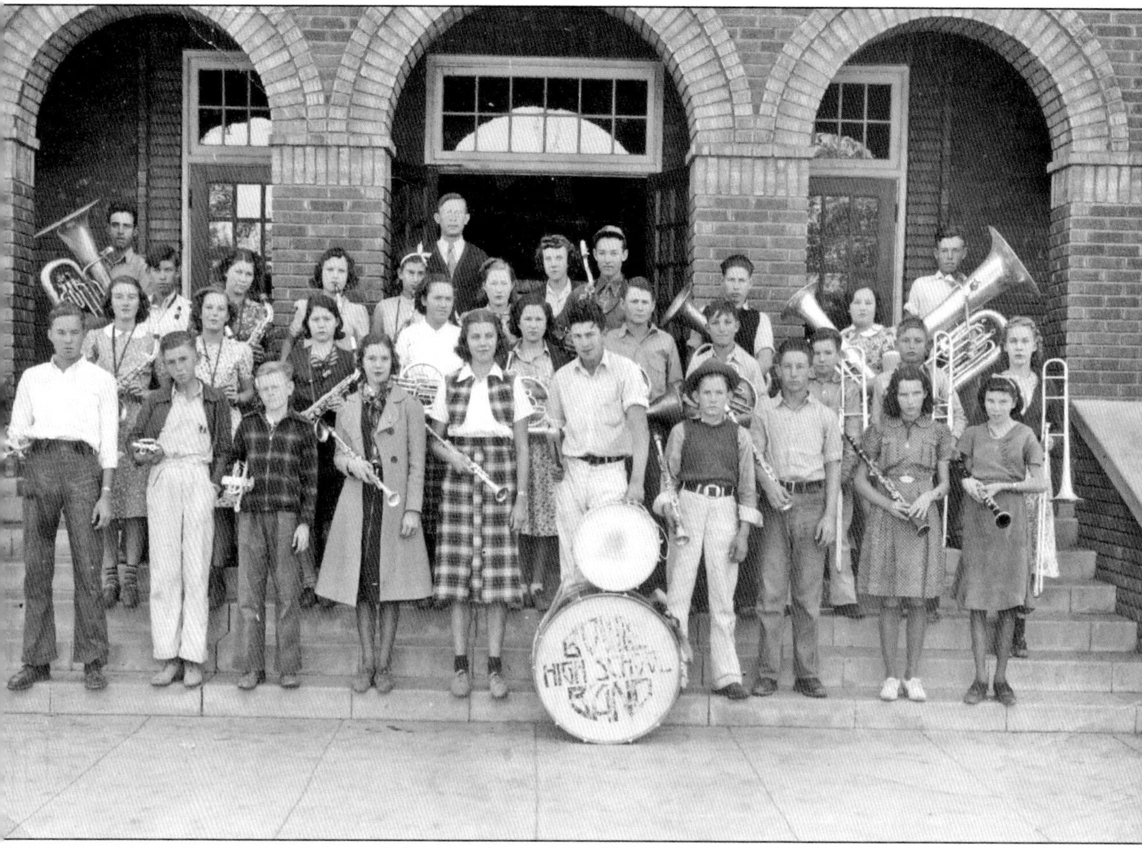

The 1938–1939 high school band was under the supervision of Lendon Enloe. The 35-piece band played over the radio twice and was in parades in Lordsburg and Willcox. The band won a rating of "excellent" at the Southeastern Music Contest in Thatcher. Band members are, from left to right, (first row) Jack Edwards, Sam McKee, Jimmie Blanton, Frances Moore, Billie Jean Bouck, Dennis Vanderpool, Julius Dahlgren, Walter Tuttle, Neva Jane Connelly, and Doralie Garey; (second row) Barbara Scott, Shirley Dillon, Juanita Martin, Vera Harmon, Faye Kelley, John Carleton, George Saner, Ernest Dahlgren, Raymond Fousel, and Frances Upham; (third row) Leo Mendez, Pete Guzman, Helen Duke, Jean Brown, Patsy Gertz, Dell Kelley, Mary Lee Gannon, Jack Spikes, Charles Martin, Dorothy Tuttle, and Hampton Eaton. (Courtesy of Raymond Fousel.)

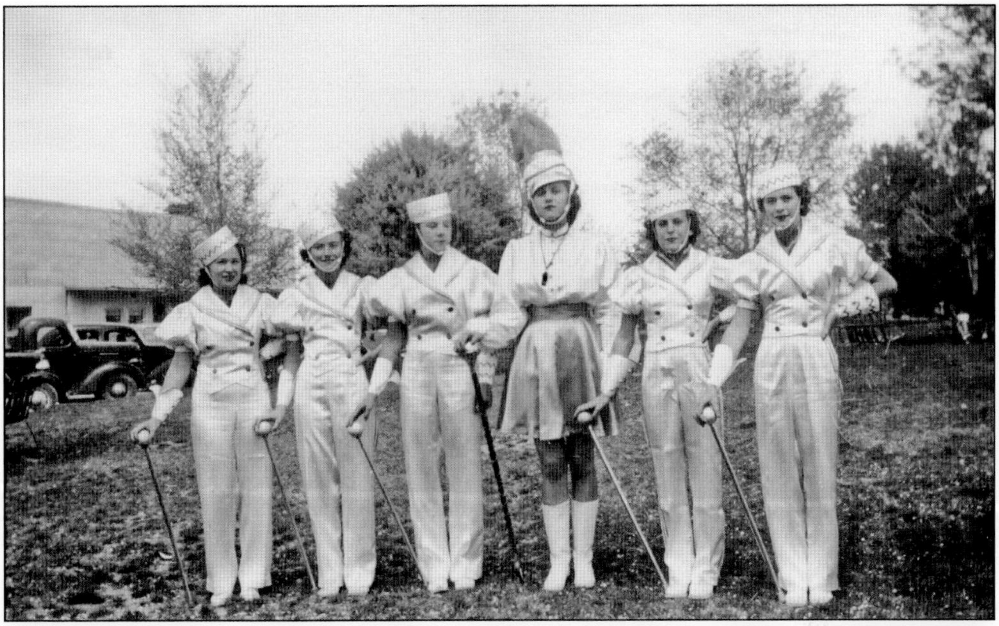

Majorettes in 1939 are, from left to right, Frances Moore, Shirley Dillan, Billie Jean Bouck, Mary Lee Gannon, Barbara Scott, and Dell Kelley, who was class secretary and the only girl in the senior class. Bouck was chosen queen of the Boy Scout Circus in 1938. (Courtesy of Barbara Blandin.)

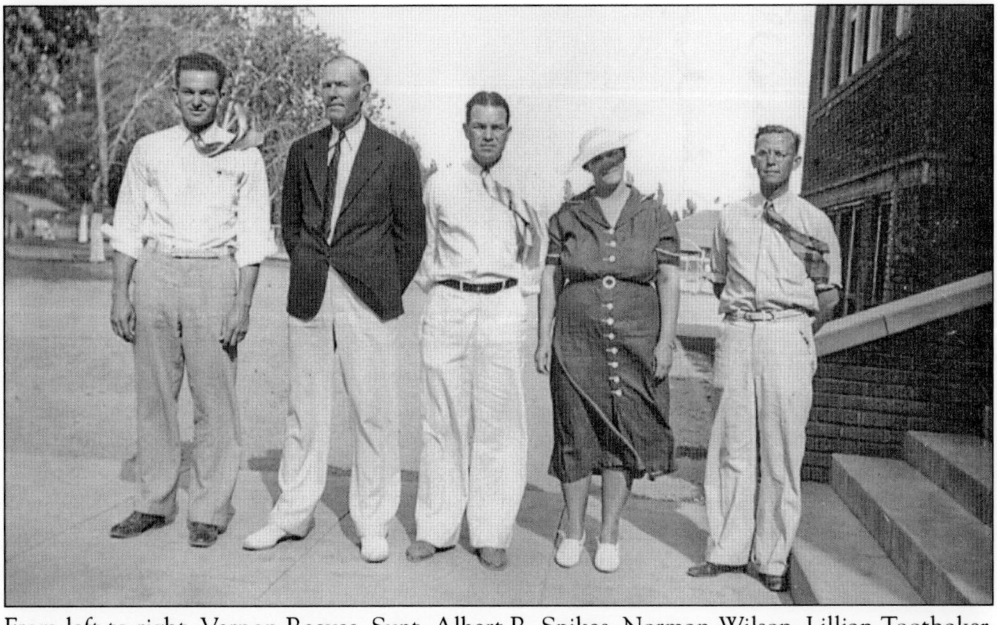

From left to right, Vernon Reeves, Supt. Albert R. Spikes, Norman Wilson, Lillian Toothaker, and Lendon A. Enloe comprised the high school staff of 1939. Reeves taught from 1937 to 1940, joined the Army Air Corps, and retired with the rank of colonel in 1967. He received 10 citations for valor. Wilson was killed in an airplane crash during a snowstorm on the Mogollon Rim in 1958. (Courtesy of Bobby Montana.)

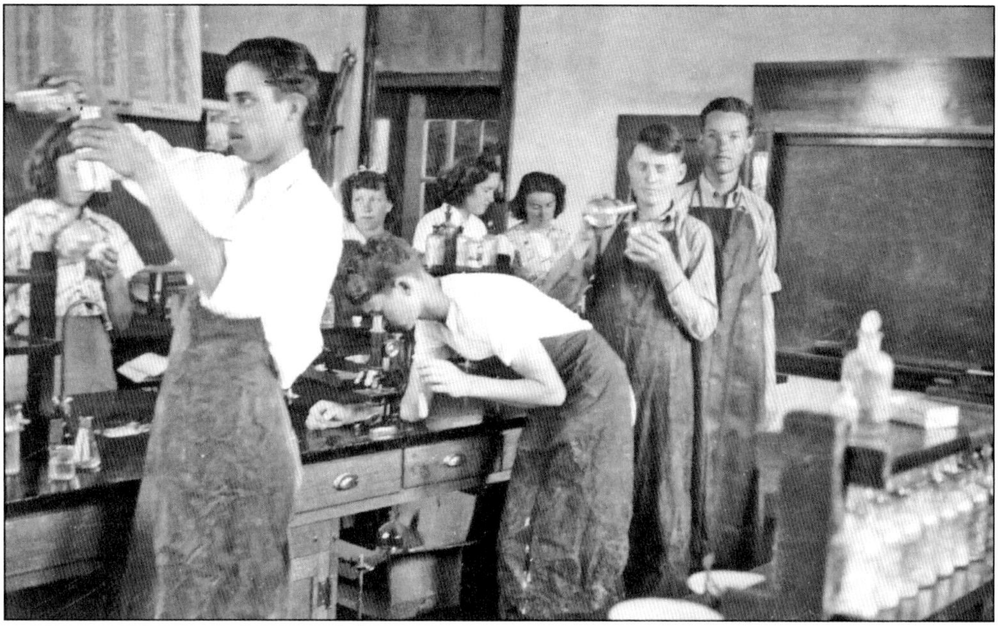

Students performing chemistry lab projects in 1939 include, from left to right, (first row) Leo Mendez, Jack Brown, John Carleton, and Jack Spikes; (second row) Lillie Saner, Dorothy Brown, Vera Harmon, and Barbara "Bobbie" Scott. (Courtesy of Welker family.)

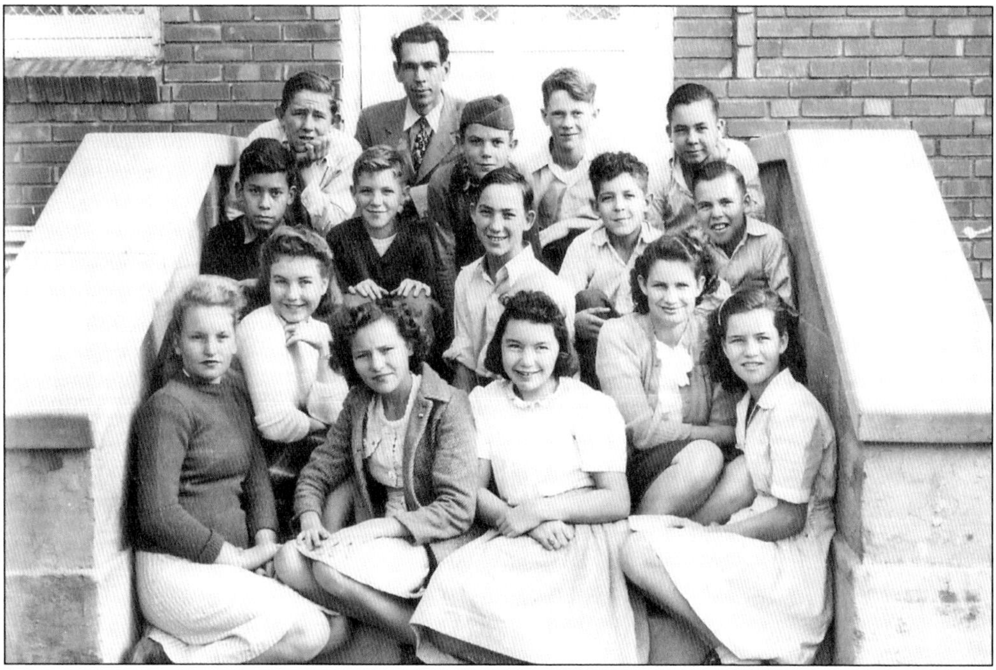

Seventh- and eighth-grade classes in 1942 pose on the steps of the school with their teacher Eugene Wakefield. They are, from left to right, (first row) Mary Doreen Fousel, Betty Woodrow, Vera Takvam, Lois Jean Bertoglio, unidentified, and Ann Takvam; (second row) Lorenzo Abalos, Donald Cawood, Arthur Saner, Gregory Chavez, and Jimmy Snyder; (third row) Charles Harmon, Leroy Brown, Hibberd Knape, and Raymond Snyder. (Courtesy of Gregory Chavez.)

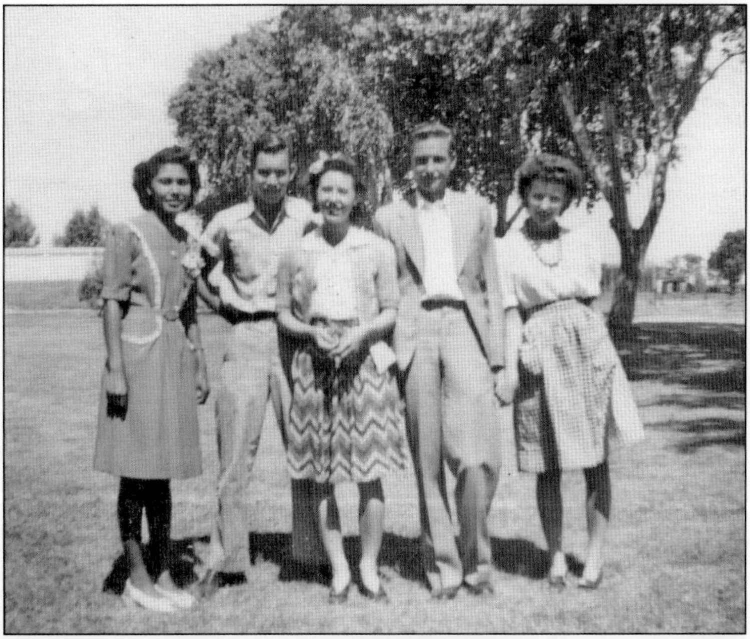

Graduates of the class of 1944 were, from left to right, Victoria Lopez, Ernie Dahlgren, Patty Doyle, Raymond Fousel, and Neva Jane Connelly, whose father owned the Desert Rose rock shop. She married William Longnecker. Raymond married Billie Jean Sheffield in 1945. (Courtesy of Sam McKee.)

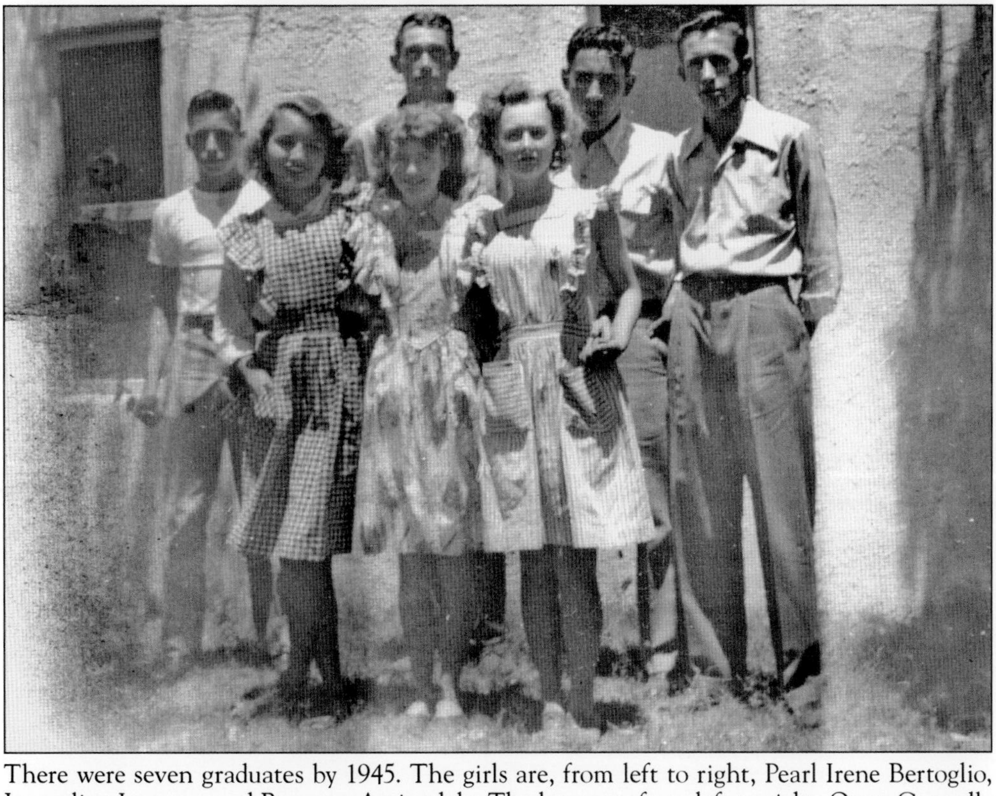

There were seven graduates by 1945. The girls are, from left to right, Pearl Irene Bertoglio, Jacqueline Lenzner, and Ramona Areingdale. The boys are, from left to right, Oscar Connelly Jr. (later killed in Farmington, New Mexico, while working on an oil rig), John Daniel Klump, Feliciano "Chano" Jacques, and Lamar Welker. Dan Klump was the first in a long line of Klumps to graduate from Bowie High School. (Courtesy of Keith Klump.)

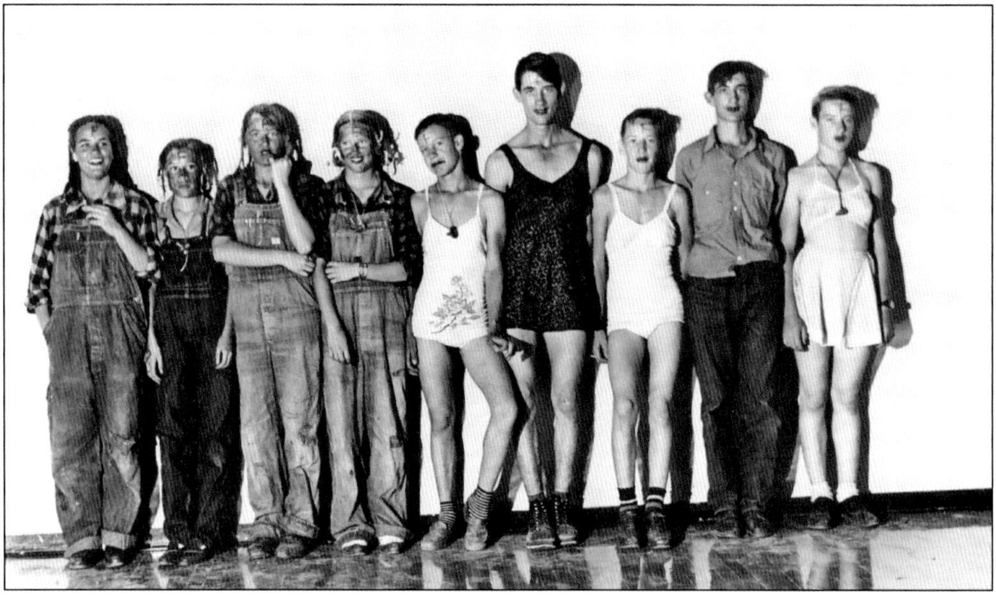

Freshman initiation must have been an interesting day in 1947. The girls are in men's clothes, and the boys are dressed in ladies' underwear, except for Wallace Klump, who probably refused to comply. Pictured are, from left to right, Edith ?, Mary Abalos, Marcia Harmon, Janice Creighton, Louis "Boog" Enloe, Richard Klump, Norman Takvam, Wallace Klump, and Billy Morris. (Courtesy of Janice Grizzle.)

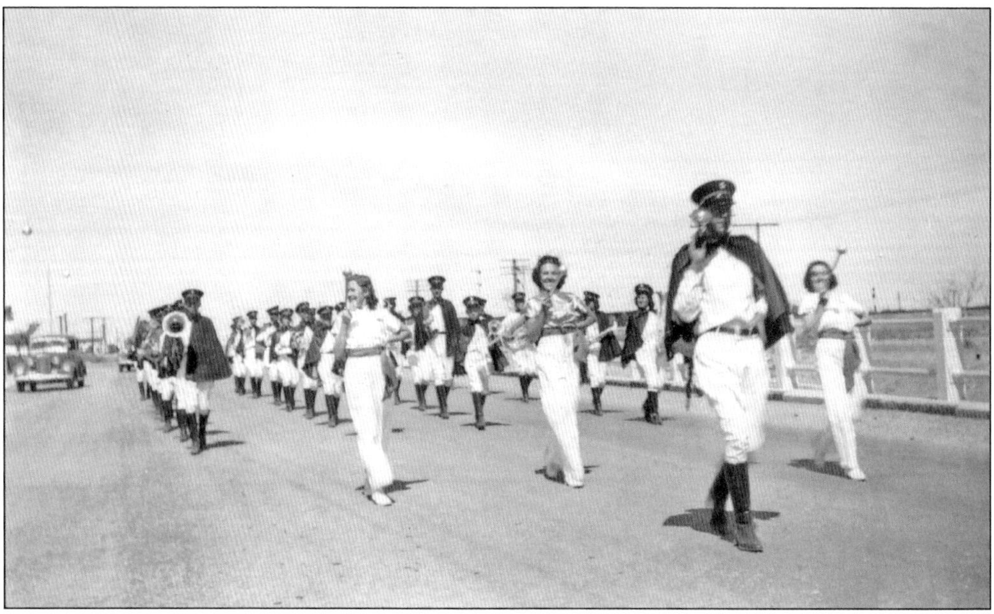

In 1939, the band, originally with 90 members, is led by drum major Eldon Harmon, as they march in the Lordsburg parade. The uniforms were royal blue with gold caps and capes, white shirts, black bow ties, white English riding pants, black belts, and black riding boots. They were the only marching band in southern Arizona dressed alike from head to toe. (Courtesy of Janice Grizzle.)

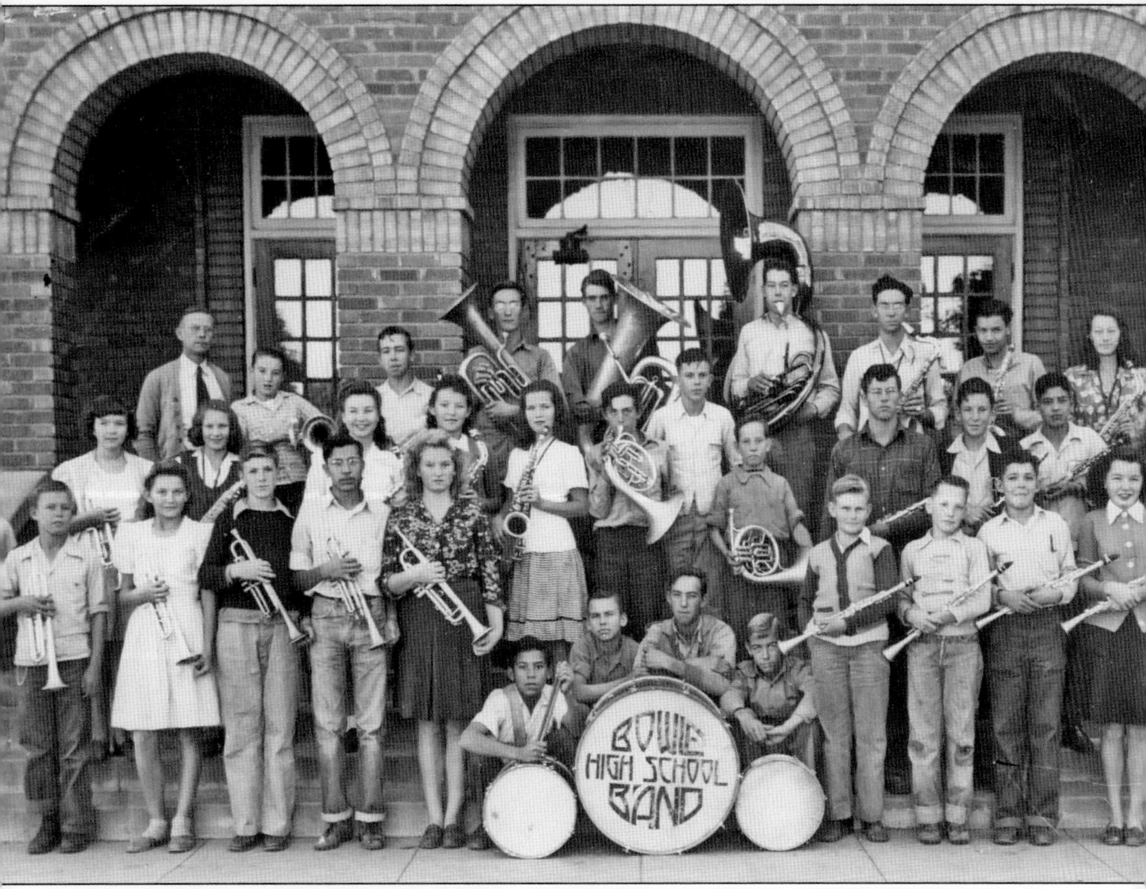

Seventh through 12th grades participated in band in 1946. The band's first concert of the year was the evening of the Christmas play. The last one would be on commencement night. Pictured are, from left to right, (first row) Louis "Boog" Enloe, Marcia Harmon, Don Cawood, Bobby Montana, Mary Fousel, Lorenzo Abalos, Jimmy Snyder, Arthur Saner, Henry Grizzle, Danny Johnson, Norman Takvam, Gregory Chavez, and Lois Bertoglio; (second row) Lillian Whitaker, Janice Creighton, Betty Woodrow, Vera Takvam, Ann Takvam, Wallace Klump, Howard Craddock, Melvin Grusendorf, Kenneth Fousel, Carlos Chavez, and Janice Welker; (third row) Lendon Enloe (band director), Billy Morris, Raymond Snyder, Victor Fousel, Richard Klump, Leroy Brown, Joe Doyle, Charles Sheffield, Gabriel Guzman, and Doris Klump. (Courtesy of Janice Grizzle.)

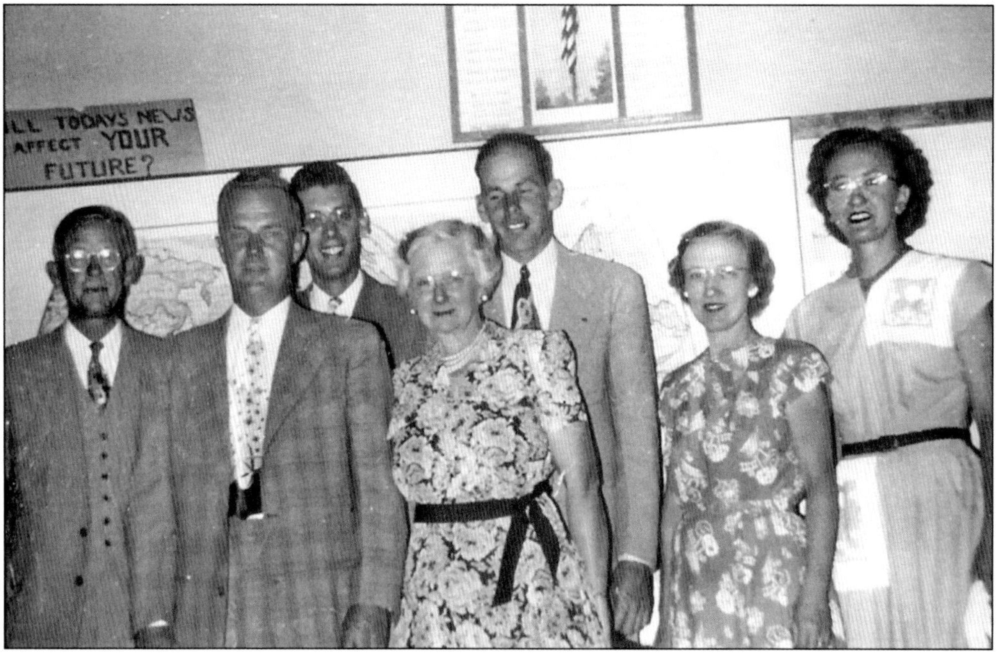

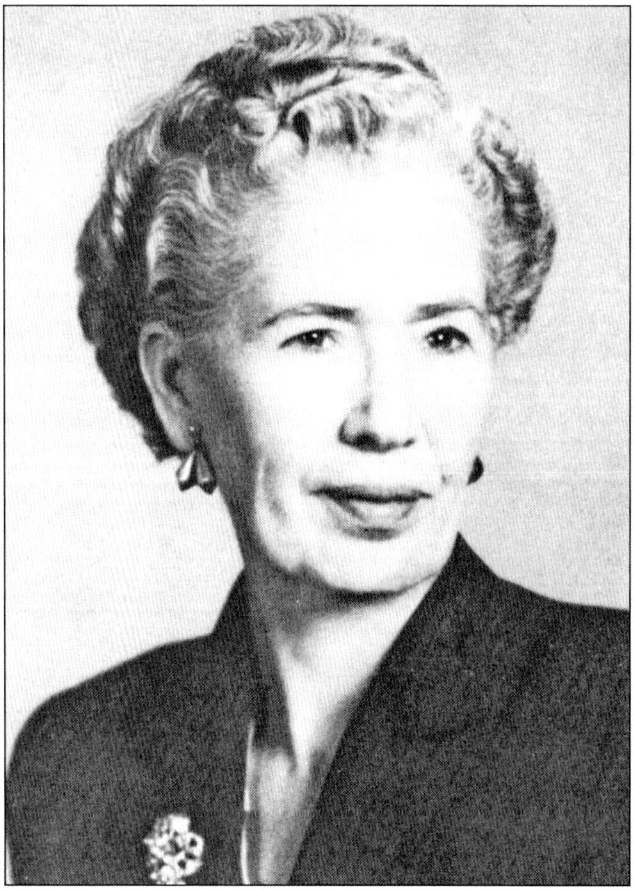

Pictured from left to right in 1950 are Lendon Enloe, who continued as superintendent of schools; Paul Orr, who taught science and was Scoutmaster (the Boy Scouts met every Tuesday in the gymnasium.); Chester McCarthy, who taught social studies; Helen McClenahan, who taught English; Paul Jones, who was the math, typing, and boys' physical education teacher; Mildred Enloe, who taught fifth and sixth grades; and Mary Wertenberger, who taught Spanish, biology, and girls' physical education. (Courtesy of Gregory Chavez.)

In 1959, Belva Ridgeway taught typing, eighth-grade English, and algebra. In 1956, she was teaching the first-grade class. Her house was purchased as the Methodist church parsonage. (Courtesy of Guy Clerc.)

In 1951, Dr. Frederick Watson Parrish was school physician. He started his practice about 1930 and died in 1959, at age 89. He had one bottle of pills he gave students no matter what ailment they had. He had one syringe with one needle that he sharpened when it got dull. Other doctors in town at various times were Dr. Morrow, Dr. Thatcher, Dr. Erhard Pelskey, and Dr. William Gillespie. (Courtesy of Guy Clerc.)

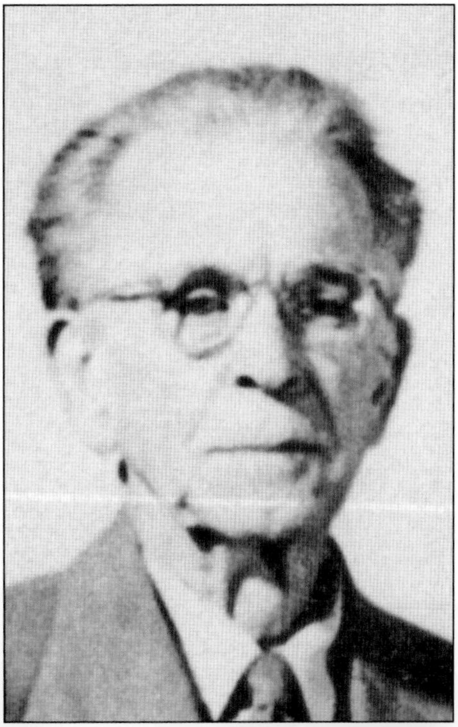

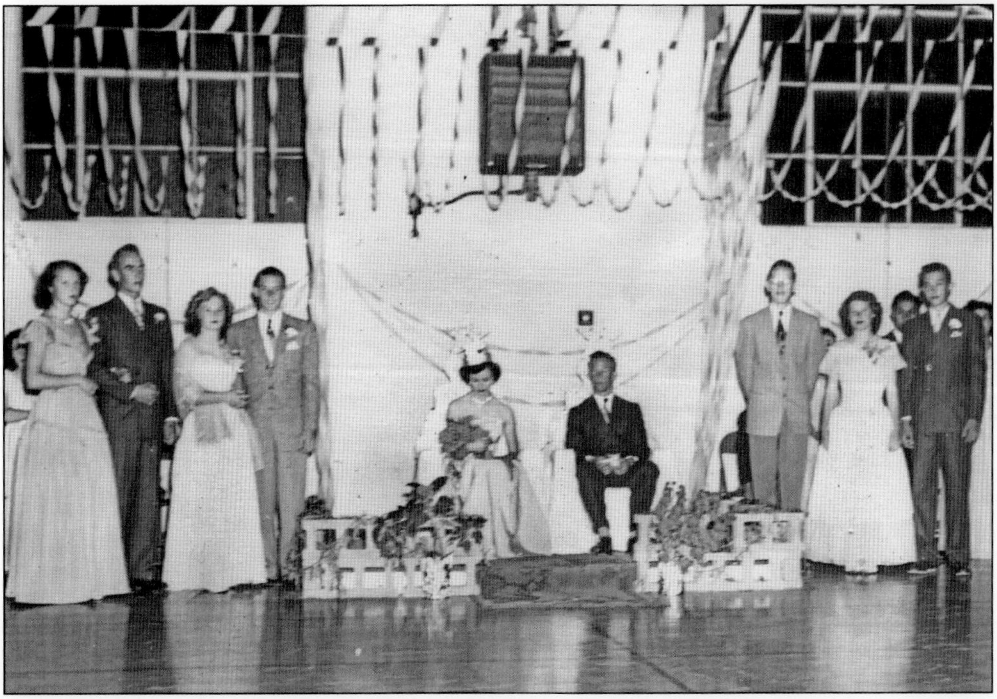

In Bowie, the whole town turns out for the junior prom, the social event of the year. For the prom of March 25, 1950, Mary McCurry and Boog Enloe were crowned queen and king. Their attendants are, from left to right, Janice Creighton, Henry Grizzle, Earlene Boyd, Billy Morris, Norman Takvam, Donella Morris, and Vic Boll. (Courtesy of Janice Grizzle.)

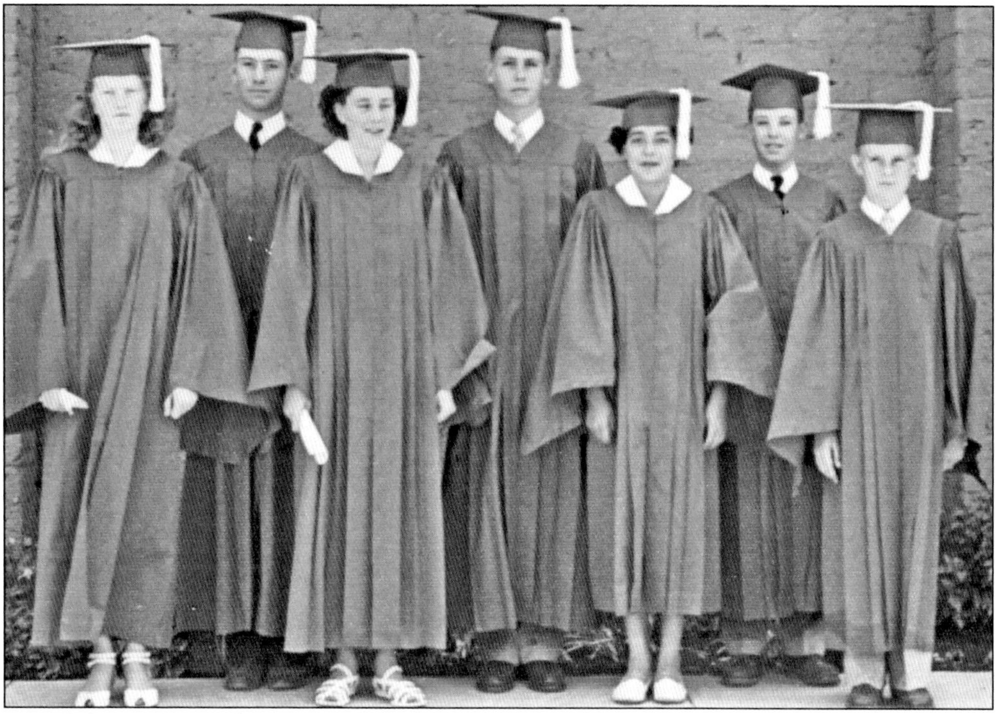

From left to right, Twila Garey, Keith Klump, Carol Robeson, Joe Lee Haire, Ida Castillo, Gayle Morris, and Gary Royster wear caps and gowns as they graduate from eighth grade in 1951. Keith, Gayle, and Gary went on to graduate high school together in 1955. (Courtesy of Twila Shelton.)

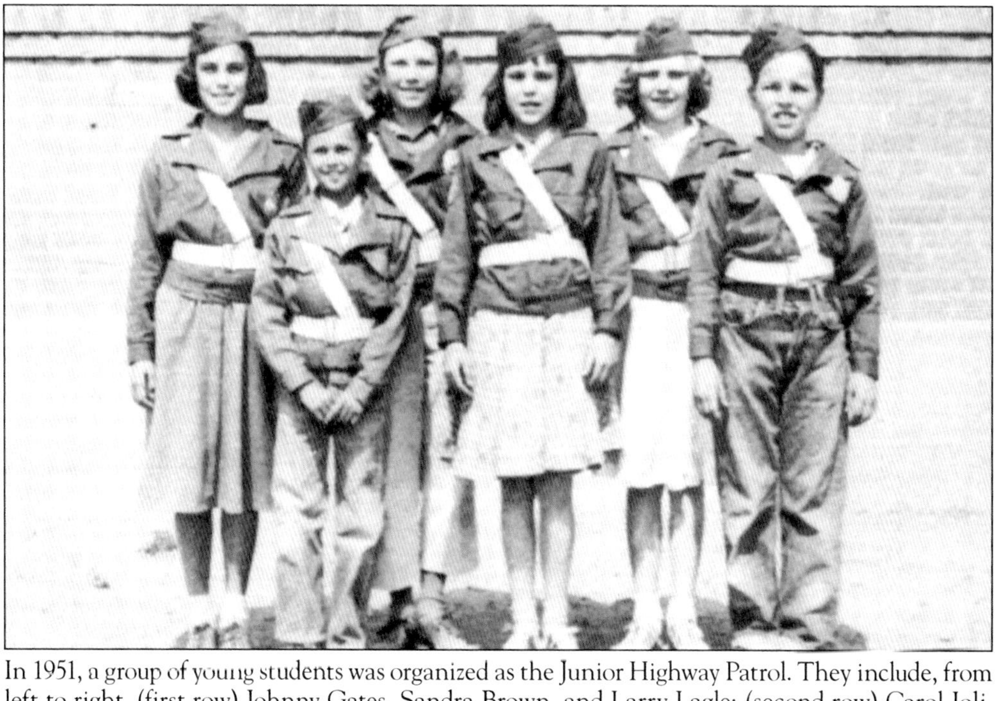

In 1951, a group of young students was organized as the Junior Highway Patrol. They include, from left to right, (first row) Johnny Gates, Sandra Brown, and Larry Lagle; (second row) Carol Ioli, Margaret Helen Cawood, and Dora Harmon. (Courtesy of Joe Ann McCurry Godbehere.)

Morris Cawood served as the president of the board of education in 1951. The Cawoods were early local settlers. His father, James, and his uncle Henry Cawood filed entry of homestead on February 26, 1912. (Courtesy of Guy Clerc.)

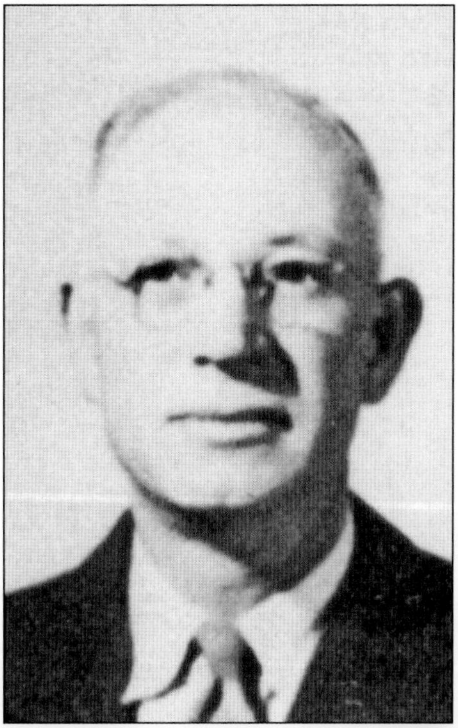

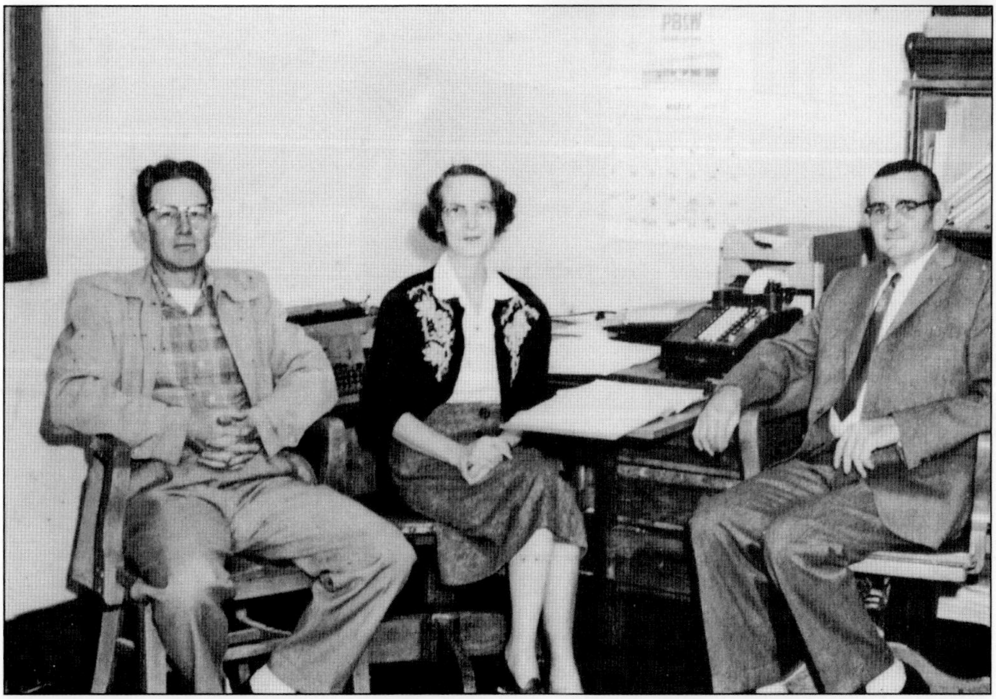

From left to right, Garland B. "Bert" Francis, Mary Tunnell, and Bill Scott were trustees on the board of education in 1958. During their tenure, the new elementary school was built and dedicated in 1961. Francis operated the Chevron station. The Tunnells had a law and real estate office. Scott owned Scott's Refrigeration. (Courtesy of Guy Clerc.)

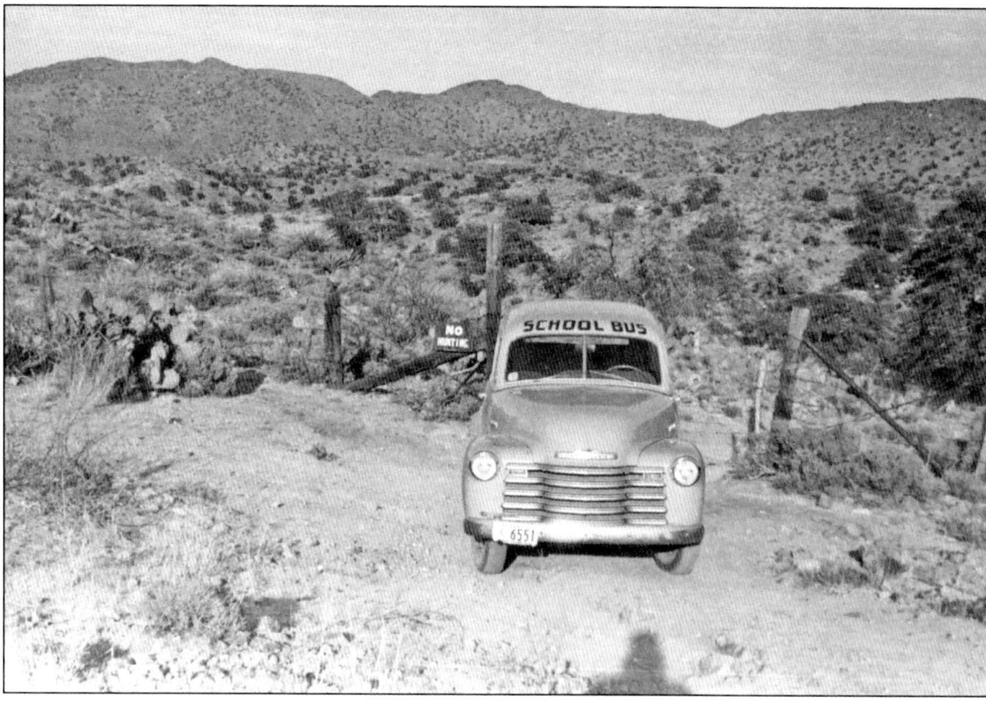

Irene Doyle drove this school bus, picking up children on the Dos Cabezas mountain route in the 1940s and early 1950s. The second year the school operated a bus route was in 1923. The legal notice for bids read that "the bus must be a motor vehicle of sufficient capacity to carry passengers in comfort, be equipped with a top, curtains, cushion, and rear door." (Courtesy of Evelyn Lathram.)

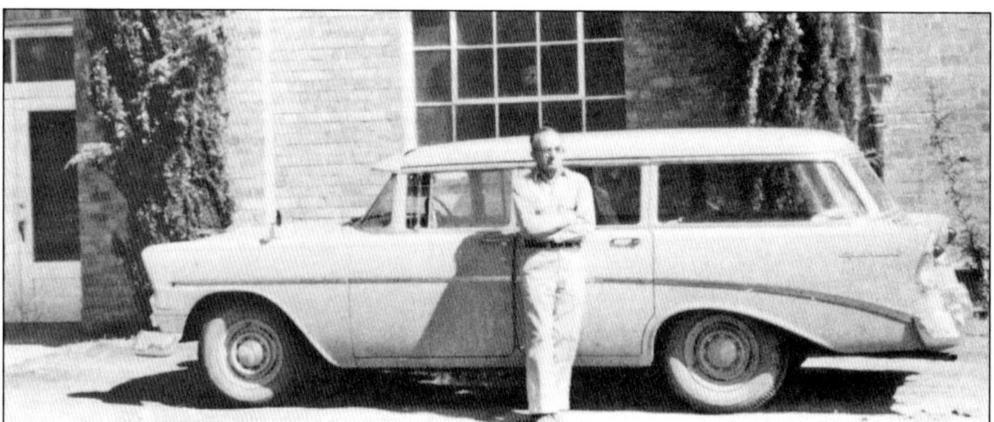

The school bus in 1958 was this station wagon, driven by Guy Clerc. Clerc was also in charge of Arizona Public Service utilities, providing natural gas to residents for the first time in May 1950. He was married to Gwendeline Saunders, and their son was Guy Clerc Jr. (Courtesy of Guy Clerc.)

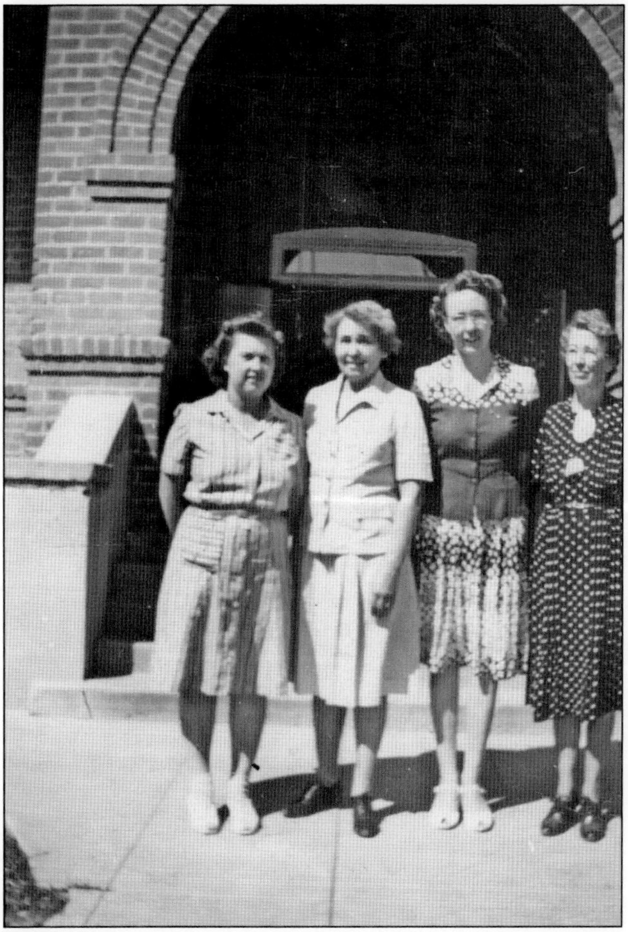

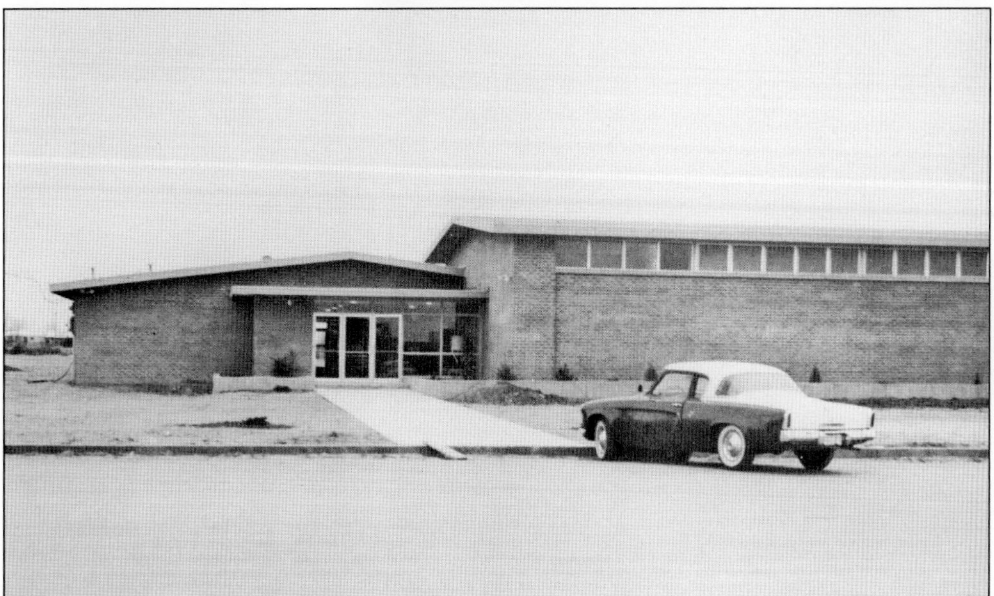

The teachers pictured are, from left to right, Mary Louise "Jimmie" Libhart, unidentified, Maybelle Whitaker, and Eva Hall. Libhart started teaching in Bowie in 1938, right out of college, and stayed here for 50 years. On April 17, 1985, the local county branch library was named the Jimmie Libhart Library and dedicated "to Jimmie, who has tenderly guided three generations of students down the 'Yellow Brick Road' and given them the treasures of Oz." Hall began teaching fourth and fifth grades in 1921, became grammar school principal in 1926, and continued in that position and in teaching until her retirement in 1949. The grammar school was named after her in 1999. Pictured below is the new elementary school, built in 1961 and named in memory of beloved teacher Mary Grace Wertenberger Doyle. (Both, courtesy of Twila Shelton.)

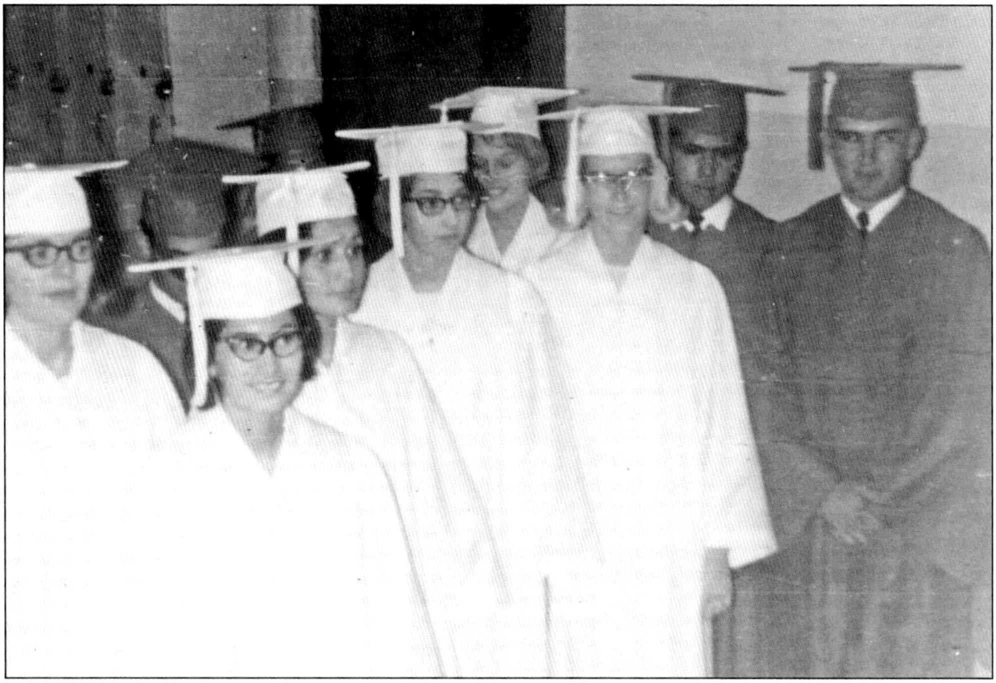

The graduates of the class of 1967 are, from left to right, (first row) Sylvia Newell, Helen Chapa, Evelyn Spikes, Nancy Nitzsche, and Glenn Jacobs; (second row) Nancy Gardner, Armando Fimbres (valedictorian), unidentified, Karen Barksdale, and George Dimas. Missing are Shirley Closson, Adan Chapa, and Robert Salas. (Courtesy of Karen Burreson.)

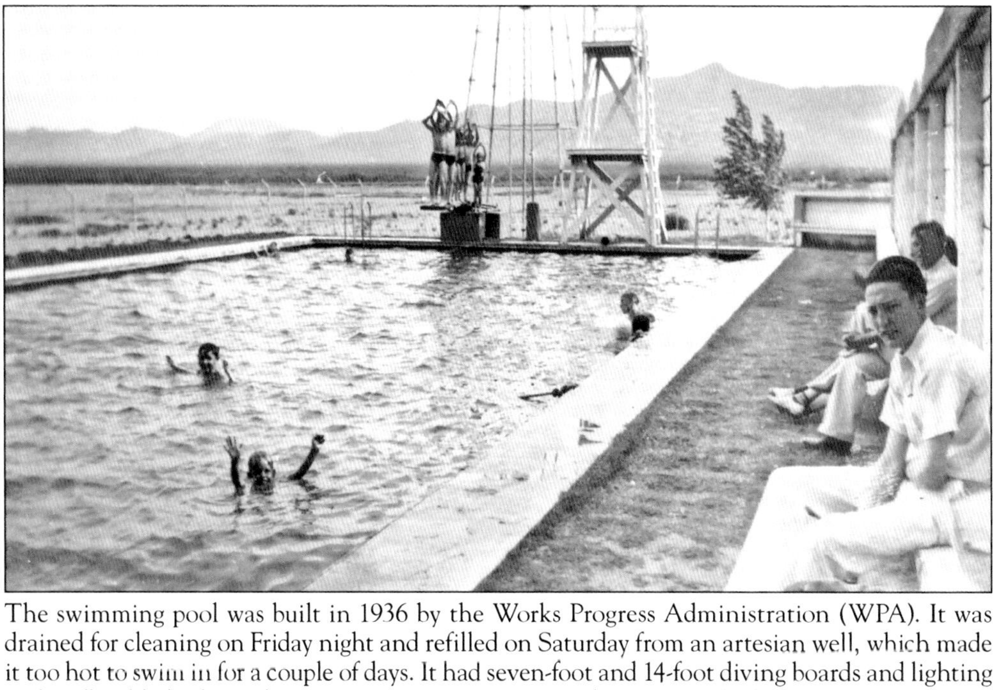

The swimming pool was built in 1936 by the Works Progress Administration (WPA). It was drained for cleaning on Friday night and refilled on Saturday from an artesian well, which made it too hot to swim in for a couple of days. It had seven-foot and 14-foot diving boards and lighting with a flood light for night swimmers. It was quite popular, even with those from neighboring towns. (Courtesy of Linda Leedom.)

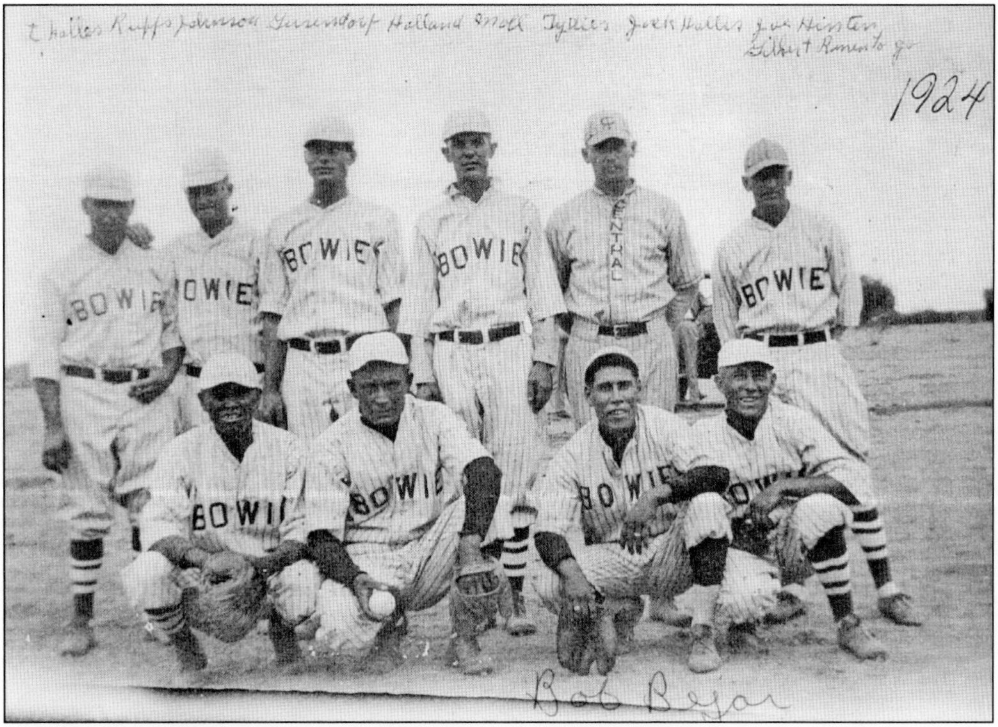

In September 1915, the newspaper reported that the men's baseball team would be known as the Green Stockings. Players in 1924 are identified on the photograph. Businessmen asked the baseball players not to practice on Central Street, between Seventh and Eighth Streets, "as such practice will result in cancellation of all plate glass insurance in Bowie." (Courtesy of Evelyn Lathram.)

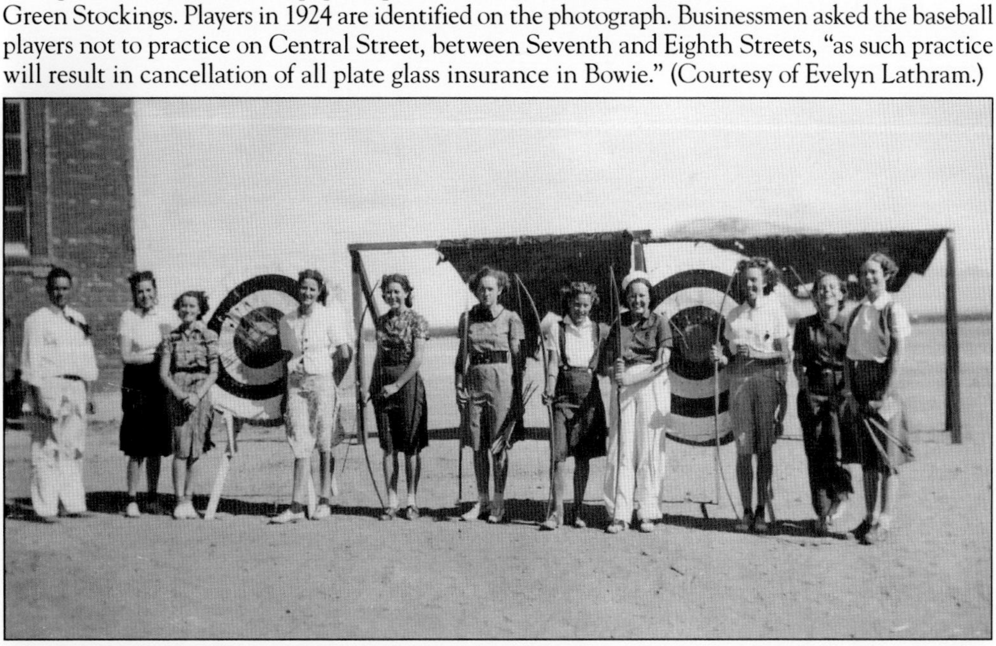

The only high school in Arizona teaching archery, Bowie won the majority of awards in the first Cochise County archery tournament in Douglas. According to the 1939 yearbook, "Among the more accurate hitters are Mary Gannon, Ruth Hannum, Frances Moore, and Dorothy Tuttle." Walter Tuttle won first place at the Western Archery Tournament in Phoenix with Sam McKee as runner-up. Bennie Saner twice won the State Junior Championship. (Courtesy of Linda Leedom.)

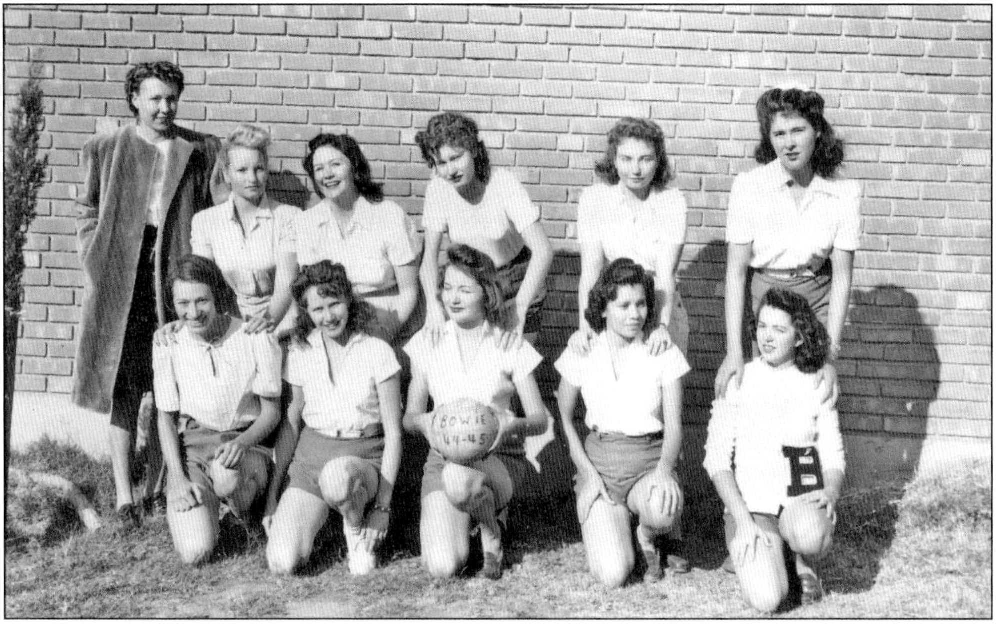

Maybelle Whitaker was the girl's volleyball coach in 1945. Players are, from left to right, (first row) Doris Klump, Patsy Garey, Pearl Bertoglio, Socorro Morales, and Jean Kelley; (second row) Mary Doreen Fousel, Billie Jean Sheffield, Eunice Garey, Betty Woodrow, and Mary Eva Mulkins, whose father, Forrest Mulkins, ran the OX Bar Ranch southeast of Bowie. (Courtesy of Raymond Fousel.)

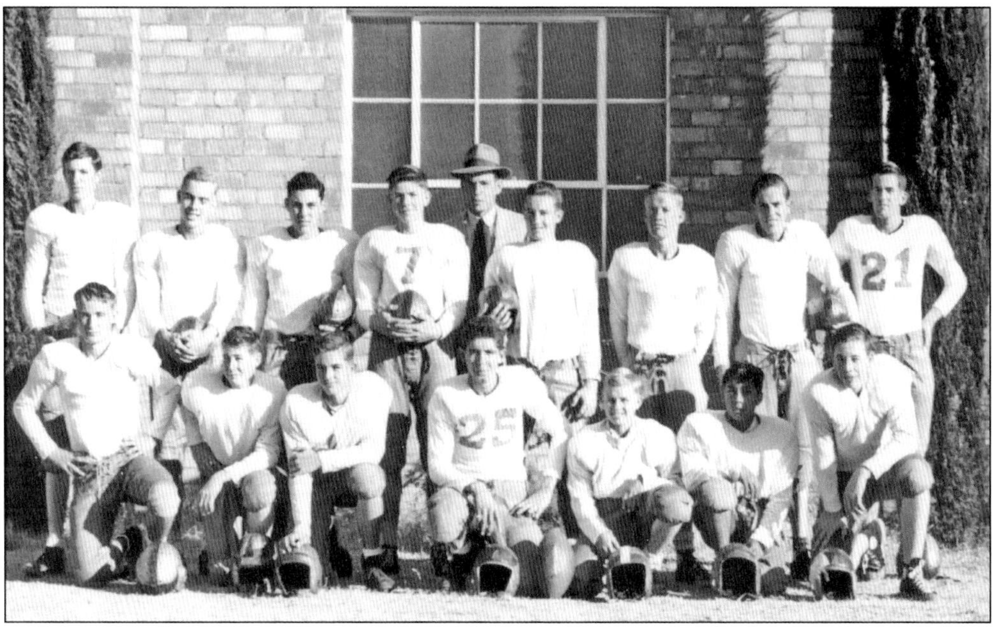

In 1949, Paul Jones coached the first football team, comprised of almost all the boys in school. They are, from left to right, (first row) Larry Areingdale, Joe Cooke, Vic Boll, Greg Chavez, Howard Enloe, Frank Tellez, and Larry Doyle; (second row) Donald Cawood, Henry Grizzle, Bill Ioli, Doug Robeson, Billy Morris, Boog Enloe, Leroy Brown, and Mickey Peddie. Mickey was the only one with football experience, having played at Fort Thomas. (Courtesy of Todd Brown.)

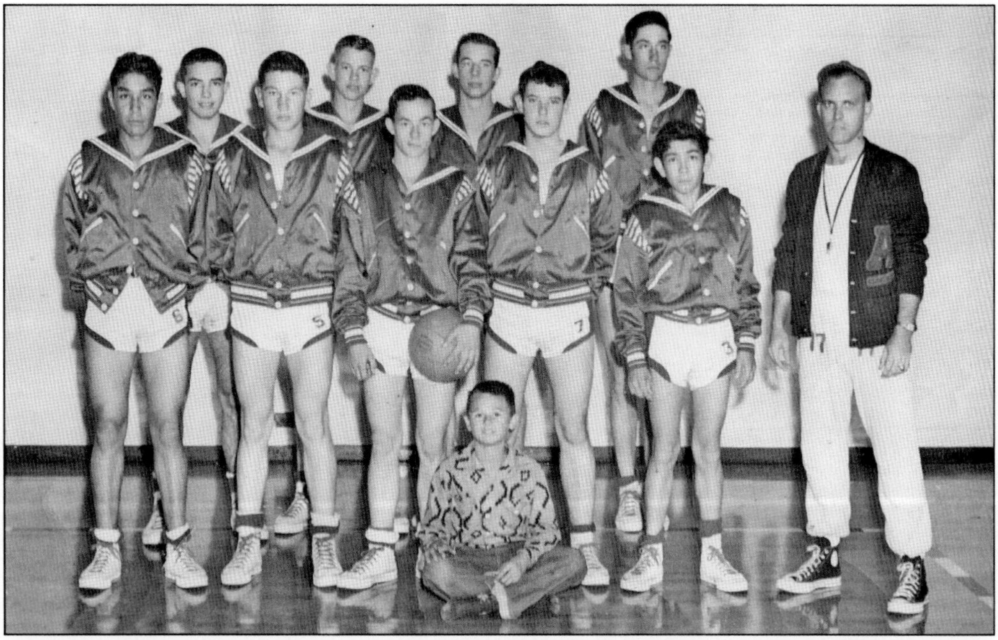

The junior high basketball team of 1949 was coached by Allie Reynolds. They are, from left to right, (first row) Frank Tellez, Clint Cohorn, Guy Clerc, Gayle Morris, and Freddie Tellez; (second row) Vic Boll, Edward McCurry, Larry Doyle, and Sherman Klump. Johnnie Gates is sitting on the floor. Klump died at age 28, of melanoma. (Courtesy of Guy Clerc.)

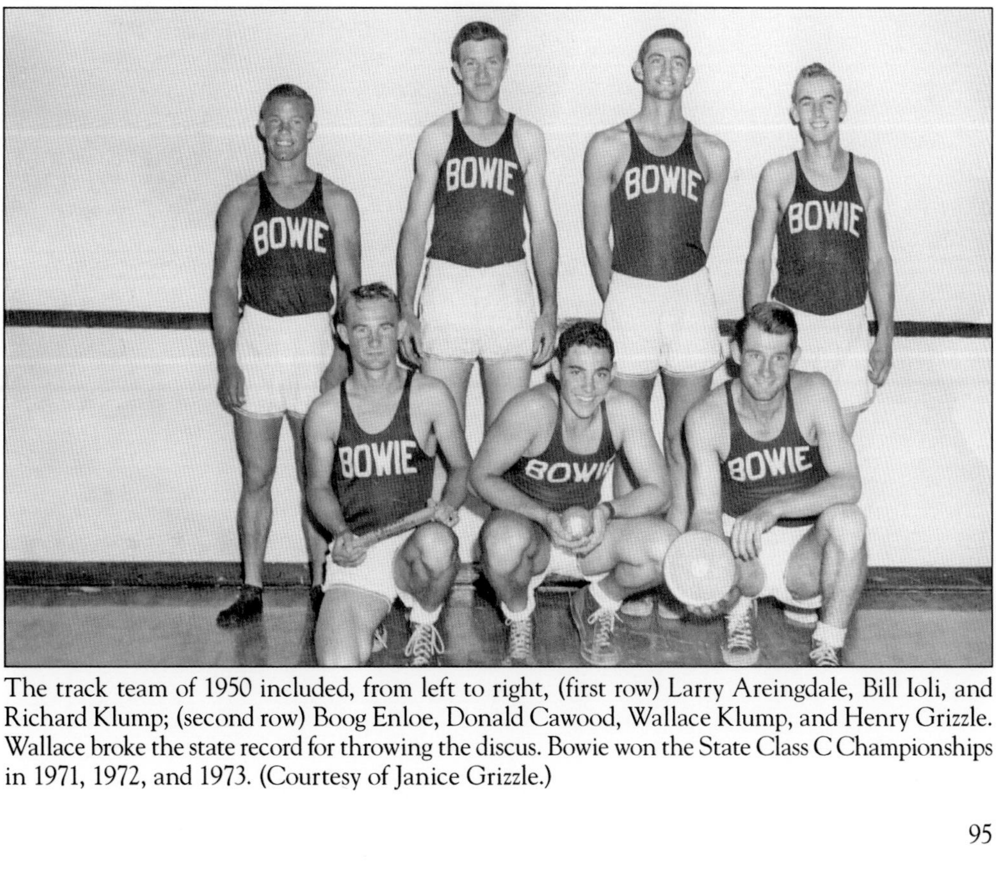

The track team of 1950 included, from left to right, (first row) Larry Areingdale, Bill Ioli, and Richard Klump; (second row) Boog Enloe, Donald Cawood, Wallace Klump, and Henry Grizzle. Wallace broke the state record for throwing the discus. Bowie won the State Class C Championships in 1971, 1972, and 1973. (Courtesy of Janice Grizzle.)

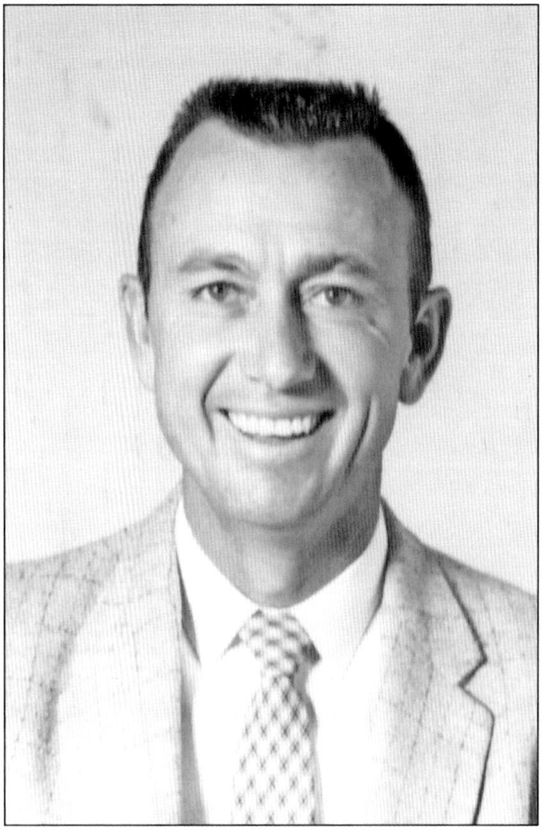

As teacher of government and health, Keith Creamer is remembered for coaching the Panthers versus San Simon Longhorns basketball game in 1961. As each Longhorn fouled out, Creamer pulled a player off the court until only Wayne Klump (at six feet, five inches) and Bob Talbot (at five feet, eight inches), of San Simon, were left. San Simon threw in the towel with the score of 73-28. (Courtesy of Joyce Creamer.)

The 1963 basketball team with Dan Turner as coach are, from left to right, (first row) Louis Newell, Julian Almodova, Velios Candelaria, Raul Castillo, Henry Castillo, and Charlie Cunningham; (second row) Turner, Bill Hall, John Ray Jacobs, Rich Hall, John Francis, Anselmo Candelaria, and Donald Brown. (Courtesy of Janice Grizzle.)

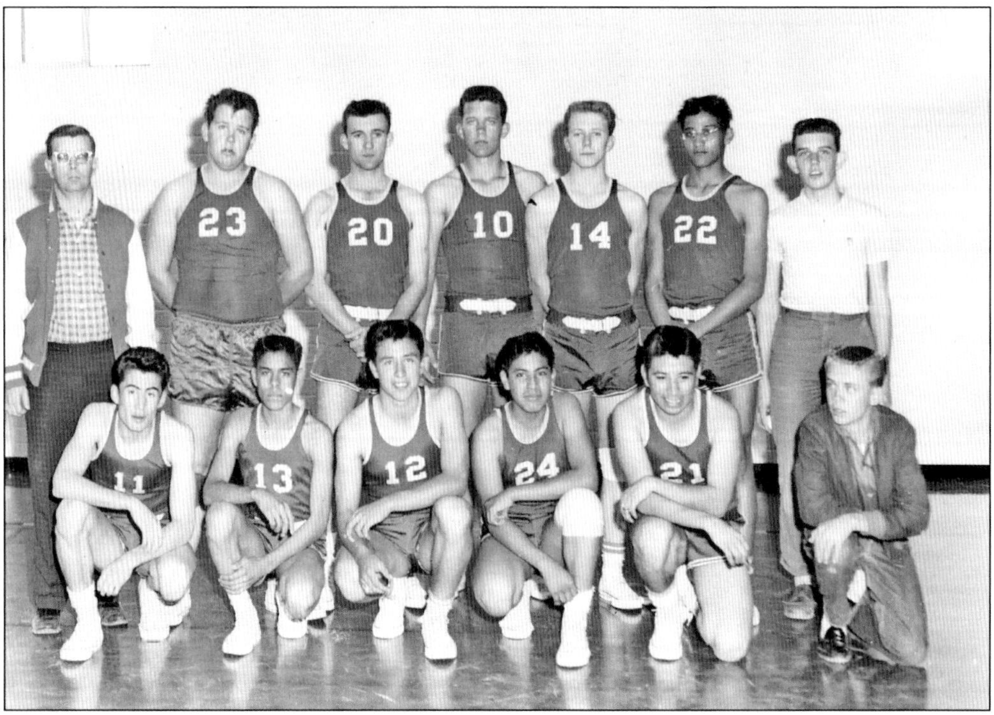

Six

Churches and Social Life

The Methodist, Catholic, and Christian churches were the first in Bowie. Only the Methodists had a resident pastor, which they shared with San Simon. The Christian church had services as early as 1912 and held them in the opera house. They had several fundraisers until they had enough money to build a new chapel, which opened for services in July 1916. Now all the original church buildings are gone, but new ones were constructed for the Methodists, Catholics, and Baptists.

The churches provided many of the social activities of the town, such as potlucks and socials. There was the Home Mission Society and the Methodist Ladies Aid Society, who fenced the church property, oiled the roof, bought 14 large window shades and screens for the windows and doors, and installed lights in 1915. In March 1916, the daughter of famous sheriff Pat Garrett who had been blind since six months old gave a musical at the Methodist church.

There were a wide variety of clubs and organizations. The Literary Club was organized October 24, 1912. Present at the first meeting were Mrs. Dawson, Bertha Wheeler, Velma Pulliam, Clara Pulliam, Wesley Ray Wheeler, Claude Wheeler, and Russell Henrich. The first brass band, led by Wesley Wheeler, had their premiere performance on Washington's birthday in 1913. There was the Women's Political Club, the Bridge Club, the Epworth League, and the Woman's Club. Woodmen of the World was organized in 1913 and had 41 members by 1917. Grover Davis was commander, and Henry Saner was advisory lieutenant. There was a local Red Cross organization during World War I with 58 members and a War Savings Stamp Committee of teenage girls. The Masonic Lodge and Eastern Star met in Willcox until they received their own charter. Their daughters belonged to Rainbow Girls. The Grammar Club started in 1930. The Lions Club and Lionesses provided civic services to the community. Lawrence Wright formed the Boy Scouts in 1918, and the Campfire Girls started in 1919.

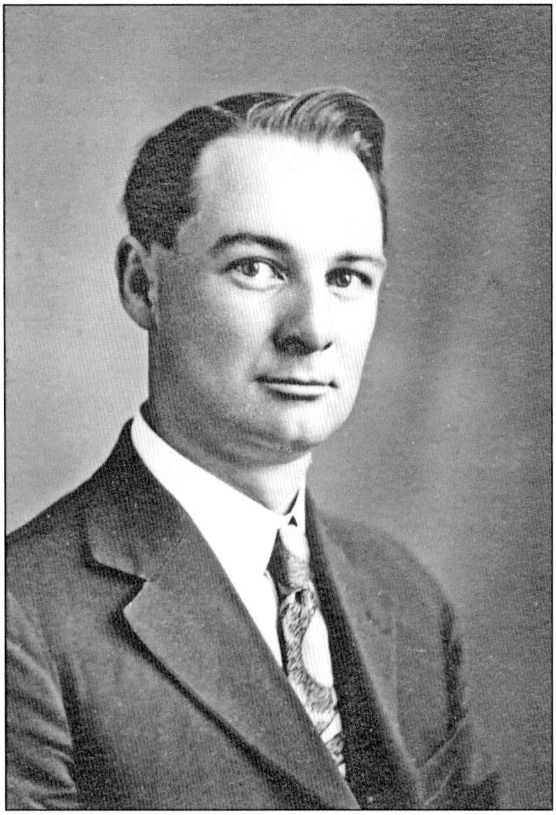

Rev. Douglas Graves Dechard arrived in November 1918 from Pandora, Texas, as pastor of the Methodist church in Bowie and San Simon. His wife, Abigail, and sons Douglas and David soon joined him. His sister Nellie married Albert R. Spikes. Preceding him, were the Reverends Roberts, Crutchfield, Wheeler, Bond, Gould, and Forman. Dechard was assigned to Prescott in October 1920 but returned from 1922 to 1923. (Courtesy of Evelyn Lathram.)

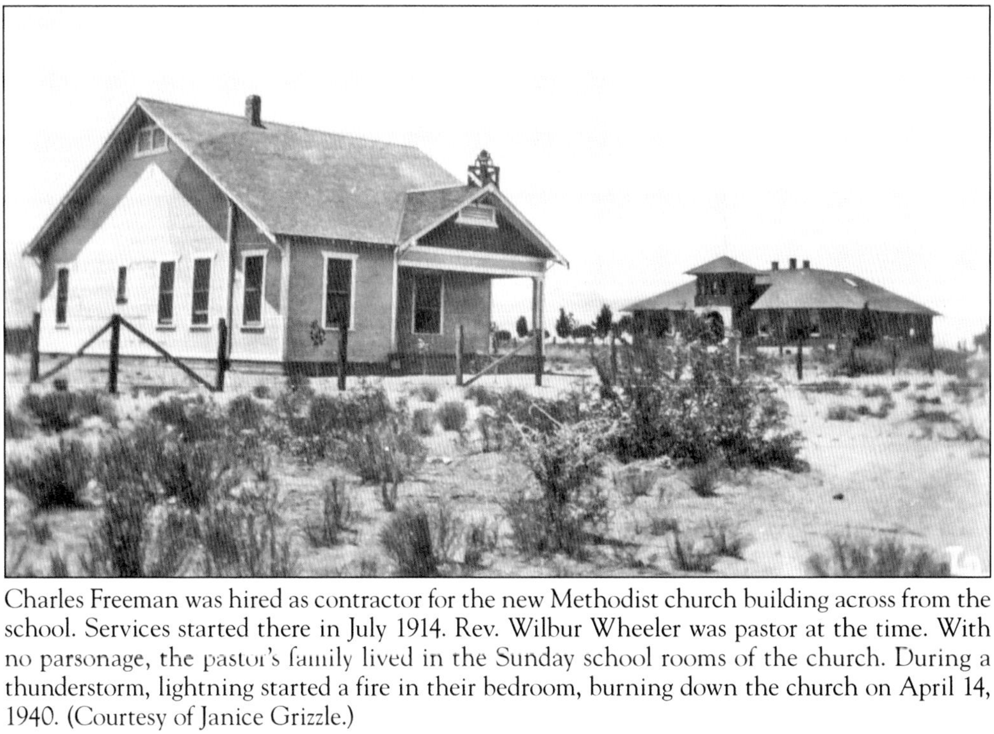

Charles Freeman was hired as contractor for the new Methodist church building across from the school. Services started there in July 1914. Rev. Wilbur Wheeler was pastor at the time. With no parsonage, the pastor's family lived in the Sunday school rooms of the church. During a thunderstorm, lightning started a fire in their bedroom, burning down the church on April 14, 1940. (Courtesy of Janice Grizzle.)

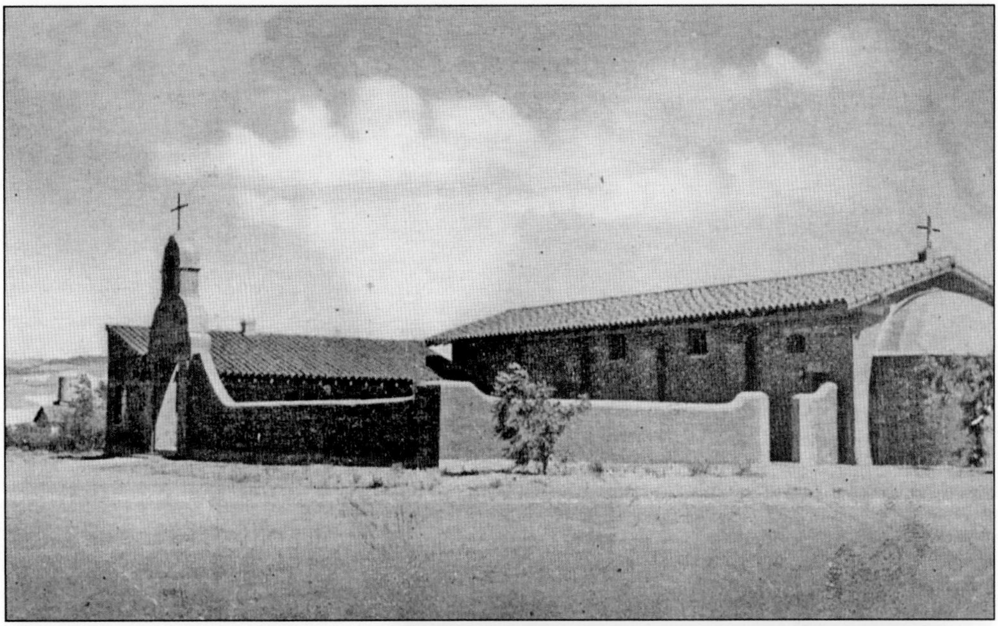

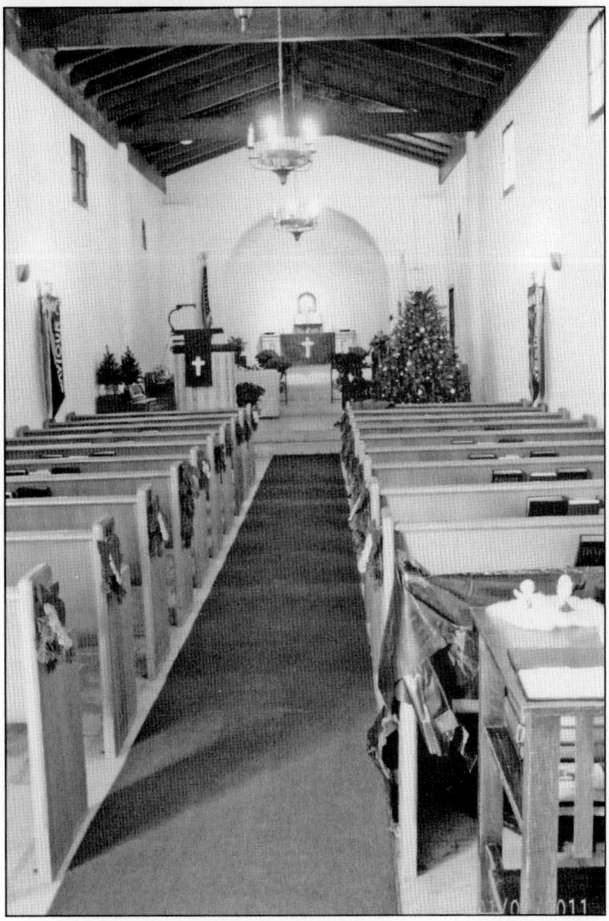

The cornerstone for the new Community Methodist Church was laid on September 11, 1941. Built of native adobe with tile roofing, it was 60 feet wide by 67 feet long. The architect was Reginald Inwood, of Los Angeles. The building committee consisted of pastor L.R. Seymour, Albert Spikes (president of the board of trustees), Morris Cawood (secretary-treasurer), Dr. Fred Parrish, Victor Boll, Larren O. Scott (superintendent of construction), and Jim Freeman, of San Simon. Native marble was used for the floor, altar, lectern, and pulpit. Levy Knape and Herbert Smith laid the floor. Ernest Harmon built the pulpit, and George Beckwith did the carvings on the altar, pulpit, and lectern. (Courtesy of Evelyn Lathram.)

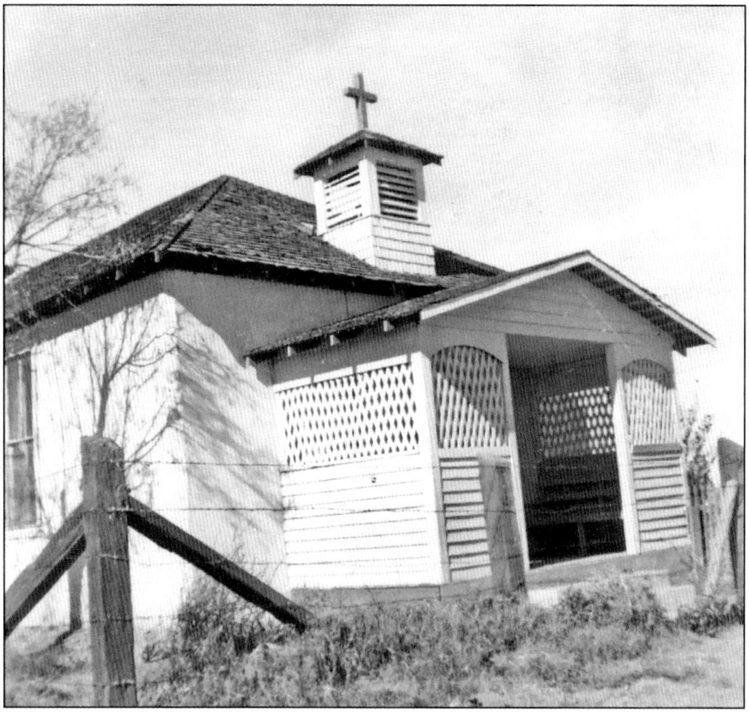

Our Lady of Guadalupe Catholic Church was first built on Cleveland Avenue. The Very Reverend Lucas de St. Jose, of Tucson, conducted the dedication ceremony on April 12, 1916. He was assisted by Rev. Father Joseph Raida, of Solomonville. In 1922, under Rev. Mariano Uron, a bazaar, supper, and dance were held with the $174.75 proceeds going towards the purchase of a piano. (Courtesy of Barbara Blandin.)

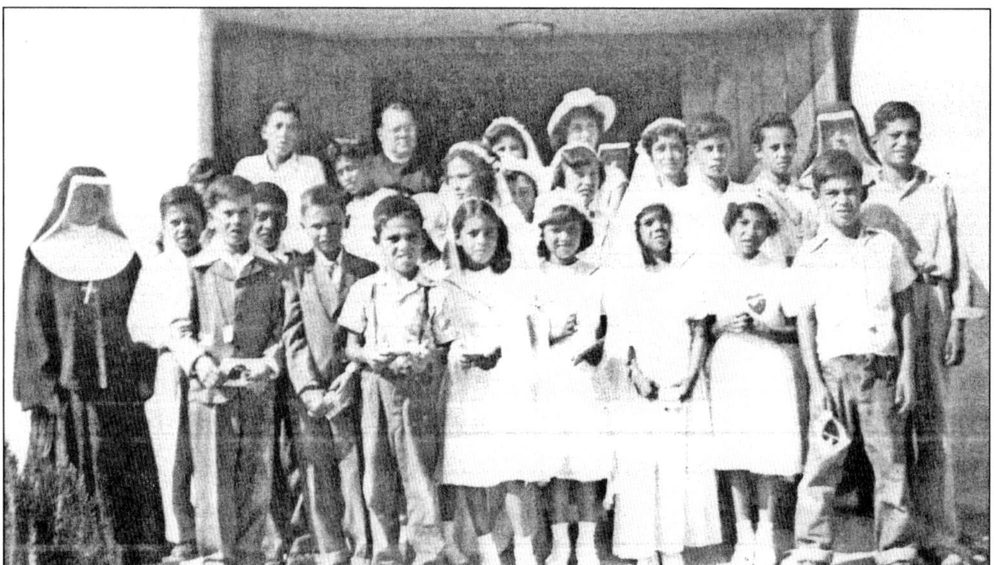

Children from Bowie are pictured after receiving their First Communion in 1950. Johnny Gates is fourth from left in the first row. Dolores Montana is second from right in the first row. (Courtesy of Bobby Montana.)

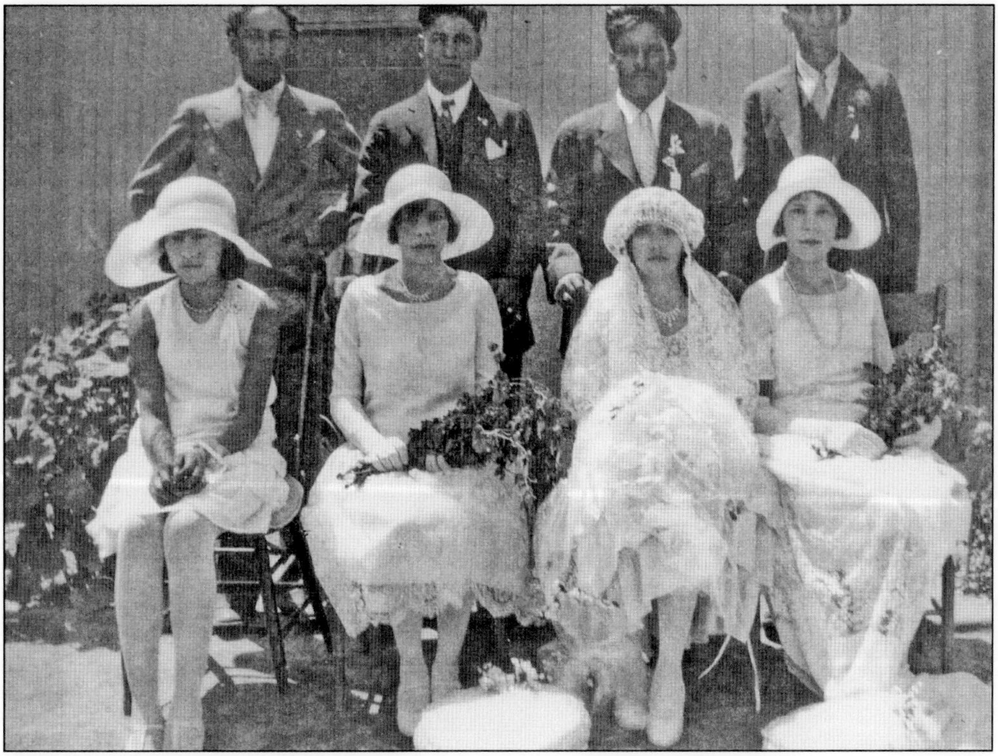

Pictured here on May 12, 1929, are, from left to right, (seated) Nellie Lopez; Natividad Garcia, the bride's sister, who married Frank Almodova; bride Felipa Garcia; and Lucia ?, a friend who married Antonio Serrano; (standing) unidentified; Emilio Chavez, who married Josephine Gonzalez; groom Jose Montana, who came to Olga in 1925; and Jose Maria Gallegos, who worked for the railroad and lived at the Arizona Eastern Railway yard. (Courtesy of Bobby Montana.)

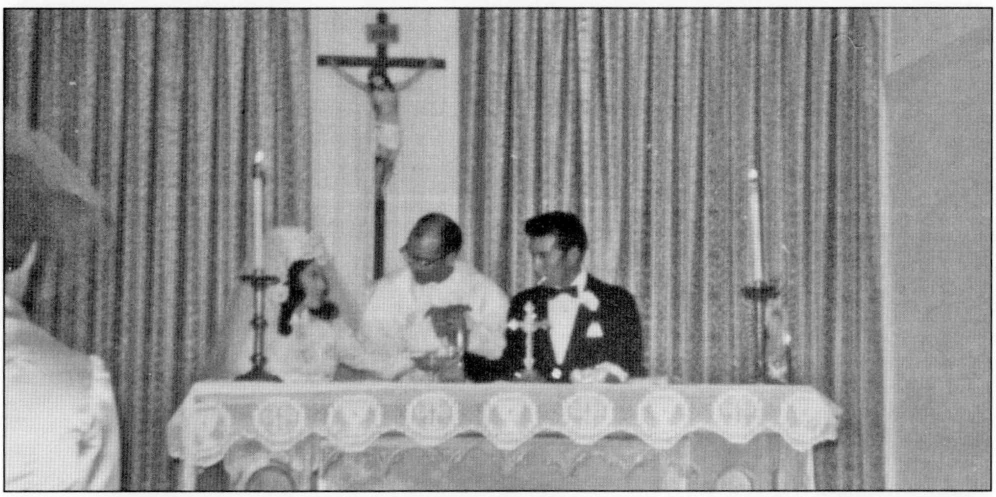

The marriage of Lorenzo Fuentes and Rebecca Mendoza was performed by Fr. Gilbert Padilla in the new Catholic church on October 25, 1969. Lorenzo came at age 12 to live with his sister Sara Vargas. Rebecca arrived when she was four. Her parents, Cecilio and Timota Reyna Mendoza, stayed in Bowie after their car broke down, and Cecilio started working for the railroad. (Courtesy of Lorenzo Fuentes.)

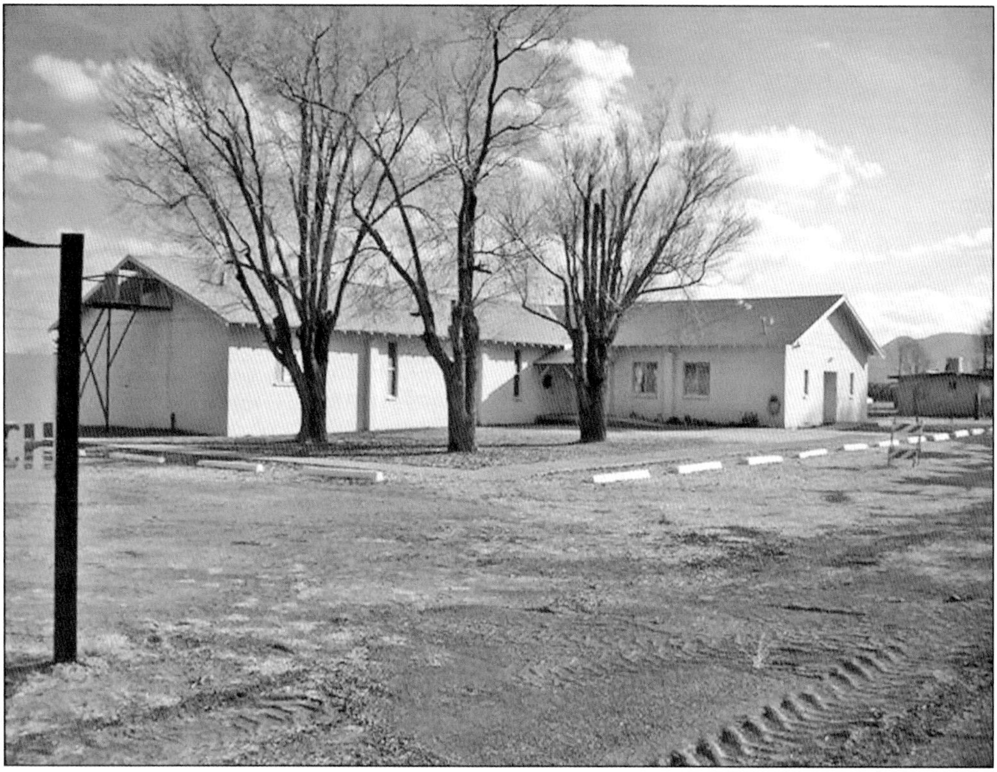

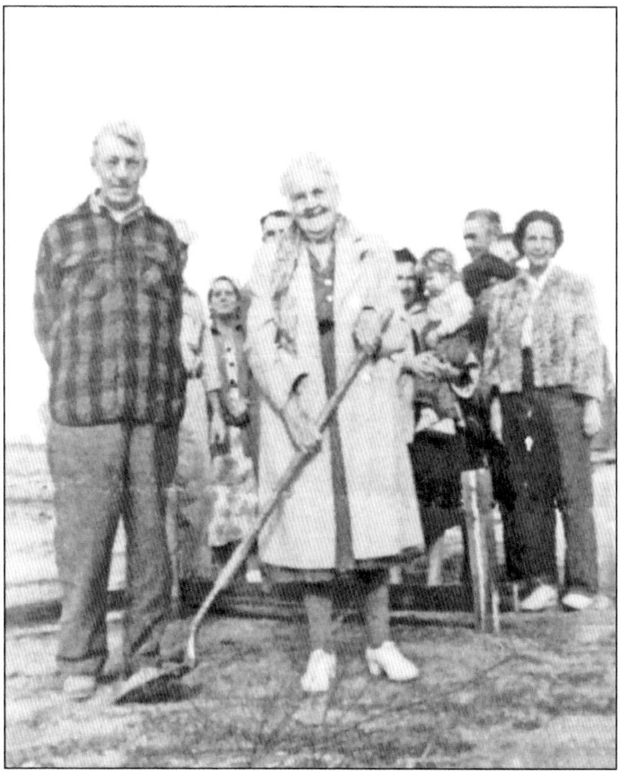

The First Southern Baptist Church was constituted on January 31, 1954, with 10 charter members: Mr. and Mrs. Edward Wharton, Leo P. and Bessie Harris, Joe and Lucille Alexander, Grace Kennedy, missionary H.D. Pack and his wife, and Meriem Gillespie. Clifford and Stella Head were baptized following the service. The congregation had been sponsored by Rev. Albert Faulk and the Willcox church. (Courtesy of Janice Grizzle.)

Digging the first shovel of dirt for the cornerstone of the Baptist church is Winnie Harwood, on December 7, 1954. The addition was built in 1967. Tennis and Ella Creighton and Henry and Janice Grizzle were members of the congregation. (Courtesy of Marjorie Kuban, Arizona Baptist Historical Commission.)

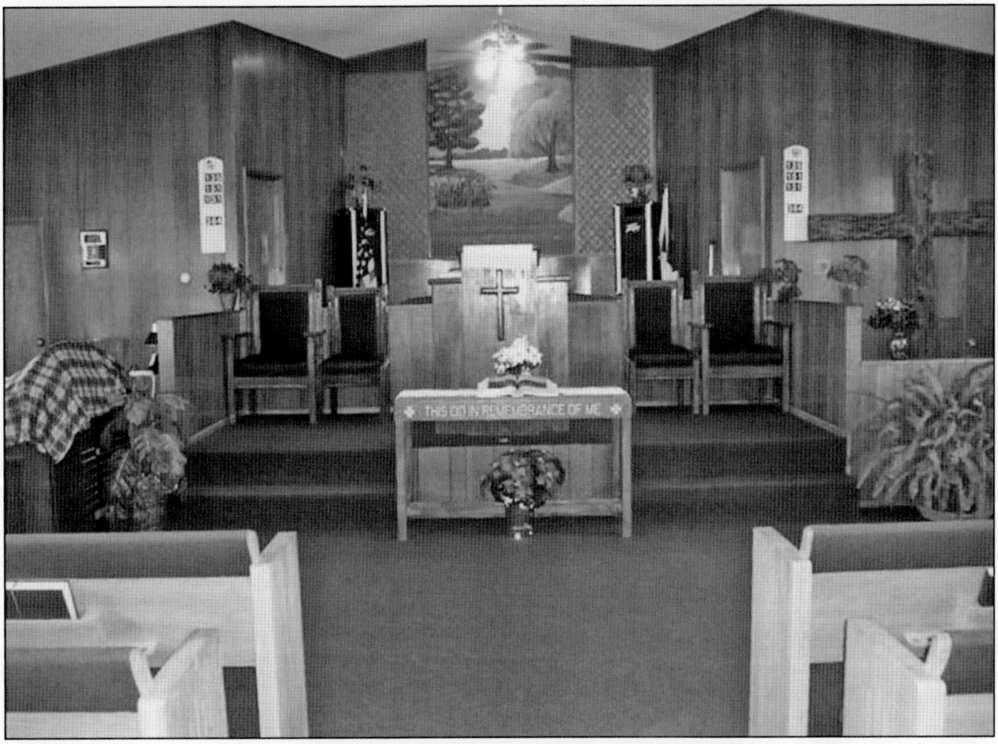

This is an inside view of the Baptist church built by Ernest Hart. Before this church was built, services were held in Upham's Lumber store. The September 23, 1928, newspaper reported a social at the Baptist church, but there had not been a church for years before the 1954 one was built. Rev. and Mrs. Hardie Connors, of Willcox, attended. (Courtesy of Janice Grizzle.)

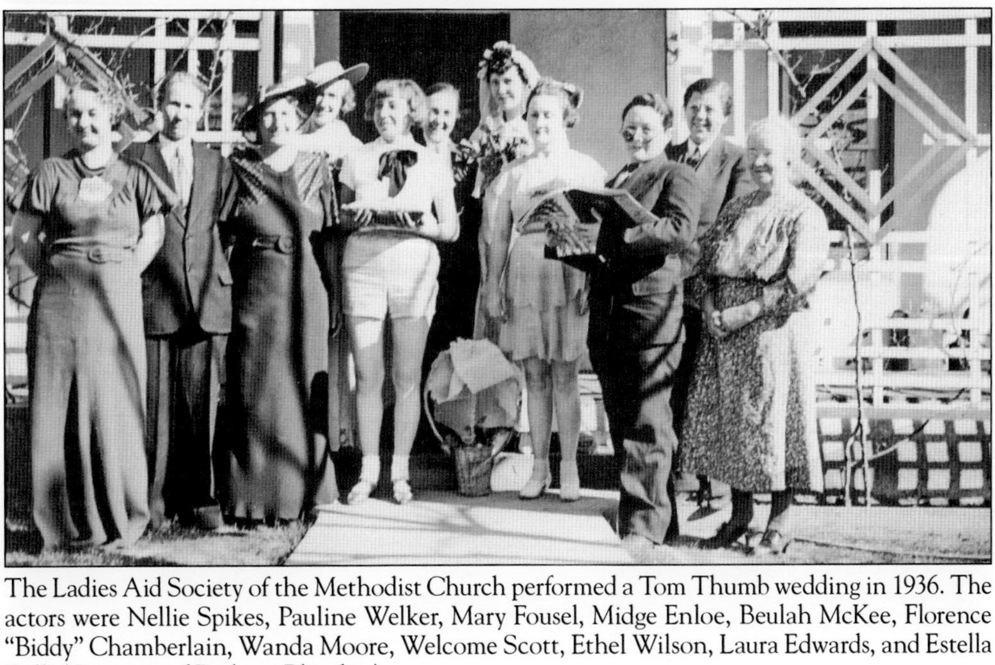

The Ladies Aid Society of the Methodist Church performed a Tom Thumb wedding in 1936. The actors were Nellie Spikes, Pauline Welker, Mary Fousel, Midge Enloe, Beulah McKee, Florence "Biddy" Chamberlain, Wanda Moore, Welcome Scott, Ethel Wilson, Laura Edwards, and Estella Boll. (Courtesy of Barbara Blandin.)

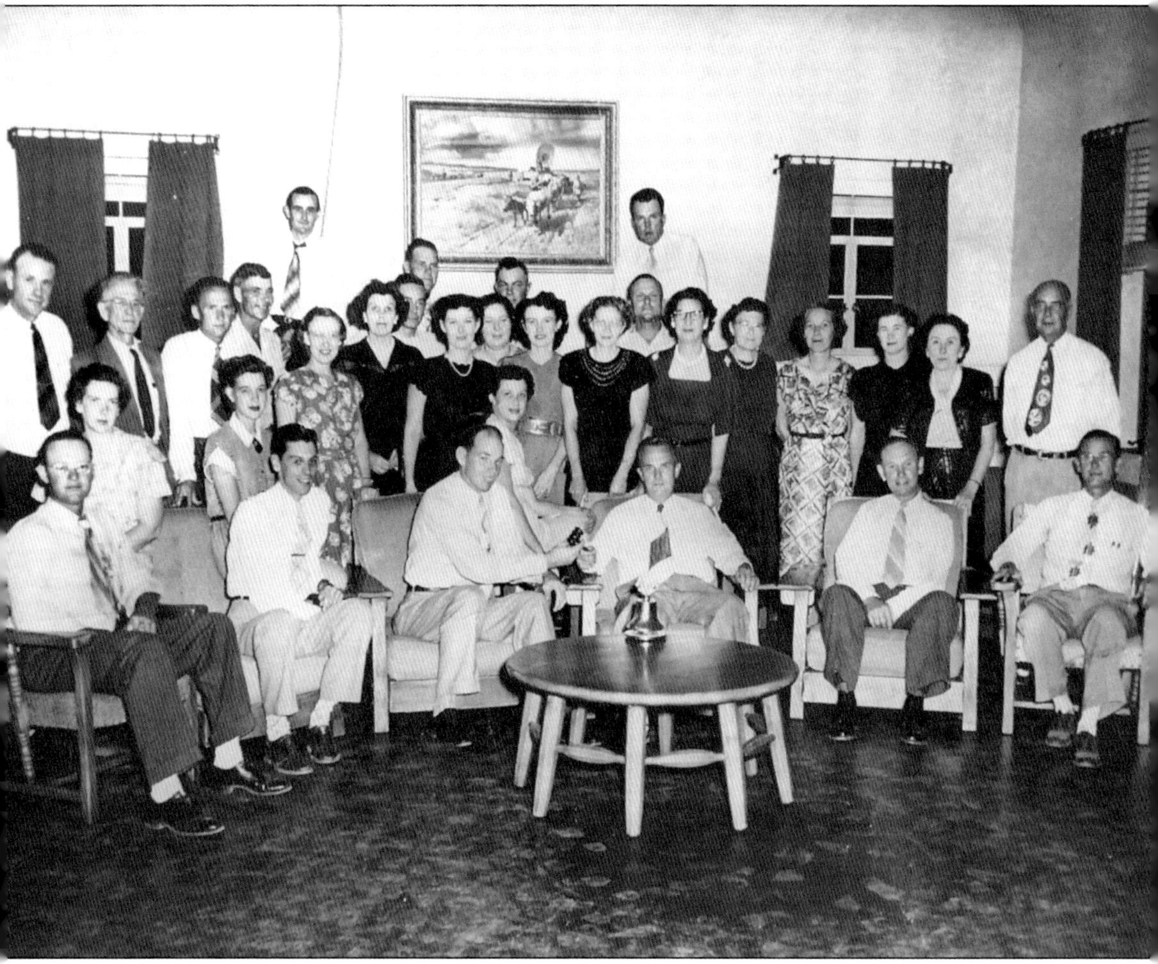

Members of the Bowie Lions Club and their wives gather at a social event around 1950. Pictured are, from left to right, (first row) Jack and Mary Lou Spikes, Chet and Virginia McCarthy, Paul Jones, Marguerite Boll, Paul Orr, Judge Tom Cooke, and Lendon A. Enloe; (second row)) Orville Robeson, Dr. Fred Parrish, Doug Welker, Carl Grusendorf, Midge Enloe, Nathalie Grusendorf, Vic Boll, Mary Jones, Gladys Robeson, Bobbie Welker, Velma Ann Lockwood, Larren O. Scott, Kathryn Orr, Opal Cook, Mary Tunnell, Jessie Scott, Welcome Scott, and Frank Tunnell; (third row) Bill Scott, Carl Olander, Dutch Lockwood, and Dave Wisener. (Courtesy of Dewain Lockwood.)

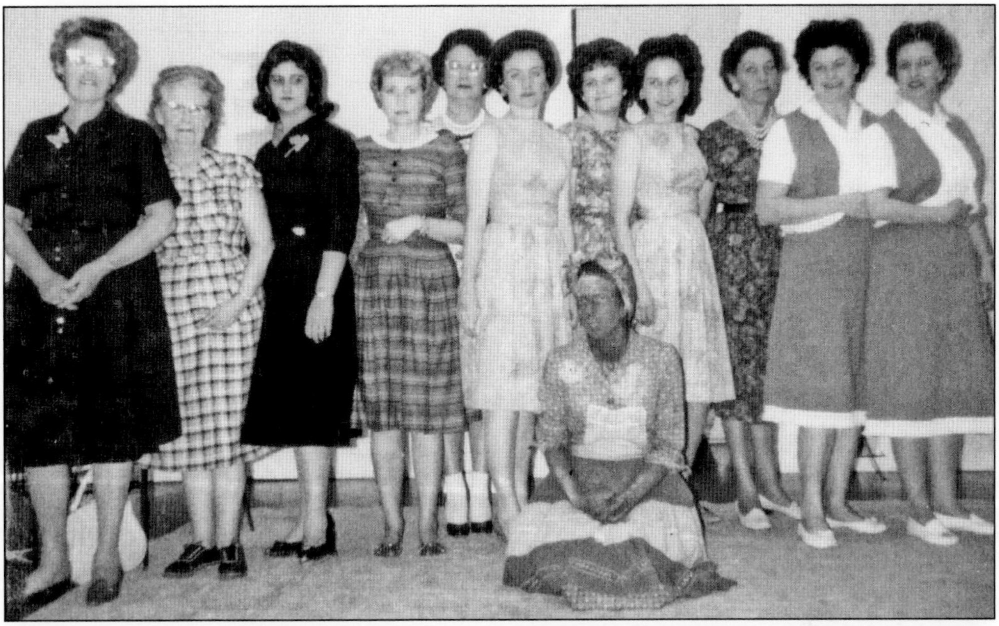

Ladies of the Lioness Club presented a play in the high school auditorium in 1962. Pictured are, from left to right, (seated) Mary Lou Spikes; (standing) Nathalie Grusendorf, Rose Cawood, Pat Walker, Mickey Cooke, Marguerite Boll, Bobbie Welker, Emily Cawood, Betty Grusendorf, Virginia Francis, Faye Creighton, and Jimmie Hilburn. (Courtesy of Barbara Blandin.)

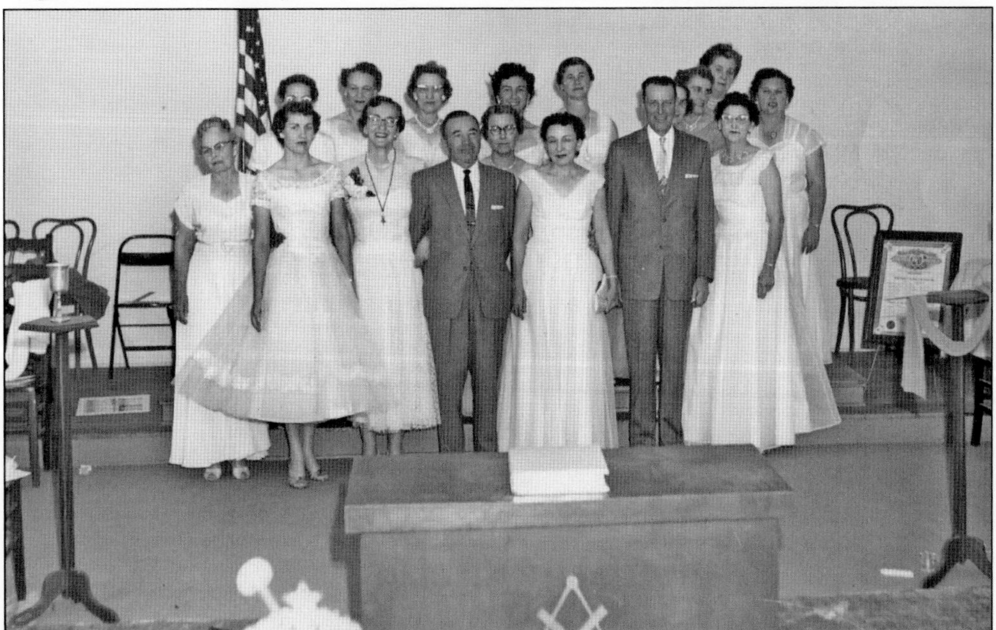

The local Eastern Star Chapter of the Masonic Lodge was organized December 13, 1923. Shown are, from left to right, (first row) Irene Doyle, Zelma Wade, Mary Doyle, Vic Bertoglio, Mamie Bertoglio (behind Vic), Alice Wasson, Joe Wasson, and Virginia Francis; (second row) Velma Ann Lockwood, Hazel Shown, Mildred Enloe, Roma Jacobs, Jessie Scott, Ella Creighton, Ruth Mefford, unidentified, and Jimmie Libhart. (Courtesy of Edna Scott.)

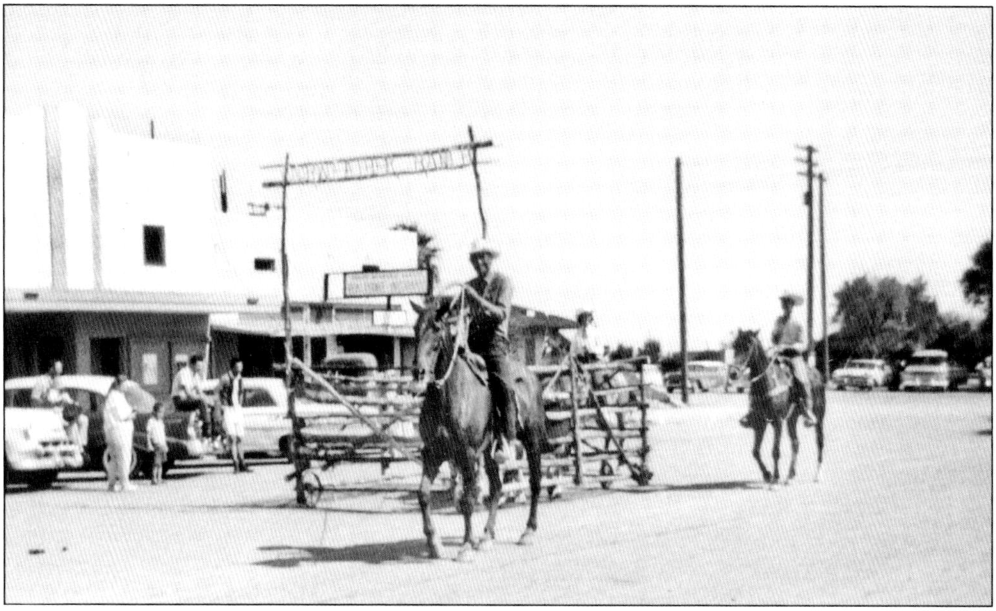

The Fourth of July is usually a big celebration with a parade downtown and fireworks on the school grounds. The Fairweather Ranch, with the FW brand, entered the parade in the 1960s with a traveling corral of cattle. Wallace, Charlene, and Keith Klump are on horseback. They are passing in front of Long's movie theater and Welker's Insurance and Real Estate Company. (Courtesy of Barbara Blandin.)

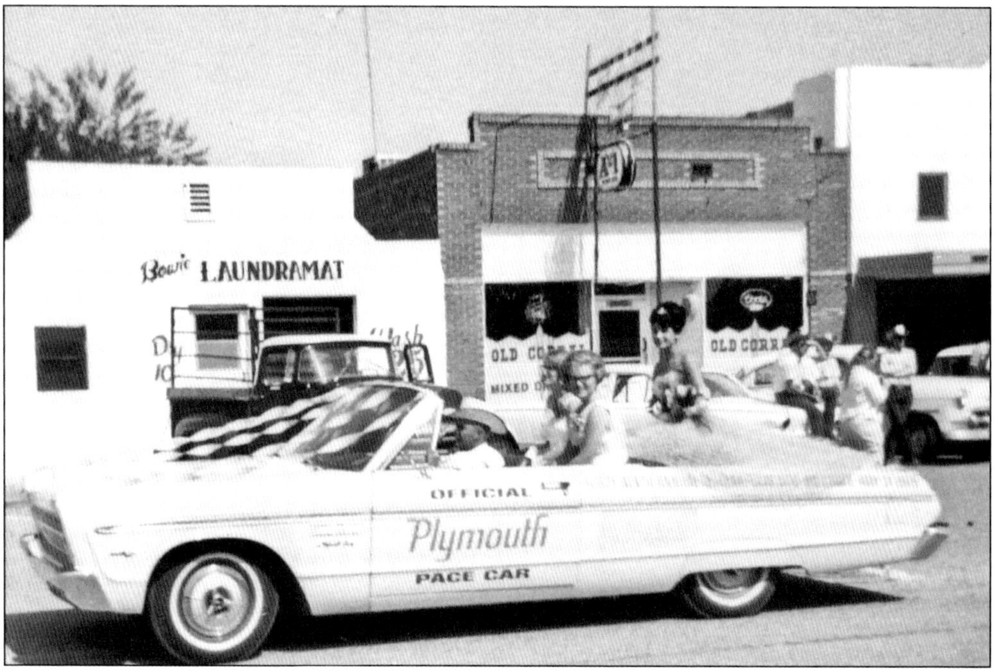

Nancy Nitzsche and Gayle Montierth ride through the Fourth of July parade in the official Plymouth pace car. The Laundromat and Tom's Old Corral bar, next to the theater, are in the background. Val and Jewell Nitzsche owned Gateway Grocery and lived in Bowie from 1956 to 1978. The Montierths have farmed here for over 50 years. (Courtesy of Barbara Blandin.)

Seven

Farming and Ranching

James Tevis planted the first orchard, which he sold to J.M. Pardue. In 1914, it was reported that the orchards had bared a constant heavy crop for 15 years without failure. Barber G.W. McDaniels filed the first homestead. Dry-land farming was very successful at first, until drought or unexpected frosts caused failure of the crops. In 1911, Lester Brenizer's well, called the "Pride of Bowie," was the start of fruit farms. It placed irrigation by pumping within reach of farmers, solving the most serious problem confronting the settlers. Brenizer's 80-pound watermelon won first place at the Arizona State Fair in 1915. A Mr. Boehm drilled wells for the homesteaders. By 1912, the Gordon-Galloway homesteads were growing maize, kaffer corn, cane, field corn, beans, alfalfa, cucumbers, squash, pumpkins, and watermelons. In 1919, J.W. Langston proved that cotton could be grown in the San Simon Valley. Later, Larren Scott grew the first long-staple Egyptian cotton. The Farmers and Merchants Clubs met in joint session to organize the Irrigation District Association on May 21, 1921. Dues were 10¢ per acre of land, paid in quarterly installments. Their first goal was to acquire rights to water for the 100,000 acres in the valley, which falls in the Chiricahua and Graham Mountains watersheds. George Maxwell was elected executive director with Joe Chambers (owner of the local dairy) as president.

Several cattle ranches surrounded Bowie. Goat ranches shipped huge amounts of mohair. T.M. Templeton raised Duroc hogs, and in 1916, Perry "Arkansas Bill" Dewalt was in town marketing his large supply of pigs, saying, "The pork business has paid very well for several years." In the 1960s, Firpo's Pork Rind Company was owned by Raul Sapien.

Foaled in 1936, Lucky Blanton was a legendary chestnut quarter horse stallion, a great rope horse, and sire of many top rope horses. He was bred by Burns Blanton, of Bowie, who produced many great cowboy horses. Eighteen Lucky Blanton foals went to the racetracks, where they won 37 races.

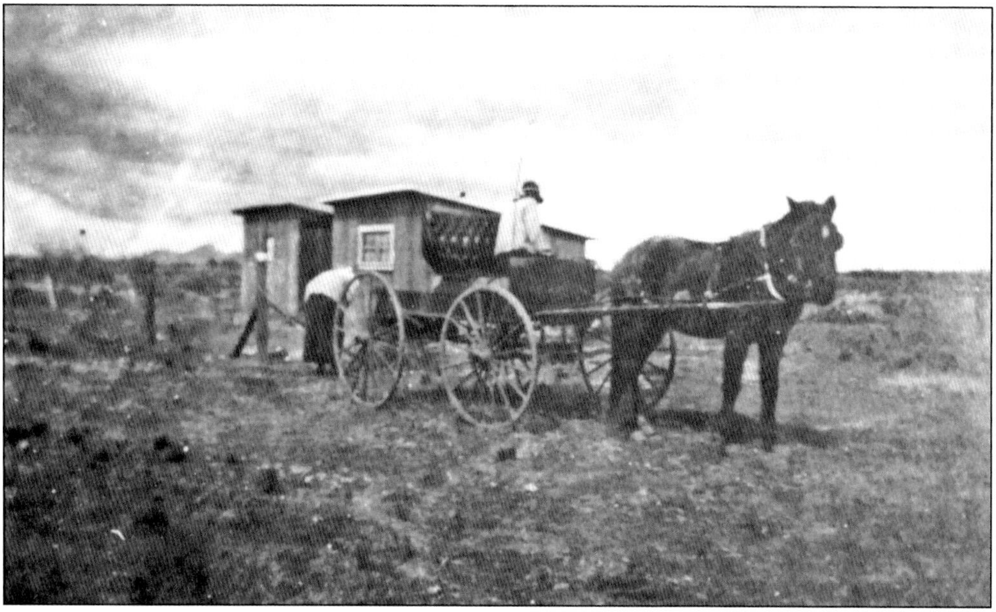

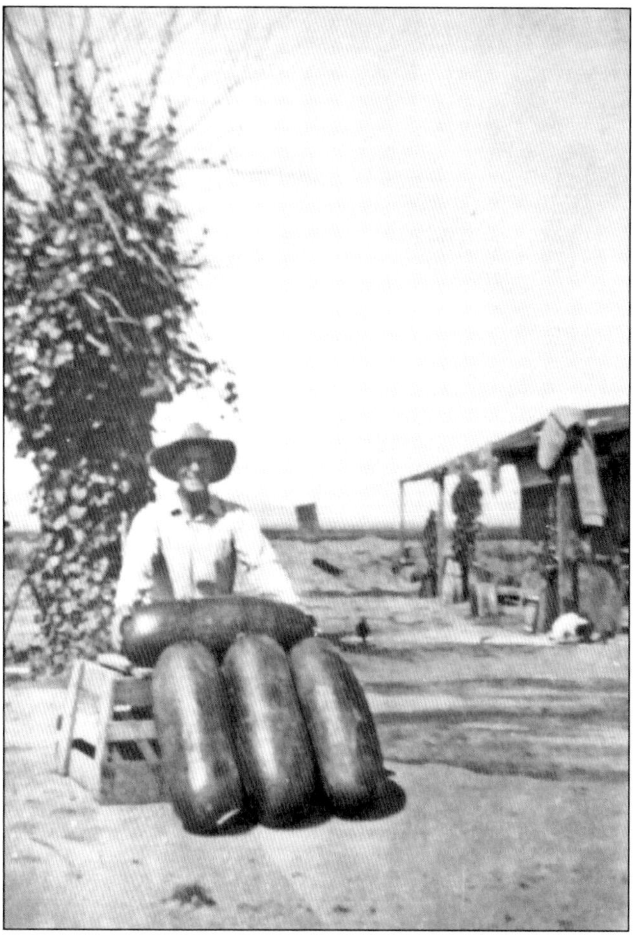

Lola Blake Tomlinson and Hattie Denniston are building a fence on the Denniston-Tomlinson homestead with a horse-drawn buggy, pulled by Old Joe. Lola and Hattie filed for homesteads on December 7, 1914. Lola was the niece of Mrs. Homer Henrich. Judge Henrich was recalled because of personal animosities between him and many residents, jeopardizing the confidence of the court and justice. Joseph Schafer won the recall election. (Courtesy of Janice Grizzle.)

Jim Blanks is showing off his prized watermelons at his farm outside Bowie. The sandy loam soil made it possible to grow several melons of this size from one plant. It was common for melons to weigh over 70 pounds each. His brother Lawrence Blanks married Hazel Sincraugh in August 1914. Her father, Harry Sincraugh, ran a barbershop and poolroom with cool drinks and tobacco. (Courtesy of Janice Grizzle.)

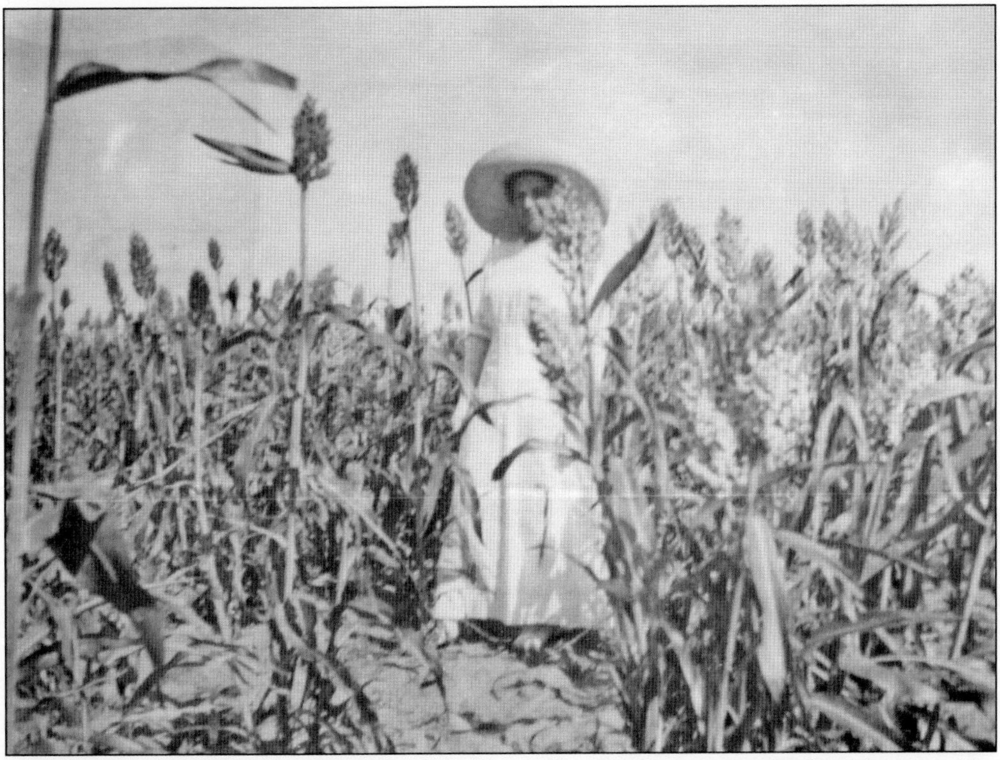

Mrs. Jesse R. Symond is standing in her field of milo maize, grown by dry-land farming. She and her husband applied for homestead on November 4, 1912, and laid the foundation for their bungalow later that same month. Mrs. Symond and Hattie Denniston were sisters. Mrs. Symond, originally from Kansas, lived in Gleeson before moving to Bowie. Jesse Symond worked for the railroad. (Courtesy of Janice Grizzle.)

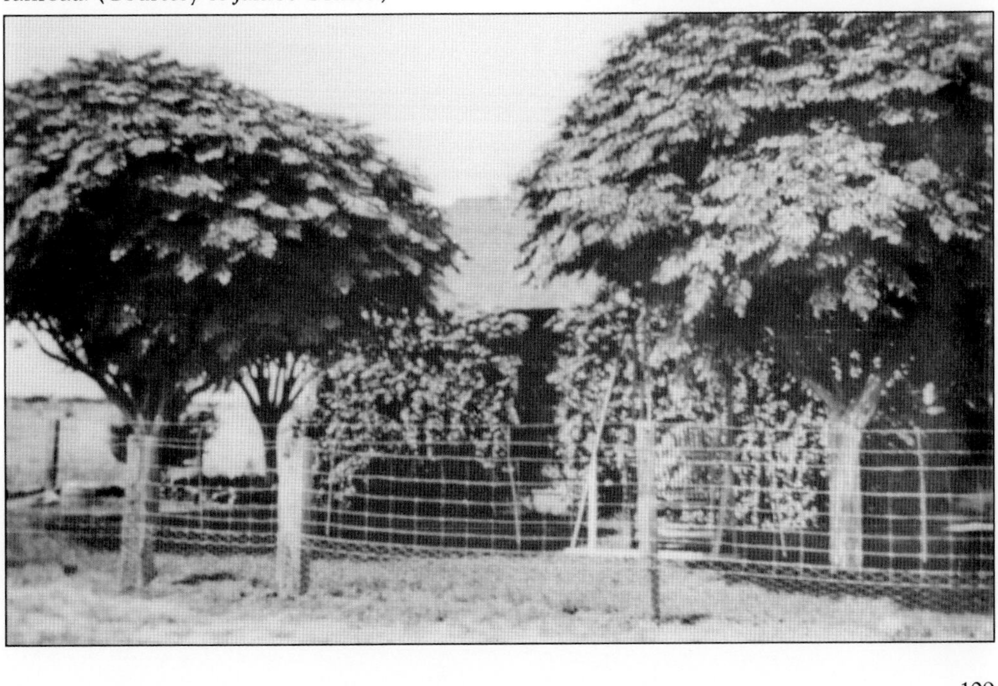

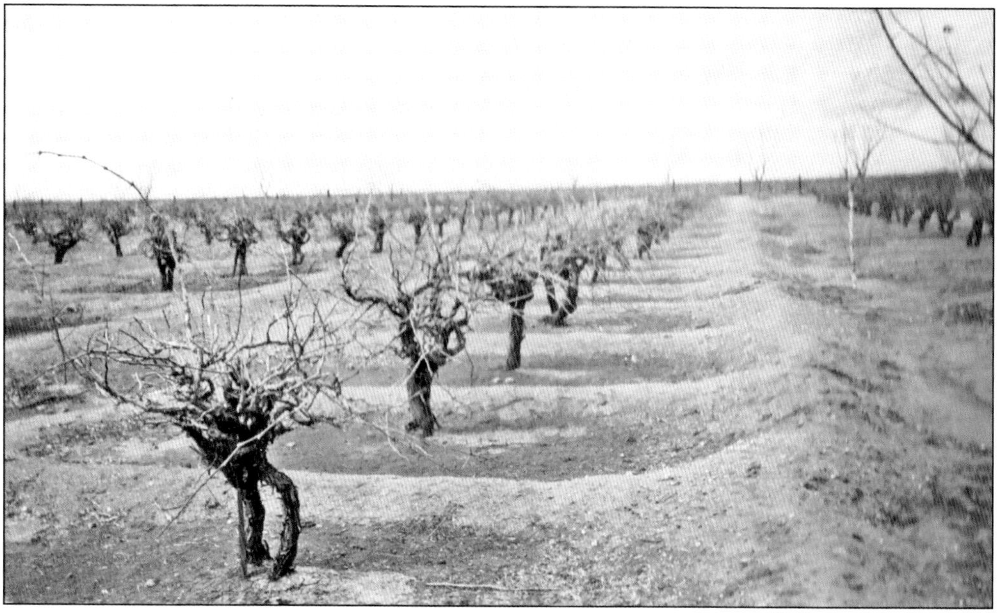

Roy Reed planted five acres of varying types of grapes in 1918. His first shipment of Thompson Seedless grapes was in August 1923, when he sent 95 boxes, each weighing 20 pounds, to Bisbee, Douglas, and Willcox. He had a unique system of dams, basins, and ditches to hold floodwater and drain direct rainfall to plants for deep moisture, even during drought, using no irrigation. (Courtesy of SSVHS.)

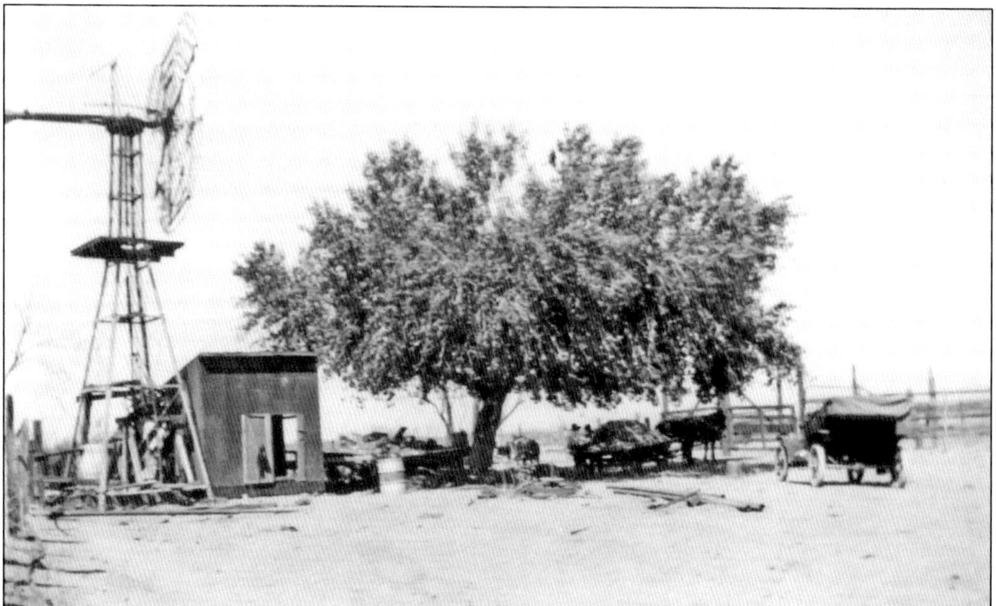

The One-Mile Ranch branded their cattle with the Z brand. This picture was taken by Lola Tomlinson and would be from about 1915. There are two different owners of record, Oscar Cockrans and Dud Prewitt. (Courtesy of Janice Grizzle.)

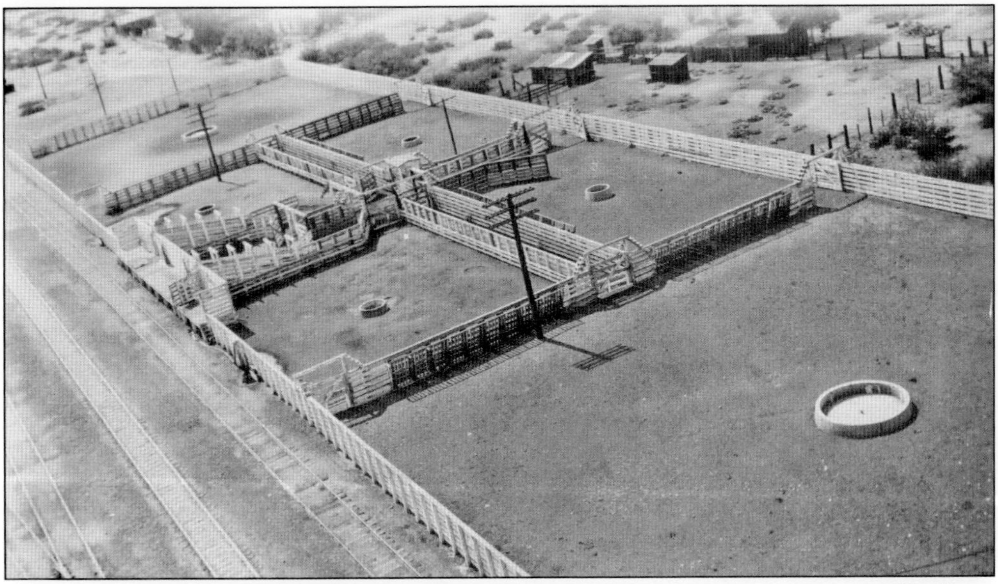

Joseph Schafer was the brand inspector working the stockyards in San Simon, Bowie, and Willcox. The ranchers got together to round up the cattle and bring them to the pens. High school boys would be excited to get out of school to help with the roundups. Southern Pacific was notified of the number of cars needed. Two cars could be loaded at one time. (Courtesy of Ed Crews.)

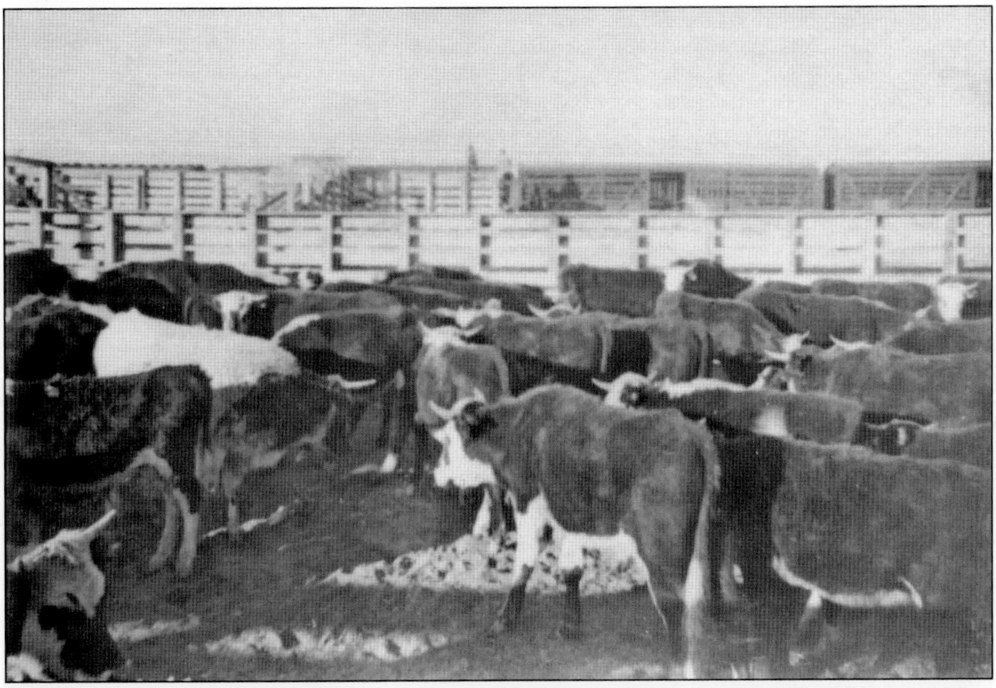

Johnson and Cook's ranch shipped a trainload of cattle in November 1916. Bowie was fast becoming a major cattle-shipping point. John Gleeson, who purchased Kaiser's Livery, shipped 10 carloads of cattle from Bowie stockyards on their way to Kansas City in September 1918. In 1921, the War Finance Company began to call in its cattle loans. Prices fell immediately, and hundreds of cattlemen went broke. (Courtesy of Janice Grizzle.)

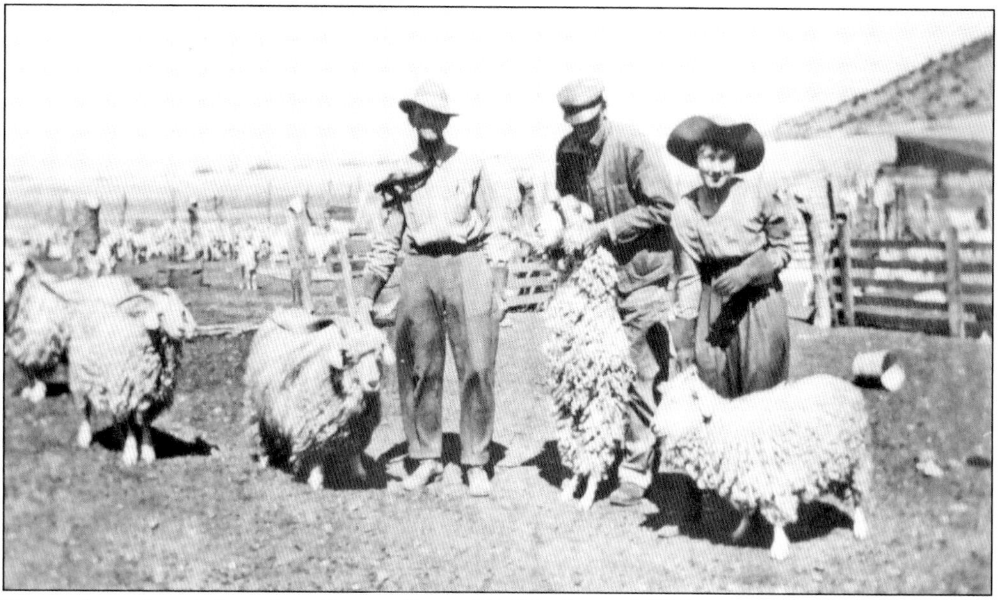

Pictured are, from left to right, Larren Scott, W. Schafer, and Welcome Scott at the goat ranch in Emigrant Canyon. In April 1923, Charles Sands shipped 48,000 pounds of mohair at 56¢ a pound. He said, "What this country needs is more goats. The five men here bring in more money to this community than all the cattlemen combined." Other goat ranchers included the Knapes, the Gojkovich family, and Oliver Saner. (Courtesy of Janice Grizzle.)

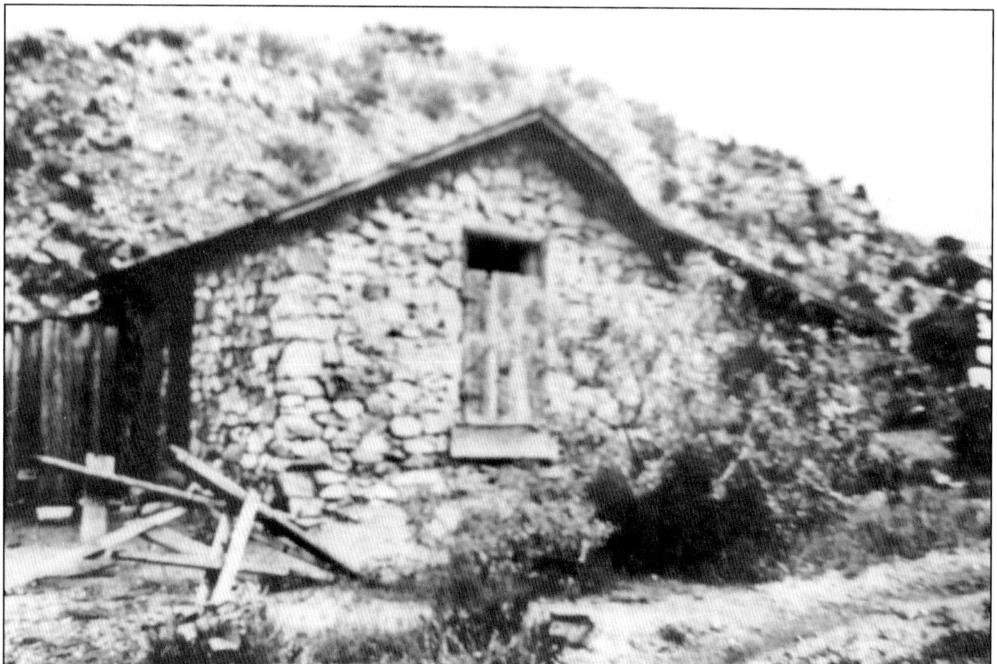

J.M. Nelson built this house in Buckeye Canyon between the Joe Lawler place and Wallace Klump's ranch house. Nelson resigned his position with Southern Pacific to drive school bus route number one. His daughter Velda was a student. (Courtesy of Janice Grizzle.)

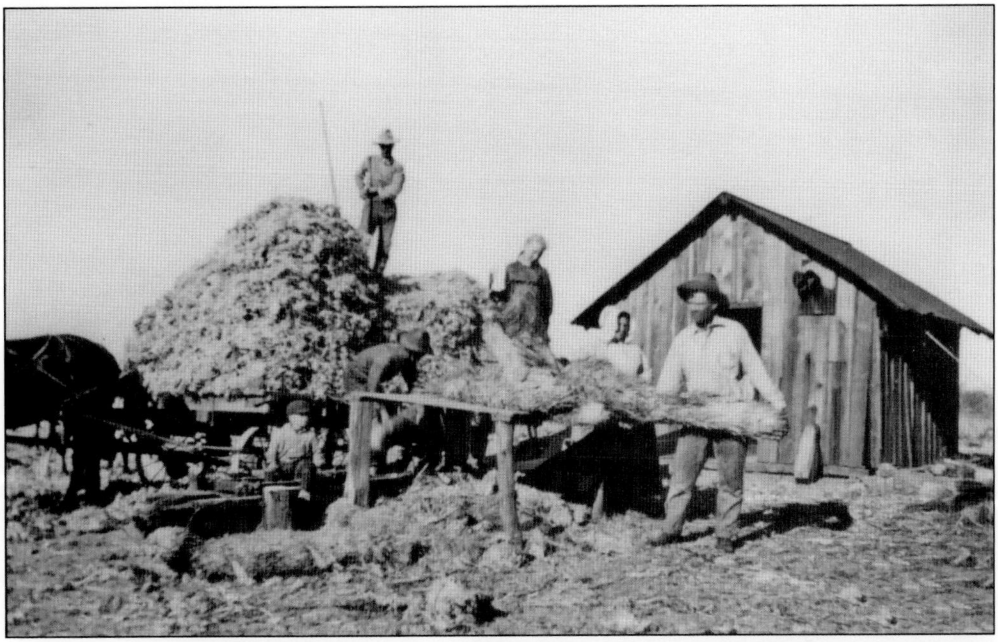

During the drought, Josie Lawhon (center) and her parents, Anna and Joseph Lawhon, had to chop soap weed (yucca) to keep cattle from starving. In the 1920s, Justice of the Peace Samuel Davis had the only soap-weed cutter in this section, making it a very valuable piece of machinery. Josie owned the HYL ranch after her parents' deaths. (Courtesy of Janice Grizzle.)

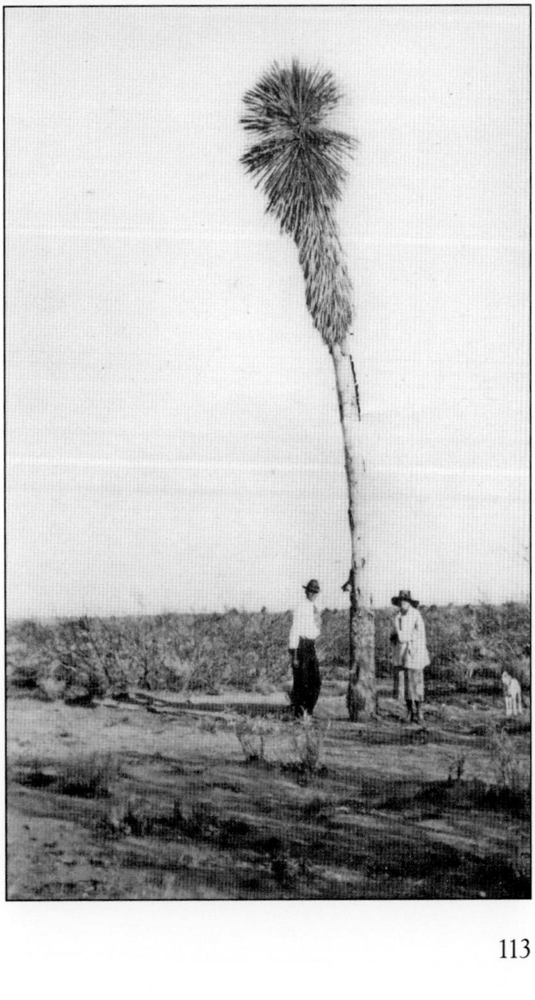

Larren Scott and his wife, Welcome, are standing beside a huge yucca plant. It is rare for one to grow to this extremely large size. This is another photograph showcasing the interesting images captured by Lola Tomlinson in the early 1900s. (Courtesy of Janice Grizzle.)

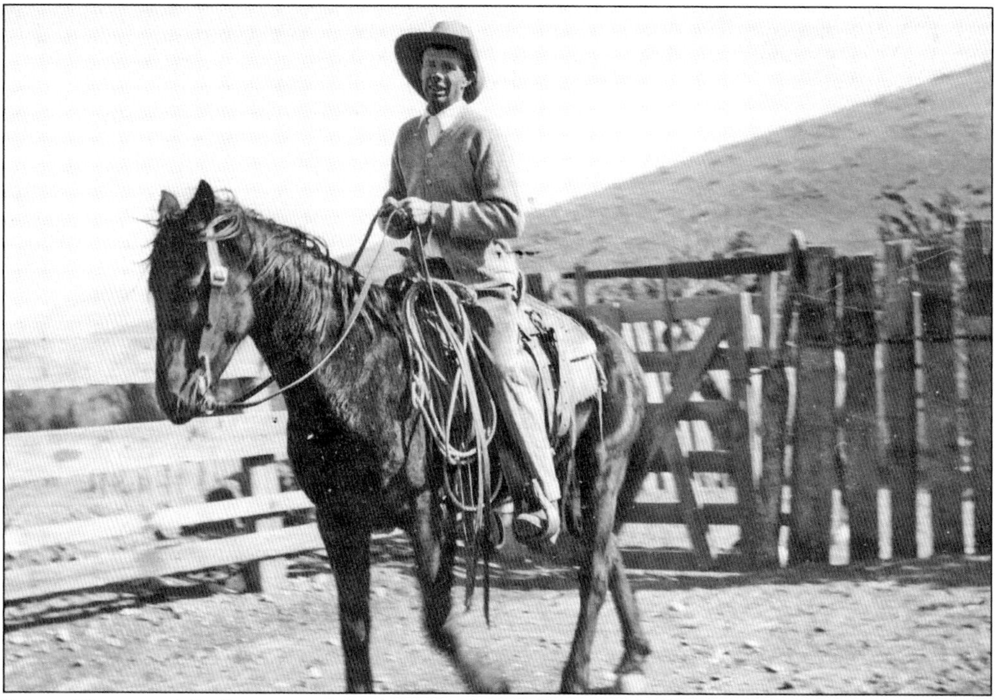

Edward Brewster Monk managed the huge cattle ranch started by his uncles in 1881. Sadly, though well educated and a prolific writer, his last years were spent in the state mental institution. He and wife, Margaret, had one daughter, Margaret Brewster Monk. His nephew Ned Hall inherited the ranch and is in the Willcox Cowboy Hall of Fame. Bowie's Monk Addition is named after the family. (Courtesy of SSVHS.)

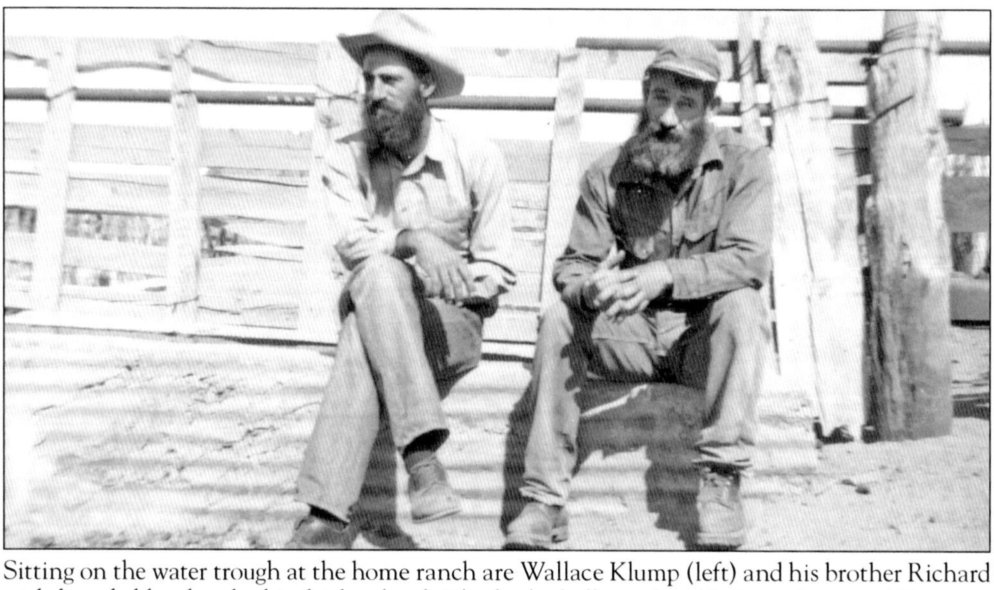

Sitting on the water trough at the home ranch are Wallace Klump (left) and his brother Richard with beards like they had in high school. The basketball coach told them they would have to shave to play. They told him that Jesus had a beard. The coach said, "Yes, but Jesus didn't want to be on the basketball team." Their grandfather John Walter Klump settled here in 1904. (Courtesy of Keith Klump.)

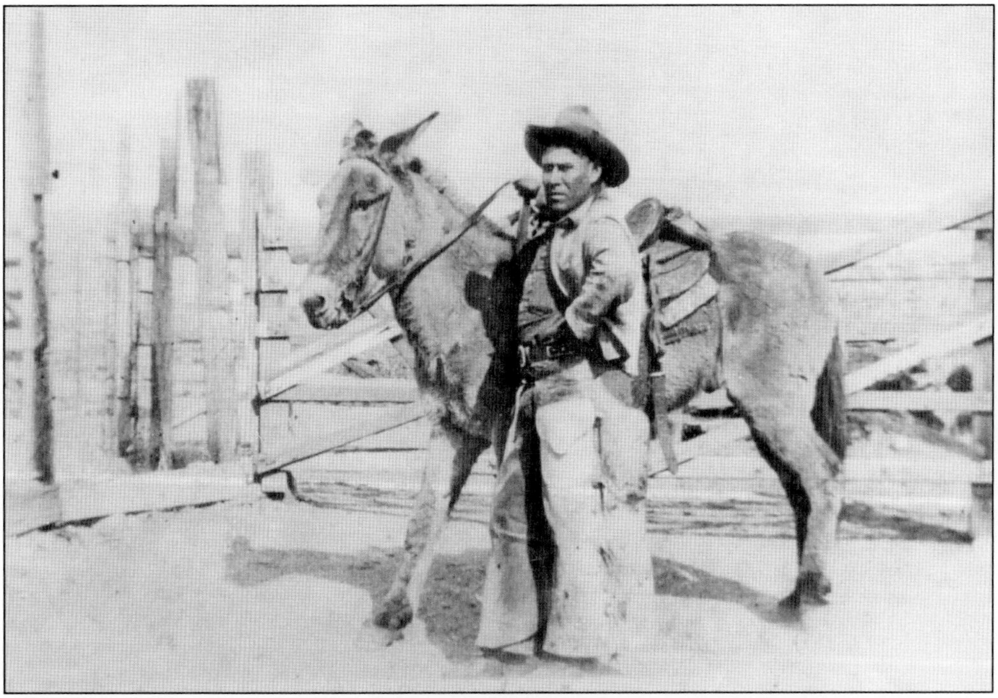

Manuel Hernandez Sr., one of the old-time cowboys, is standing beside his mule and dressed in typical cowboy gear. Some of the best cowboys in the Southwest were the Mexican vaqueros. The going rate for day workers in early times was $1 a day for the cowboy and another $1 a day if he supplied his own horse. (Courtesy of Bowie Justice Court.)

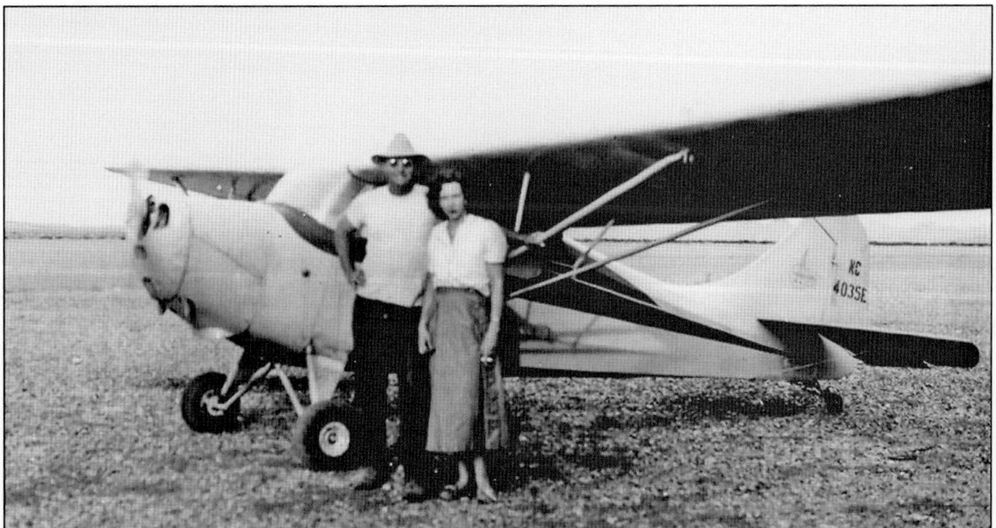

Jack Dechard Spikes and wife Mary Lou surveyed their farm and the Staple Bar ranch by airplane. Jack was grand master of the Masons of Arizona, headed Bowie Water Company, and ran 66 marathons in his later years. They had three children: Evelyn, Jim and Dan. Mary Lou taught high school math and typing, as well as first grade. She served on the board of education for several years. (Courtesy of Evelyn Lathram.)

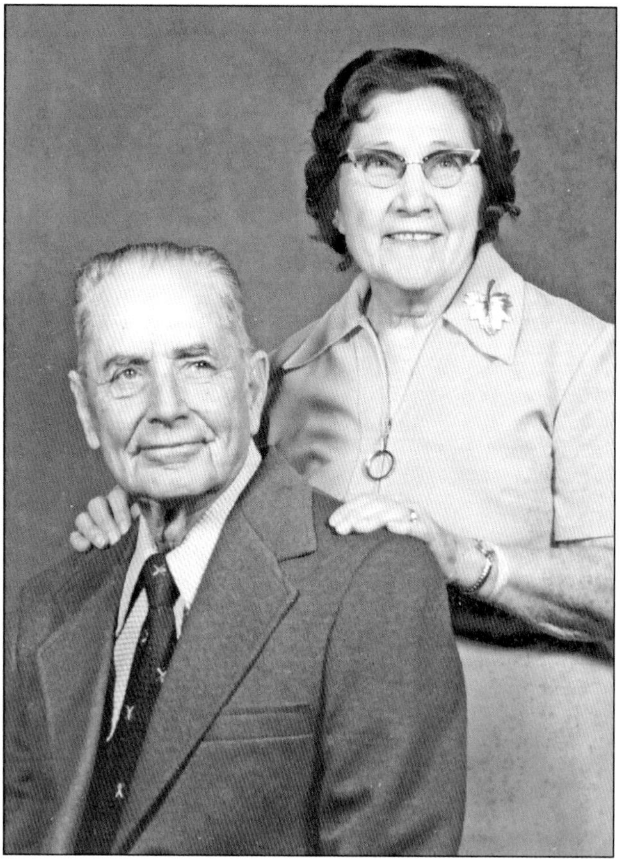

Tennis and Ella Creighton came in 1940 and purchased the UX Ranch, located northwest of Bowie. Creighton was also a government trapper and livestock inspector. Their children Janice and Neilan both graduated from Bowie High School. Neilan married Fay Minor, and Janice married Henry "Jack" Grizzle. The Grizzles' three children, Joyce, Victor, and Diane, also graduated from Bowie. Joyce married "Bo" Hall, who has a successful career as a sports coach. Victor married Geri Hamilton. Diane married Kim Gierke, a teacher at Bowie High School. The Creightons sold the UX in 1971 and moved to Christoval, Texas, to operate another cattle ranch. The UX ranch was photographed from the top of Fisher Hills in 1950 before the government built Creighton Dam. The house was moved into town and is the Baptist parsonage. (Courtesy of Janice Grizzle.)

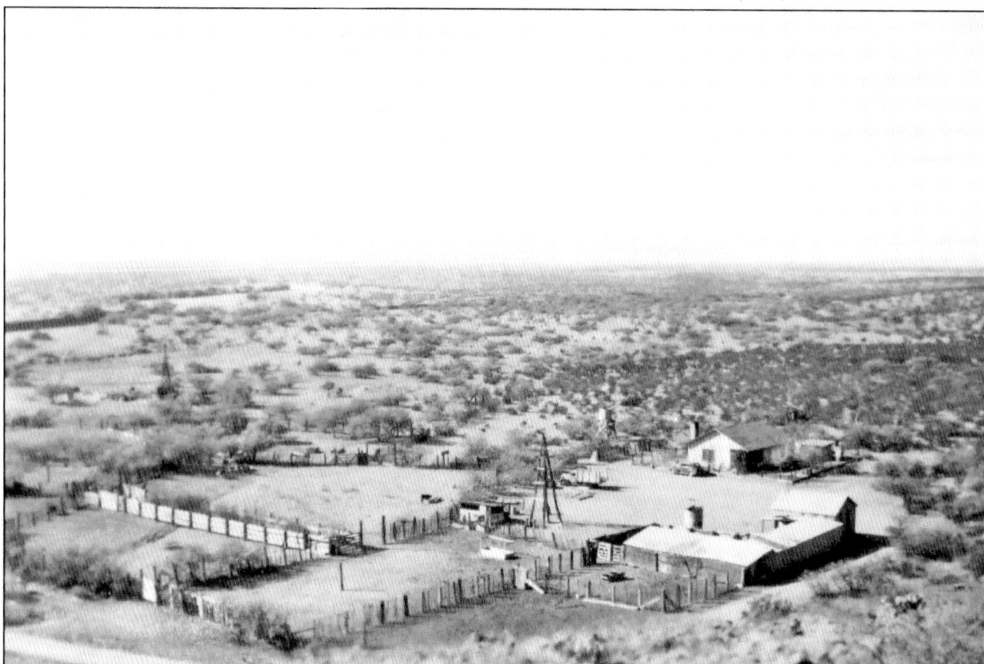

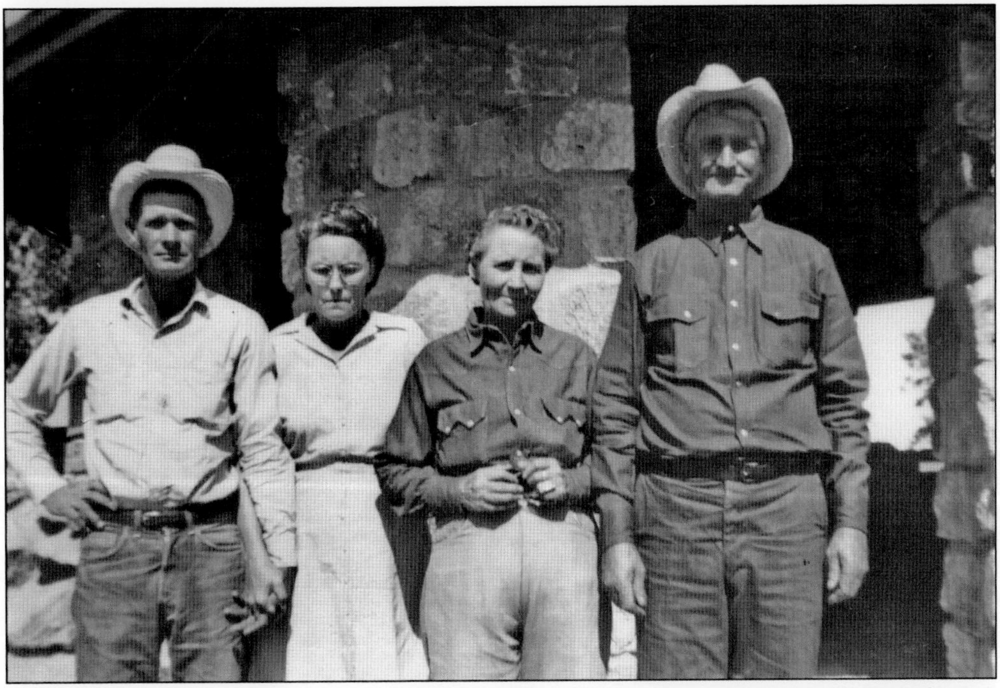

Andrew and Sallie Garrett with Minnie "Ma" and Lee Bartlett worked together on Tom Shown's ranch, which Shown purchased from Donald and Lorraine Riggs. The Garretts worked at the old Schafer Ranch from August 1949 to 1954. Andrew died at only 44 years old. The Bartletts owned a ranch at the edge of Bowie. (Courtesy of Anna Mahan.)

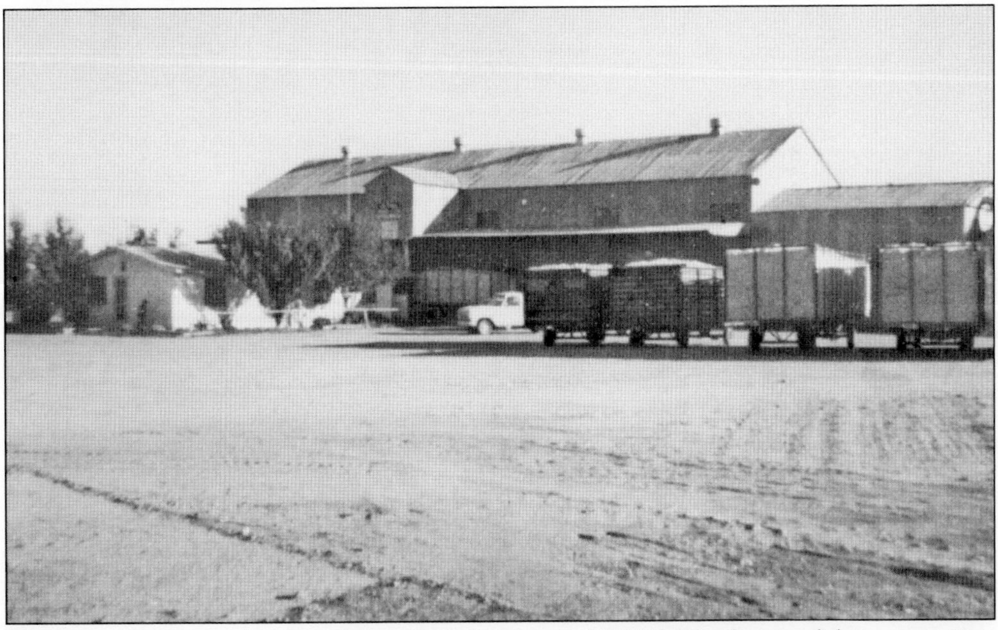

The Bowie Gin was a division of Casa Grande Cotton Oil Mill. The farmers did not get serious about growing cotton until April 1924, when a meeting was held in the Cochise County Agricultural Agent's office in Willcox with extension agronomist W.B. Showers. Cotton was hauled to Safford for years, until Vaughn Hilburn built the first cotton gin. (Courtesy of Jim Spikes.)

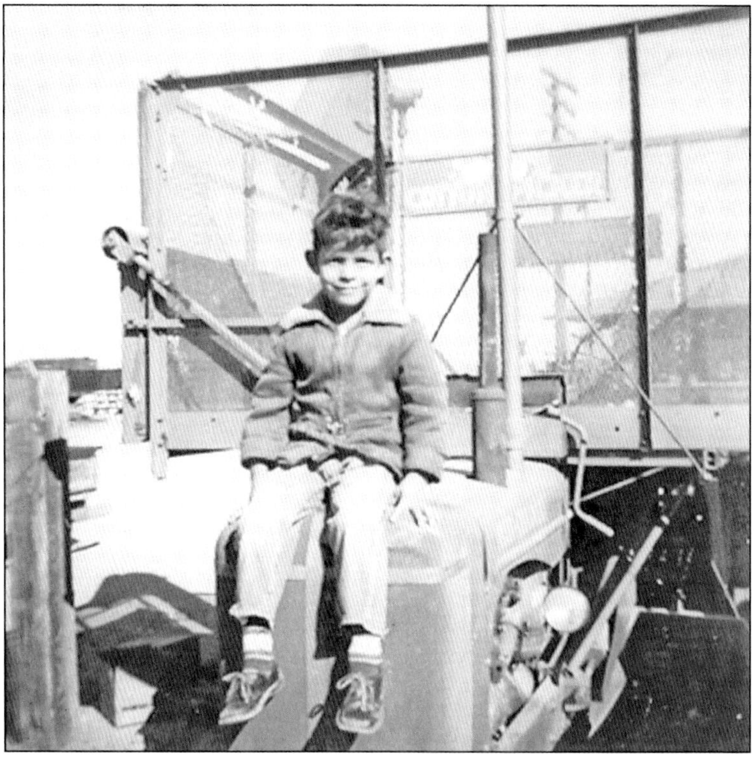

This picture, taken across the street from the depot, shows Elias Rodriguez after his dad, Efren, picked him up and sat him on the cotton picker. Efren and Epifania Rodriguez came in 1953 and worked for Vaughn Hilburn and Cooke Farms. Their children were Efren III, Geronimo, Elias, Juan, Mario, Yolanda, and Mary Sue. (Courtesy of Elias Rodriguez.)

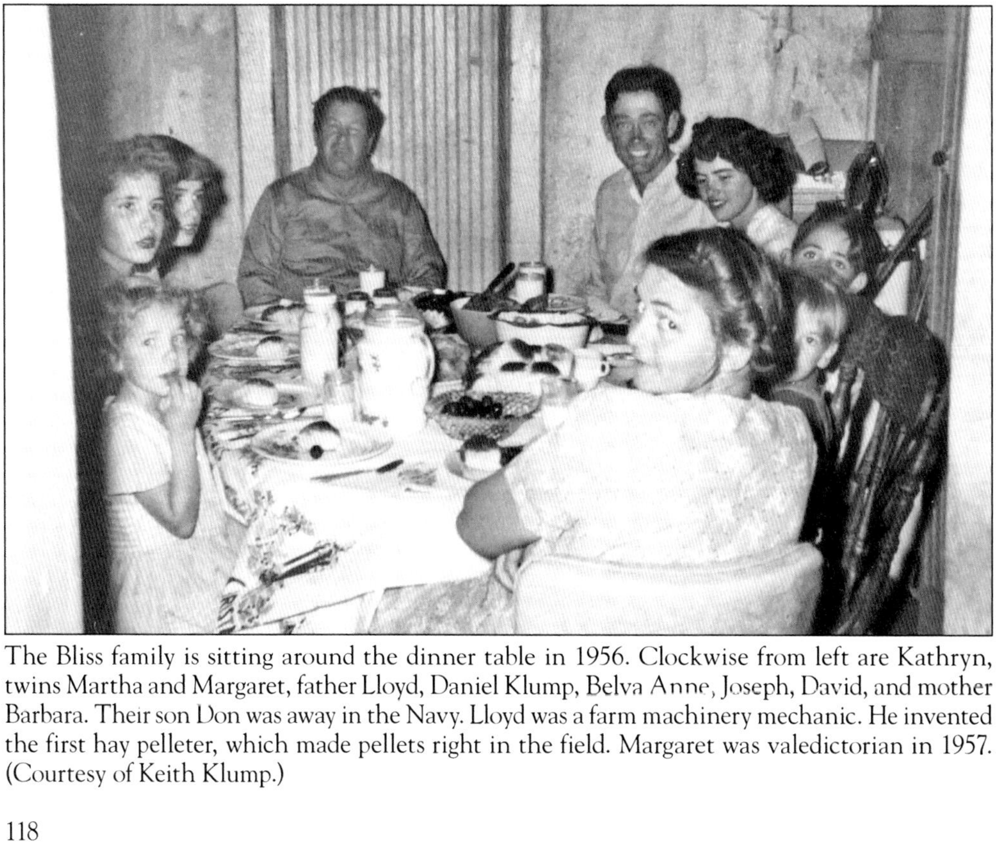

The Bliss family is sitting around the dinner table in 1956. Clockwise from left are Kathryn, twins Martha and Margaret, father Lloyd, Daniel Klump, Belva Anne, Joseph, David, and mother Barbara. Their son Don was away in the Navy. Lloyd was a farm machinery mechanic. He invented the first hay pelleter, which made pellets right in the field. Margaret was valedictorian in 1957. (Courtesy of Keith Klump.)

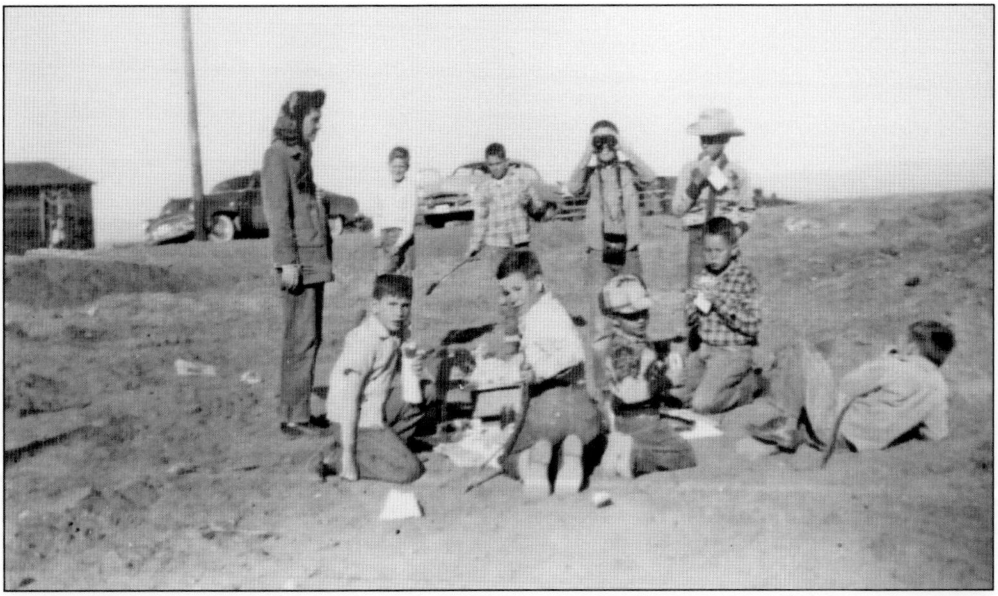

Lindsey Cohorn owned the first commercial farm in 1951. El Paso Natural Gas ran a gas line through Apache Pass, making large acreage irrigation possible. Roma Jacobs assisted Willie Pearl Cohorn with a wiener roast for son Tony on his 11th birthday. Friends attending were Roger Boll, Martin Scott, Dewain Lockwood, Scottie Welker, Jerry Jones, John Ray Jacobs, and Glennie Jacobs. (Courtesy of Tony Cohorn.)

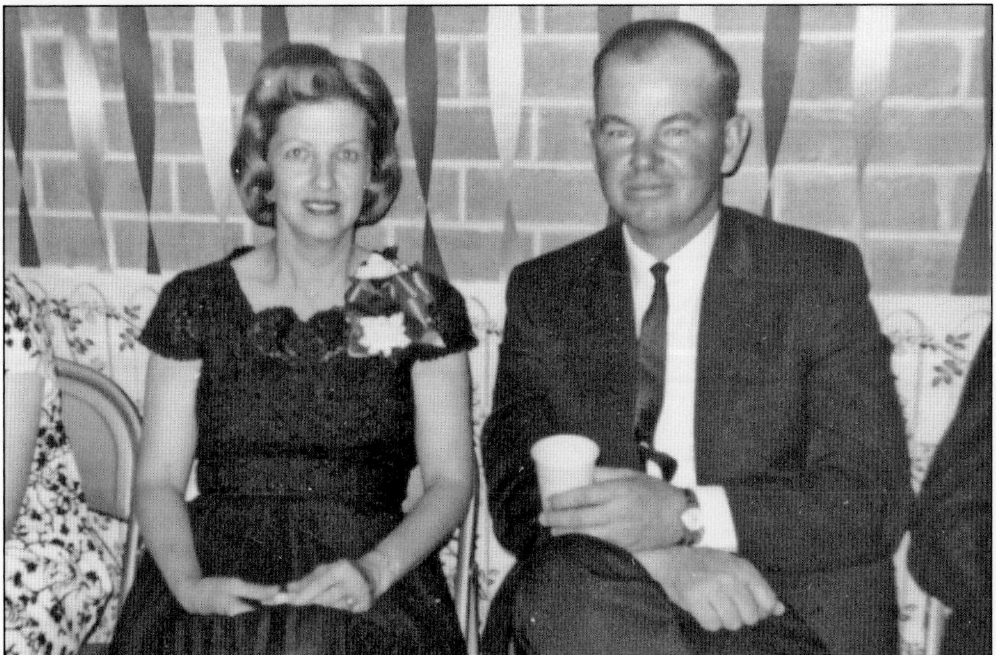

Jimmie and Vaughn Hilburn were farmers with four daughters, Frances, Patricia, Virginia, and Kathy. He was a brother to Bill and an uncle to Kent Hilburn. Tomato crops were shipped by train with the whole town pitching in to sort, cull, pack, and load the tomatoes onto the boxcars. (Courtesy of SSVHS.)

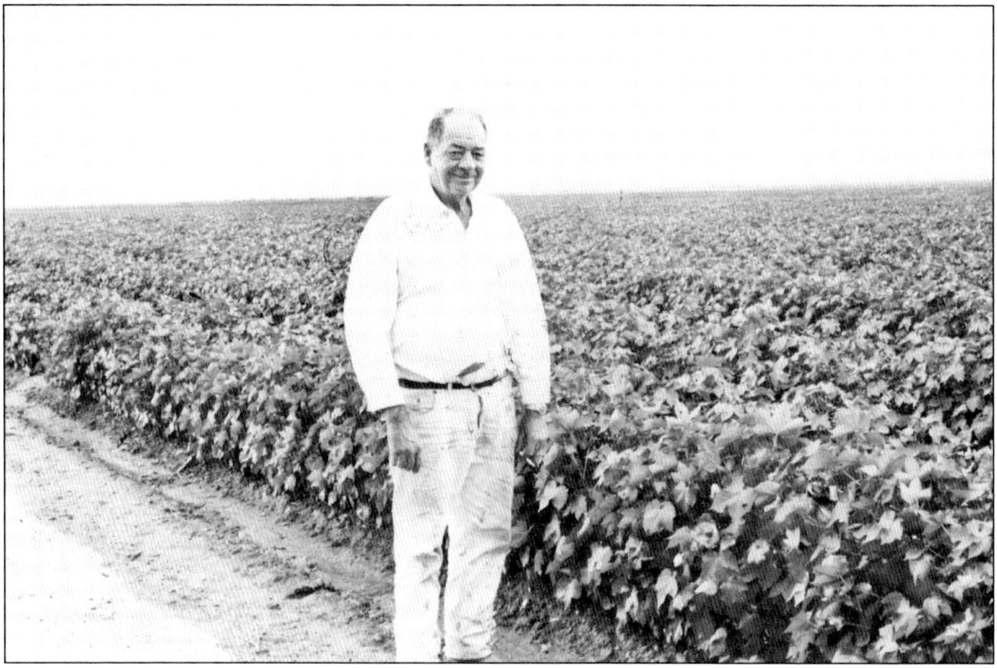

Above, Leland Jones is standing in a field of cotton in August 1979. He was superintendent of Kent Hilburn's farming operation. Below, Kent Hilburn is inspecting his cotton crop. He came to Bowie in 1973 from Seminole, Texas. He farmed the largest acreage in the Bowie area in the 1970s. He planted 2,500 acres of cotton, 300 acres of milo, and 800 acres of pecans. (Both, courtesy of SSVHS.)

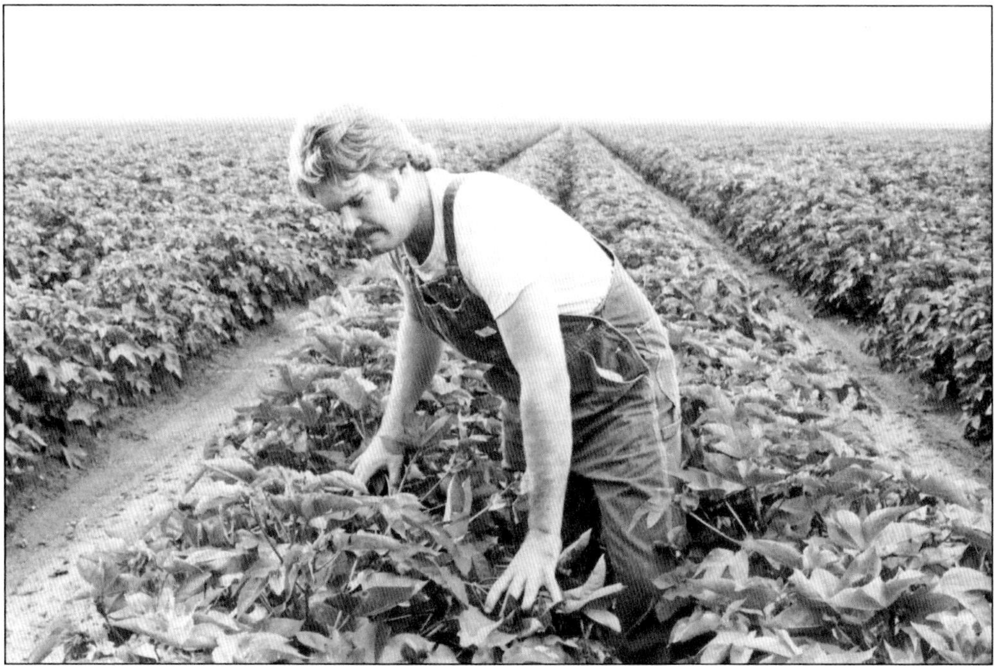

At right, Harold Wardlaw, in 1979, had 140 acres planted in pecan trees with plans for planting another 110 acres the next year. Below, Tom Shown came from Yuma and became a successful farmer in the Bowie valley. He sold out to Bill and Druecilla Hilburn, who built a large, beautiful home on the property. Hollis Roberts bought it in 1988 with 430 acres of pecans. Current owners are Dick and Cody Eastman and family, of Fort Bowie Vineyards, who grow grapes, pecans, and pistachios. (Both, courtesy of SSVHS.)

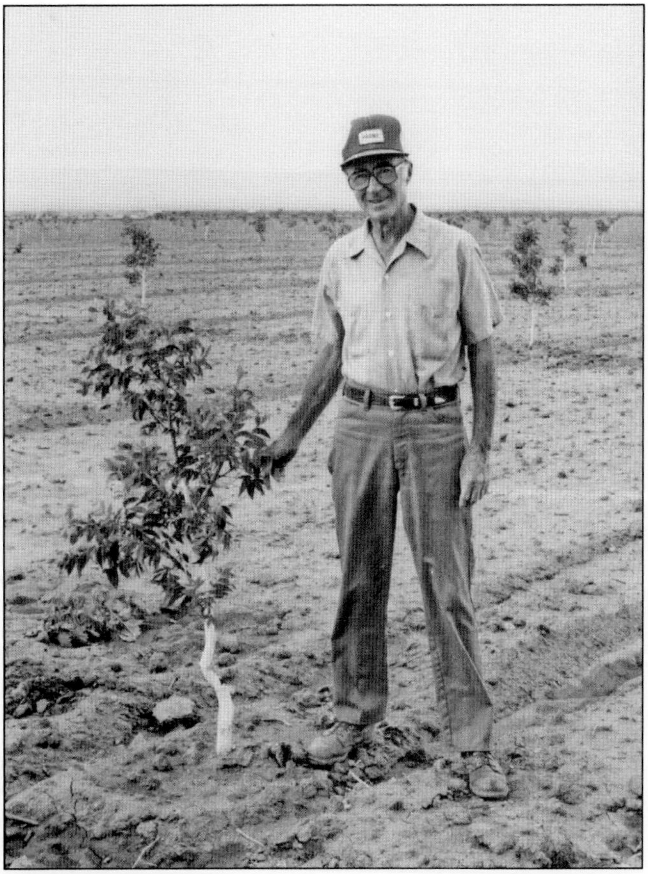

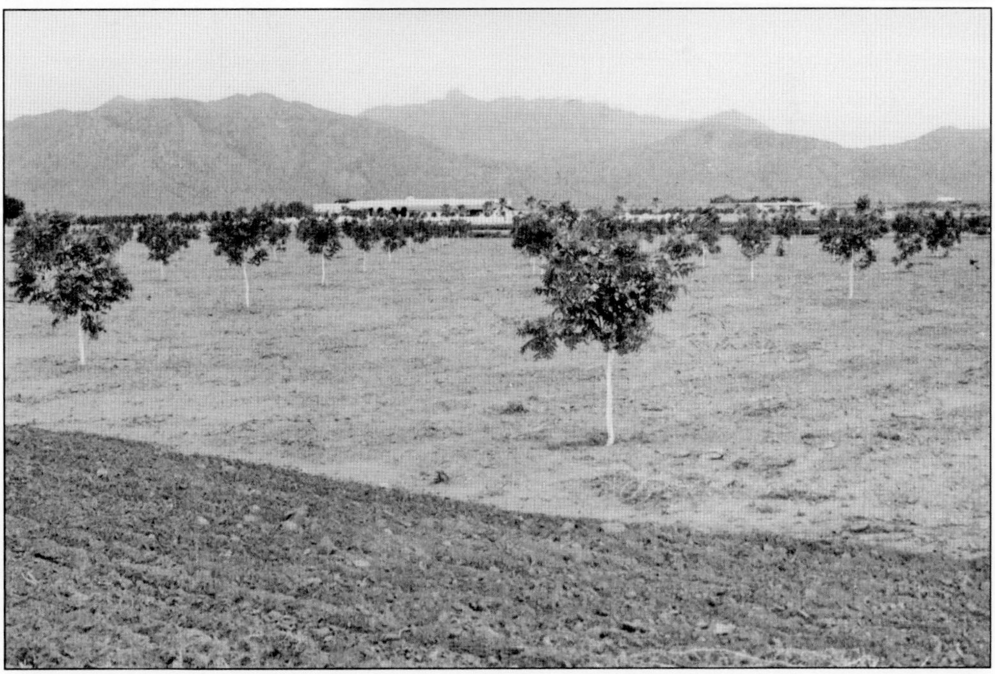

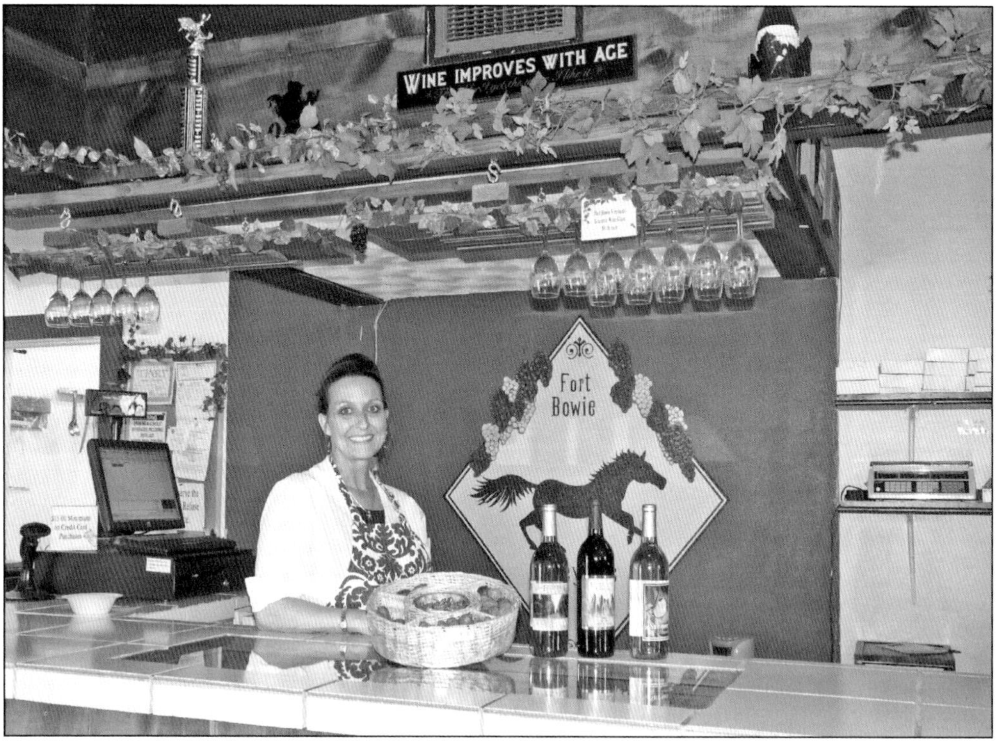

Fort Bowie Vineyards opened this store and delicatessen behind the post office. It has a delightful array of their prize-winning wines, nuts, and other gift items. Shanda Lloyd is behind the counter and ready to fill orders. The store is located in the original Masonic Lodge building, where the Masons and the Eastern Stars held their meetings and events. The marker on the building states, "Bowie Lodge number 33 and Order of the Eastern Star number 29," and gives the date as 1950. (Courtesy of Peta-Anne Tenney.)

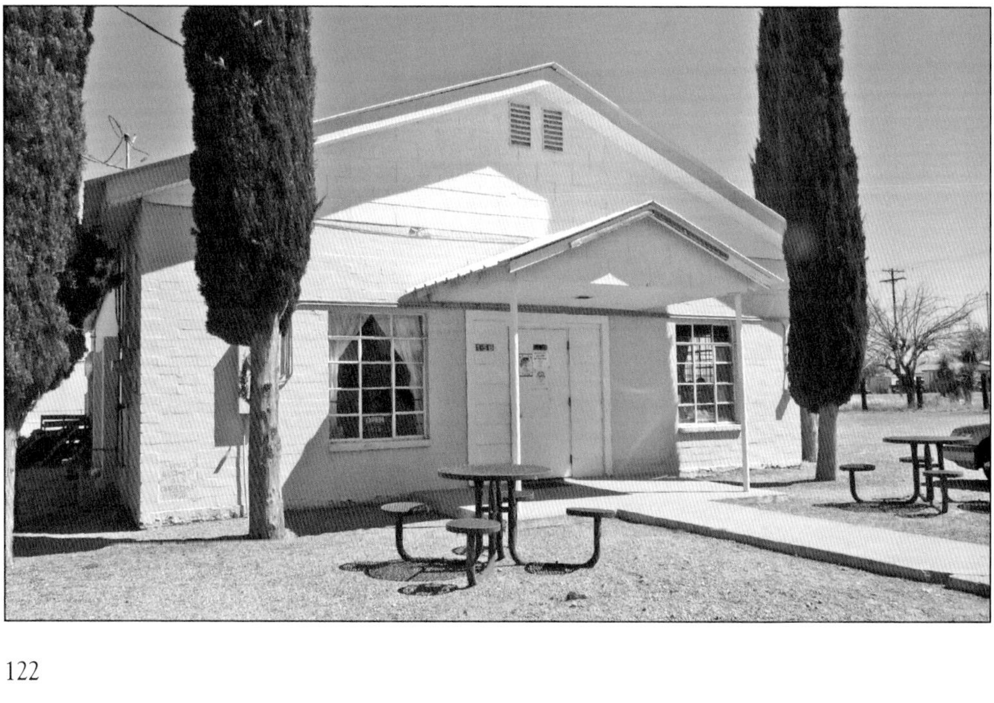

Eight

Bowie Today

Bowie has beautiful school buildings with the residents very active in the school and community events held there. The post office is the popular place to gather and get the news of the day. Around the corner is the library, where residents can get a good book to read. There are a couple of stores and places to eat. Several pioneer families live in nice homes and have a strong love for and a bond with Bowie. The chamber of commerce continues to promote the town through publications and the Internet. The Welker-Scott Memorial Park, a nice respite, was dedicated to William Ira Welker and Larren O. Scott on May 27, 1996. The town struggles to survive with few job opportunities, except the vineyards, pecan, and pistachio orchards. However, the sun shines practically every day of the year, and the climate is just perfect.

A favorite getaway for picnics and hiking is the Masonic picnic grounds with massive formations of granite outcroppings known as the Indian Bread Rocks.

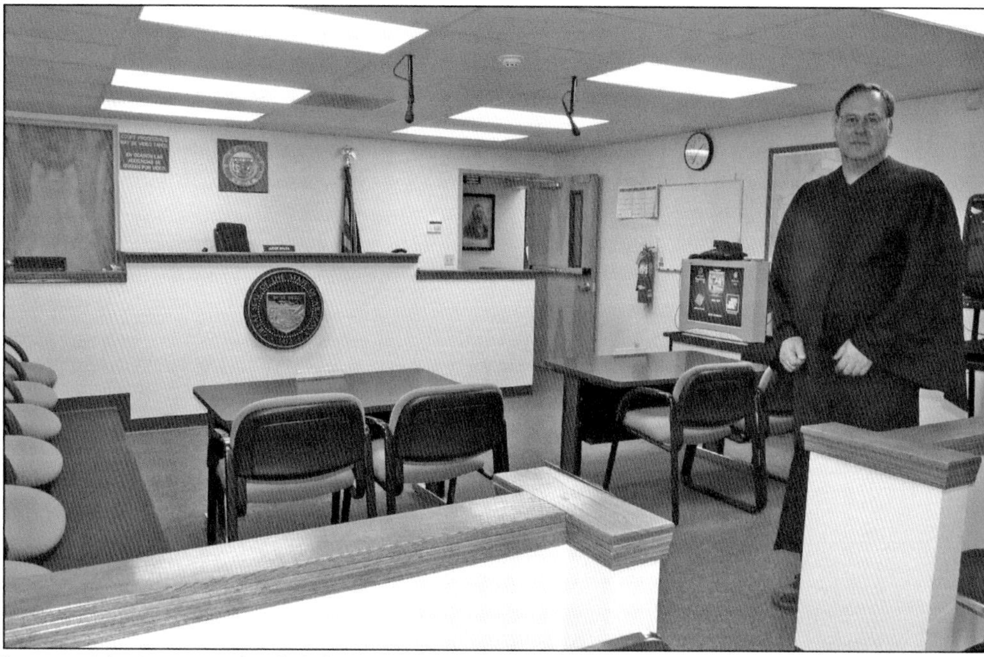

Justice of the Peace Michael Skiles stands in the modern courtroom, located in the former Variety Store building. Named after Josephine Lawhon on September 6, 1996, it is located next to the old courthouse and jail that is now the Jimmy Libhart Library. Linda Hale was the first judge to preside here. (Courtesy of Peta-Anne Tenney.)

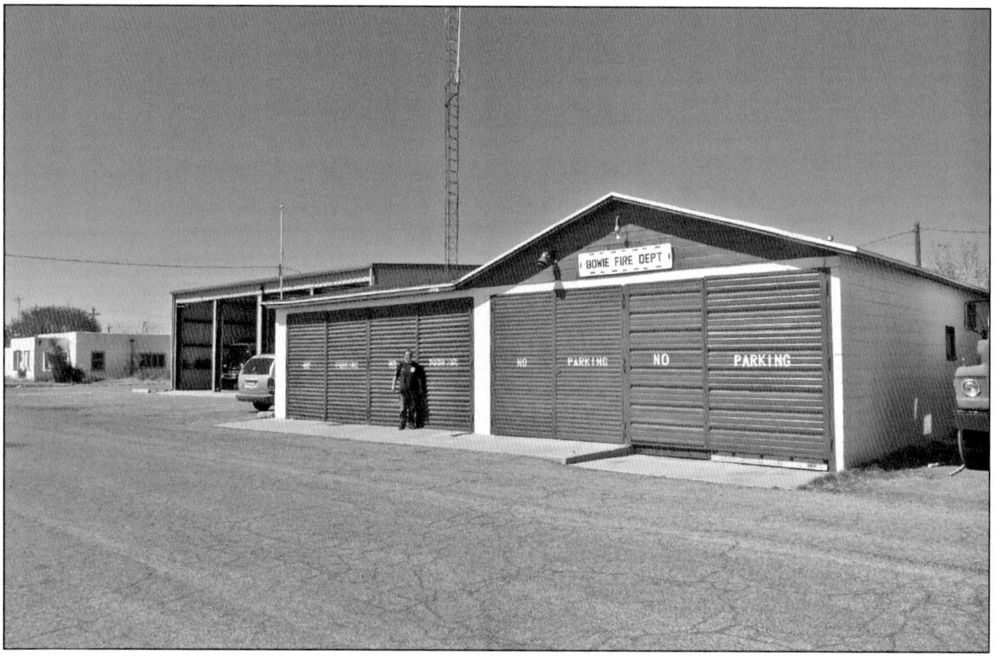

Bowie is very proud of its fire department. Chief Raye Bright, pictured, was successful in securing grants in 2010 to add three vehicles to the fleet. They are a 2,500-gallon water tender, an ambulance, and a fast-response brush-rescue truck. Others on the force are Ben Yeatman and Tenzy Patt. (Courtesy of Peta-Anne Tenney.)

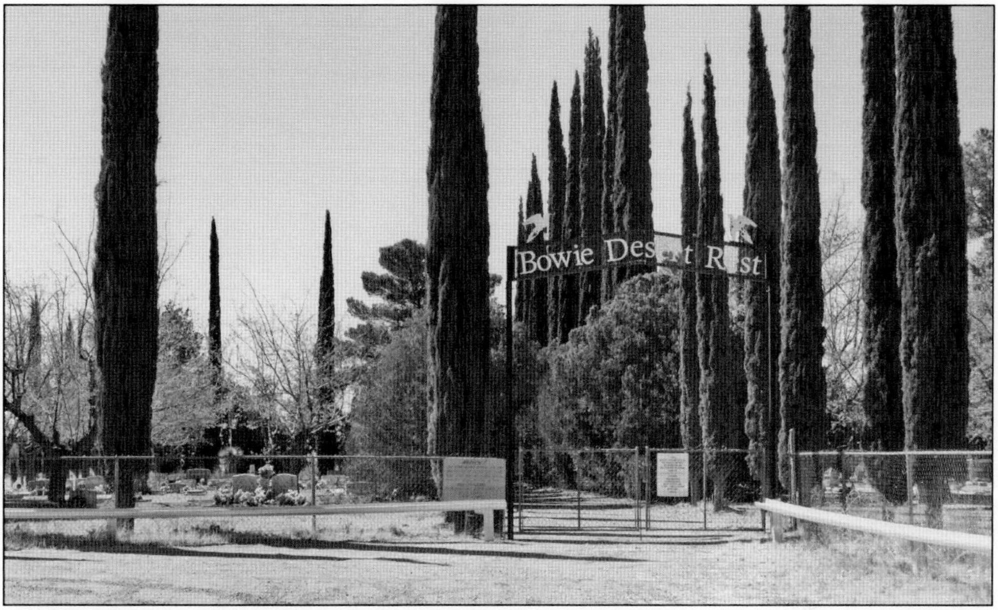

Compliments are received from all over the county, as well as from visitors, about the beautiful Desert Rest Cemetery. It is the most beautifully kept in all of Cochise County and holds over 100 years of Bowie history. Community organizations developed and maintained the water lines. It is completely maintained by volunteers. (Courtesy of Peta-Anne Tenney.)

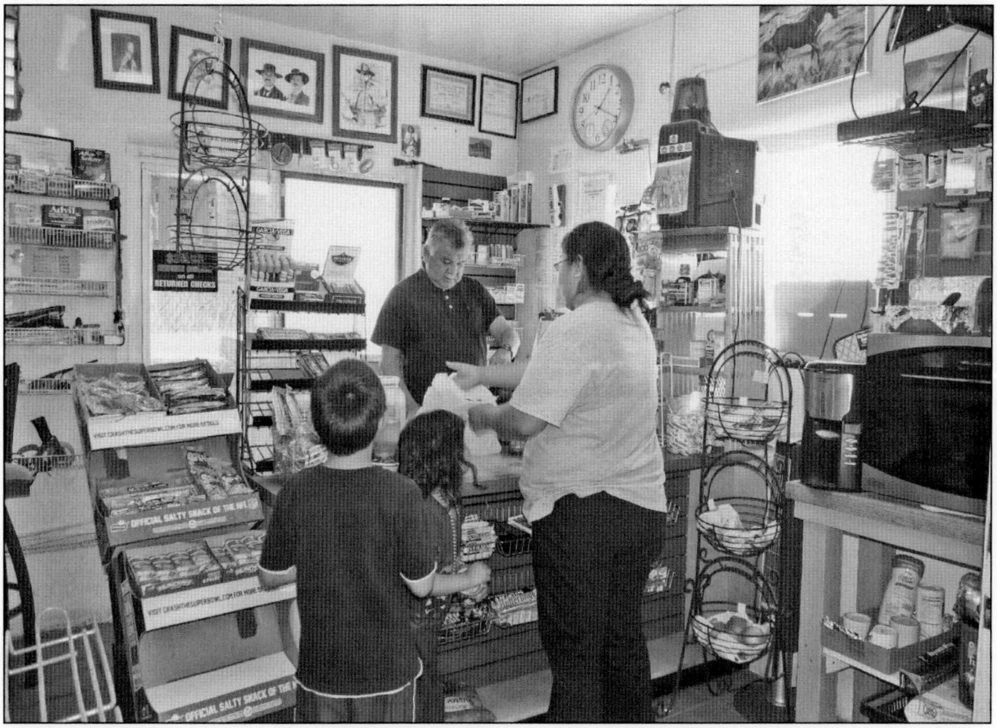

Cross the Street Mini Mart, with drive-through window, is located in the old Royster service station. Owner Phil Tapia is behind the counter, serving customers Beatrice Nunez and Patrick and Christiana Hernandez. (Courtesy of Peta-Anne Tenney.)

About Sulphur Springs Valley Historical Society

Founded in 1974 to preserve the heritage of Willcox and the surrounding area, the Sulphur Springs Valley Historical Society was successful in getting the original business buildings and homes listed in the National Register of Historic Places and creating a historic district. They began to document the history of these buildings, applied for grants, and raised funds to help in their preservation. After renovating the 1880s Schwertner family home and the Southern Pacific Railroad depot, the historical society opened the Chiricahua Regional Museum and Research Center in 1999. Located at 127 East Maley Street, the museum features the history of the Chiricahua Apache people, plus ranching and mining history, and the history of Willcox and the surrounding towns. The research center archives includes books, photographs, newspapers dating from 1894, family histories, displays from the Toggery store, and the Judge Edward R. Monk family collection.

Operated completely by volunteers, with funding by donations and memberships, the museum is open Monday through Saturday. The research library is open Wednesdays and Thursdays and by appointment.

About the Authors

Kathy Klump, a third-generation Arizonan, was selected as an Arizona Culture Keeper in 2008. She is president of the Sulphur Springs Valley Historical Society and librarian for the Chiricahua Regional Museum and Research Center. She is a cofounder of the Friends of Elsie S. Hogan Community Library. Her husband is a cattle rancher whose family came to southeastern Arizona in 1904. They are the parents of six children.

Australian-born Peta-Anne Tenney has lived in Willcox since 1985. In Australia, she was known nationwide for her equine photography. She and her husband, Todd, started the Paint Horse Association of Australia and published the *Australian Western Horsemen* magazine. She was inducted into the Australian Paint Horse Hall of Fame in 2008. She and Todd have two sons.

Bibliography

Burreson, JoDell. *Reflections*. Bowie, AZ: Self published, 1994.
Burroway, Alma. *Marble Camp*. Unpublished manuscript housed at Arizona Historical Foundation Hayden Library, Arizona State University, Tempe, AZ.
McChristian, Douglas C. *Fort Bowie, Arizona: Combat Post of the Southwest, 1858–1894*. Norman, OK: University of Oklahoma Press, 2005.
Miller, Joseph. *The Arizona Story*. New York: Hastings House, 1952.
Myrick, David F. *Railroads of Arizona*. San Diego, CA: Howell-North Books, 1981.
Tevis, James H. *Arizona in the '50's*. Albuquerque, NM: University of New Mexico Press, 1954.
Theobald, John and Lillian. *Arizona Territory Post Offices and Postmasters*. Phoenix, AZ: Arizona Historical Foundation, 1961.
Van Orden, Jay. *Geronimo's Surrender: The C.S. Fly Photographs*. Tucson, AZ: Arizona Historical Society, 2001.